Britain and the Spanish Anti-Franco Opposition, 1940–1950

Also by David J. Dunthorn

SPAIN IN AN INTERNATIONAL CONTEXT, 1936–1959 (*co-editor with Christian Leitz*)

Britain and the Spanish Anti-Franco Opposition, 1940–1950

David J. Dunthorn
Visiting Lecturer for Modern European History
University of the West of England
Bristol

First published 2000 by
PALGRAVE
Houndmills, Basingstoke, Hampshire RG21 6XS and
175 Fifth Avenue, New York, N.Y. 10010
Companies and representatives throughout the world

PALGRAVE is the new global academic imprint of
St. Martin's Press LLC Scholarly and Reference Division and
Palgrave Publishers Ltd (formerly Macmillan Press Ltd).

ISBN 0–333–91796–0

This book is printed on paper suitable for recycling and made from fully managed and sustained forest sources.

A catalogue record for this book is available from the British Library.

Library of Congress Cataloging-in-Publication Data
Dunthorn, David J. (David Joseph)
    Britain and the Spanish anti-Franco opposition, 1940–1950 / David J. Dunthorn.
        p. cm.
    Includes bibliographical references and index.
    ISBN 0–333–91796–0 (cloth : alk. paper)
    1. Great Britain—Foreign relations—Spain. 2. Spain—Foreign public opinion, British—History—20th century. 3. Government, Resistance to—Spain—History—20th century. 4. Public opinion—Great Britain—History—20th century. 5. Great Britain—Foreign relations—1936–1945. 6. Great Britain—Foreign relations—1945–1964. 7. Franco, Francisco, 1892–1975—Adversaries. 8. Spain—Foreign relations—Great Britain. 9. Spain—Foreign relations—1939–1975. I. Title.
    DA47.8 .D86 2000
    327.41046—dc21
                                                    00–040456

10   9   8   7   6   5   4   3   2   1
09   08   07   06   05   04   03   02   01   00

Printed in Great Britain by Antony Rowe Ltd, Chippenham, Wiltshire

To my wife and family

Contents

Acknowledgements

This study began as a PhD thesis under the supervision of Professor Glyn Stone and Dr Martin Thomas of the School of History, University of the West of England, and Professor John Young of the Department of Politics, University of Leicester. I am grateful for their advice and guidance, intellectual rigour and generous bestowal of time. Needless to say, the conclusions arrived at in this study and any errors it may contain are my own. I thank, too, Professor Paul Preston of the London School of Economics and Political Science and Dr Michael Richards of the University of the West of England, who examined the original thesis. Before his departure for the Department of History, University of Auckland, New Zealand, I also received valuable advice and encouragement from Dr Christian Leitz.

The progress of my research in England depended on the efficient service of the Public Record Office, Kew, the libraries of the University of the West of England and of Bristol University, the Bodleian Library, Oxford, Cambridge University Library and the British Library, London. The annual conferences of the British International History Group gave my research further stimulus, and discussion of a paper I delivered in 1997 provided a valuable opportunity for refining my thoughts.

In Spain I was treated with unfailing courtesy and generosity by all whom I consulted. In particular, I thank Dª Elisa Carolina de Santos Canalejo, Director of the General Archive of the Spanish Ministry of Foreign Affairs, D. Ignacio Ruiz, Director of the Archive of the Prime Minister's Office (*Presidencia del Gobierno*) and Dª Luisa Auñón Manzanares of the Central Archive of the Ministry of Relations with Parliament and the Government Secretariat, D. Fernando Piedrafita Salgado, Director of the Fundación Universitaria Española, and Dª Isabel Balsinde, the Fundación's Librarian, and D. Aurelio Martín of the Fundación Pablo Iglesias; all in Madrid. I thank, too, Dª María Luisa Conde Villaverde, Director of the Archivo General de la Administración, Alcalá de Henares. The staff of the National Library, Madrid, were efficient and cheerful. And even though my request to consult the Fundación Francisco Franco in Madrid proved ultimately unsuccessful, it was listened to with characteristic courtesy.

I am, finally, deeply grateful to my wife, Mary, for her patient understanding during my four years' suspension of essential *tareas domésticas*.

Note

To avoid confusion, 'republican' will be used to denote all Spaniards who supported the *Frente Popular* governments against the nationalists in the Spanish Civil War, while *'republican'* will be used to denote only members of the actual *republican* parties of the Second Republic, such as *Izquierda Unida, Unión Republicana*, or the *Partido Republicano Federalista*. Accordingly, after the Civil War, the socialists and anarcho-syndicalists were part of the 'republican' opposition but not members of the *'republican'* parties.

Introduction

> Relations with Spain, in this period, have been mainly a senti-
> mental subject, hardly worth serious consideration.[1]

In the spring of 1939, as the Spanish Civil War came to its end, the British government hoped for cordial relations with the newly established regime of General Francisco Franco y Bahamonde. It had, it believed, reason to be cautiously optimistic. During the Civil War the British government had not intervened to save the Second Republic, and, on 27 February 1939, together with France, Britain had given the Franco regime *de iure* recognition. It was also assumed in London that the new Spanish administration would turn to Britain for assistance in rebuilding the country's war-torn economy.[2] In return the British government hoped for Spanish neutrality in any future European conflicts. Yet these expectations of closer Anglo-Spanish relations did not survive World War II. Neither the British public nor its governments in 1945 could easily forget that until the very last months of the war the Spanish government had provided moral and material help to Britain's enemies.[3] The uncompromising suppression of political dissent in Franco's *New Spain*, the dictatorship's signal failure to meet the 'tests of freedom' of the British Prime Minister, Winston Churchill, and, above all, the continuing identification of the regime with fascism ruled out any immediate Anglo-Spanish *rapprochement* in the aftermath of the World War.[4]

Ideally the British government wanted a liberal democratic alternative to the Franco regime, in the form of a constitutional monarchy or a parliamentary republic.[5] This preference, however, had to be balanced against the need for stability in the Iberian Peninsula. Direct action to remove Franco – whether military, economic or even diplomatic – risked, in the view of the British government, destabilising the whole Iberian Peninsula at a moment when the northern Mediterranean littoral from France to the Balkans was already unstable and a prey to communist subversion. A revolution in Spain would undoubtedly have threatened Britain's imperial lines of communication along the length of the Mediterranean. There was, too, the danger that a move against Franco would leave Gibraltar or Tangier vulnerable to Spanish retaliation. Yet, inaction also carried with it a measure of risk. A totally passive policy towards the Franco regime was likely to alienate a public opinion, both domestic and international, which was becoming increasingly hostile towards the Spanish Dictator. Were he to remain in power, moreover, it was feared that internal discontent might still eventuate in revolution in Spain and the consequent destabilisation of the rest of Western Europe. Thus, Spain at the end of World War II placed Britain's foreign policy makers in a dilemma, for whichever policy they adopted – action or inaction – the predicted outcome remained a probable breakdown of order in the Iberian Peninsula.

The British government, however, was not alone in its desire to remove Franco; there was also the Spanish anti-Franco opposition. By the end of World War II its *democratic* component was, broadly speaking, divided into two camps – republican and monarchist.[6] The republican opposition structured itself around the surviving political organisations associated with the former *Frente Popular*. In Spain and in German occupied France its efficient functioning was impeded by police repression, and so for most of the World War its effective centre had been located in Mexico. In contrast, the monarchist opposition was made up of individuals and small groups, often without formal political affiliation and tending to act independently of each other. During the World War one group had formed in Switzerland around Don Juan de Borbón y Battenberg, the exiled Pretender to the Spanish throne, while a second group of exiles established itself in Portugal. In Spain itself the monarchist opposition constituted only a small minority within the regime's larger monarchist 'family', most of whom accepted collaboration with the nominally monarchist Franco.[7] The republican and monarchist oppositions were each characterised by serious internal divisions. The fact remained, however, that if the two rival camps overcame their differences to constitute a viable alternative to the Franco regime, acceptable to the majority of Spaniards and to the Army, then it was just conceivable that Franco might relinquish power without a fight. The transition from dictatorship to liberal democracy would be accomplished peacefully, revolution avoided and Britain's dual requirement of change and stability satisfied. In short, there was a chance, albeit slim, that the democratic Spanish anti-Franco opposition could provide a solution to Britain's 'Spanish problem'.

It was, therefore, clearly in Britain's interest not to ignore the existence of this opposition. What was less clear, however, was the extent to which mutual cooperation was possible. On the one hand, any chance, however remote, of Franco's painless removal could not be lightly passed over. On the other hand, British encouragement of a disunited opposition, before it represented a credible alternative to Franco, constituted a serious intervention into Spain's internal affairs, with the concomitant risks mentioned above. For the Spanish opposition, Britain's attitude was no less important. Its policies and organisation were directly influenced by the assumptions it made about British intentions and requirements, and to a considerable extent its credibility depended upon British recognition. There were also wider implications. The Spanish historian, Javier Tusell, has suggested that the lack of effective collaboration between the wartime Allies and the Spanish opposition is a significant factor in any explanation of the Franco regime's longevity.[8] It can be argued, therefore, that the relationship between Britain and the Spanish opposition was crucial to the latter's success or failure and, ultimately, to Franco's survival in the immediate post-war period. It is this relationship that forms the subject of this study.

In general it was the Spanish opposition that provided the dynamic in relations between it and the British government. The first aim of this study is, therefore, to provide an account of the evolution of the Spanish opposition during the 1940s. Thus, Chapter 1 describes the consolidation of the republican opposition and the emergence of the monarchist opposition in the period leading up to 1945, while in the third and subsequent chapters the Spanish opposition, and Britain's reaction to it during the years 1945 to 1950, are covered in parallel accounts.

Here it is repeated that British interest focused on the *democratic* components of the Spanish opposition, since these alone had the potential to generate a liberal democratic transformation of Spain to British satisfaction. On the republican side they included the small *republican* parties, in particular *Izquierda Republicana*, *Unión Republicana* and the *Partido Republicano Federalista*, all three of which were committed to democratic principles, though divided internally between those who advocated the unconditional restoration of the Second Republic and those who accepted the establishment of a modified democratic regime sanctioned by popular vote. Included amongst the democrats were also – at first sight surprisingly – the libertarians.[9] In its early days their principal organisation, the anarcho-syndicalist *Confederación Nacional de Trabajo* (CNT) had subscribed to Mikhail Bakunin's doctrine of social revolution through workers' direct action. But by the 1940s the majority of its leadership in Spain had lifted the proscription on libertarian involvement in the political process and accepted cooperation with the non-communist opposition to bring about democracy in Spain. However, by far the most important component of the democratic republican opposition was the *Partido Socialista Obrero Español* (PSOE), the largest party of the Spanish left both during and after the Second Republic. By the end of World War II the majority of its members were reformist and strongly anti-communist, although a dissident minority often pressed for cooperation with the communists. The PSOE's influence was extended through its trade union affiliate, the *Unión General de Trabajo* (UGT), which by the 1940s was equally reformist except, again, for a minority pro-communist faction. It would be from the moderates of both these socialist organisations that the initiative would eventually come for a republican *rapprochement* with the Spanish monarchist opposition.

Given its preference for democracy and its preoccupation with stability in the Iberian Peninsula, it followed that the British government had little time for alternatives to the mainstream democratic Spanish opposition. These included, first, the *Partido Comunista de España* (PCE), which was held to be an instrument in the service of Moscow and a fomenter of social revolution.[10] Nor, for similar reasons, was British cooperation with the internal guerrilla resistance to Franco considered a practical option, despite the fact, emphasised by the British historian, Paul Preston, that until as late as 1951 it probably constituted the most serious opposition to the Franco regime.[11] There seemed little point, either, in dealing with the exiled nationalist organisations of Basques, Catalans and Galicians, whose programmes, though undoubtedly democratic, were nevertheless rejected by the rest of the Spanish republican opposition and thought likely by the British Foreign Office to lead to the break-up of the Spanish state.[12] Again, freemasonry, which Franco and his advisers were convinced lay at the heart of all opposition to his regime, is considered irrelevant in this study and its relationship with the Spanish opposition taken as coincidental rather than causative.[13]

British interest in the Spanish monarchist opposition was also conditional upon the latter's express commitment to liberal democracy. Unlike their republican counterparts, Franco's monarchist opponents were generally late converts to the democratic ideal. Under Spain's restoration monarchy of 1874 Kings Alfonso XII and XIII had colluded in a corrupt, oligarchic 'liberal' system for 57 years, until widespread discontent brought it to an end in 1931.[14] By the time of the military *coup* against the Second Republic five years later, however, even the Alfonsist monarchy was judged by many monarchists to have been excessively liberal and they looked instead to the 'traditional' Spanish monarchy of the 16th century as an alternative to republican democracy. It was not, then, frustrated *democratic* ambition which provided the incentive for the emergence of a monarchist opposition to Franco in the early 1940s. Rather, the monarchist opposition – centred on Don Juan after the death of Alfonso XIII in February 1941 – sprang from disappointment at Franco's delay in restoring the monarchy *per se*. *Juanista* conversion to democracy came only with the realisation that victory in World War II was going inevitably to the western democracies. Not until late 1945 would the British government receive a clear indication that Don Juan was fully committed to a democratic, constitutional monarchy modelled on those of Northern Europe.

One group of monarchists was never reconciled to democracy – the *Comunión Tradicionalista*. Its origins dated back to the death of King Fernando VII in 1833 when the succession of his only child, Isabel, was challenged by his brother, Carlos María Isidro de Borbón, on the pretext that the Salic Law disqualified her, as a woman, from becoming queen. However, Carlism – as Carlos Isidro's cause became known – stood for far more than dynastic rivalry and came to articulate the reaction of many Spaniards deeply opposed to the values of nineteenth-century liberalism and the modernisation of Spain. Three civil wars were fought in a vain attempt to replace the liberal monarchy with the traditional Catholic monarchy of Carlos Isidro. After its final military defeat in 1876 Carlism waned but reappeared during the Second Republic under the new name of the *Comunión Tradicionalista*. In 1936 the extinction of the Carlist line threatened the movement's dynastic survival but its reactionary ideology lived on sharing many of the ideological premises of Francoism. What little traditionalist opposition there was came from the perception that the Franco regime had betrayed those ideals which only a traditionalist restoration could guarantee.[15] Clearly, traditionalism could never satisfy Britain's insistence on a *democratic* alternative to Franco and, as with the non-democratic republican opposition, it will receive only tangential treatment in this study.

The second aim of this study is to provide an account of the British governments' reactions to the Spanish opposition as it evolved in the 1940s. Chapter 2 shows how Anglo-Spanish relations during World War II of necessity pivoted round Britain's critical dependence on Spanish neutrality and the belief that any move to replace Franco with a regime favourable to the Allies would have driven him straight into the Germans' arms or else precipitated a *Wehrmacht* invasion of the Iberian Peninsula. Consequently, until the removal of the German threat to Spain with the Liberation of France in 1944, overt cooperation with the Spanish opposition was considered at best irrelevant and at worst perilous. Only as the war-time strategic factor lost its immediacy could the terms of Britain's relationship with Spain change. It was then, after the general election of July 1945, specifically to the new Labour government of Clement Attlee and to his Foreign Secretary, Ernest Bevin, that responsibility for Britain's relations with the Spanish opposition fell for the rest of the decade.

Chapter 3 shows how in 1945 the British government had first to respond to three major developments in the Spanish opposition: the Pretender's public commitment to democracy, the re-formation in exile of the institutions of the Second Republic – notably a government-in-exile – and a republican-monarchist *rapprochement* in Spain itself. From the British perspective, however, the new Spanish republican government-in-exile seemed determined to perpetuate the divisions of the Civil War, Don Juan's democratic monarchism generated no apparent enthusiasm among monarchists in Spain, and the internal republican monarchist talks collapsed of their own accord. In 1946, as Chapter 4 makes clear, the Pretender moved from Switzerland to Portugal and, later in the year, republican-monarchist talks resumed in Spain. If this did little to change the British government's attitude towards the Spanish opposition, its complacency was nevertheless shaken by two unexpected initiatives at international level. In March the French government signalled its anti-Franco opposition by closing France's border with Spain, and the following month, at Poland's request, the 'Spanish question' came before the United Nations (UN) Security Council. Its deliberations, as will be seen, culminated in the General Assembly resolution of December 1946 recommending the withdrawal of member states' ambassadors and ministers plenipotentiary from Madrid. The prospect of a second UN resolution a year later calling for much stronger measures against Spain revived British fears for the stability of the Iberian Peninsula and of Western Europe.

For the moderate socialists of the exiled Spanish opposition, the UN December resolution was an empty gesture, proving only that reliance on international solidarity with *republican* ambitions was mistaken. So, Chapter 5 shows how the Spanish exiled socialist leadership increasingly looked to some form of republican-monarchist agreement, rather than to the republican government-in-exile, as a means of gaining international support for action against Franco. In the summer of 1947 this change of republican strategy, coinciding as it did with British preoccupation over Spain, was exploited by the British Foreign Secretary in an attempt to pre-empt UN demands for more definite action against Spain. Thus, it will be seen how in October Bevin arranged for talks in London between the two principal spokesmen of the republican and monarchist oppositions and how, in their four meetings, significant progress towards an agreement was made. As has been emphasised, however, Spanish and British commitment to the London talks was based on mutually exclusive objectives; for the Spanish participants a republican-monarchist agreement was a means of *furthering* action against the Franco regime, while for the British government it was a means of *forestalling* it. When, therefore, as Chapter 6 demonstrates, the threat of direct UN action against Spain was lifted in late 1947, the British government retreated once more to a policy of inaction. The Spanish opposition regained the initiative and, after prolonged negotiation, successfully concluded a republican-monarchist pact in August 1948. In the meantime, though, the logic of Britain's position had not been lost on the Spanish Pretender and three days before the conclusion of the pact, and unbeknown to its negotiators, Don Juan and Franco were apparently reconciled at a meeting on board the Dictator's yacht in the Bay of Biscay. Chapter 6 shows how attempts continued throughout 1949 to breathe life into the still-born republican-monarchist pact but, with the onset of the Cold War, the West's anti-Francoism finally lost what little conviction it ever had and with it went the Spanish opposition's hopes of British support. In May 1949 a UN resolution proposing the reinstatement of ambassadors to Spain only narrowly missed being carried and on 4 November 1950 the 1946 resolution was finally rescinded. Shortly afterwards Britain returned an ambassador to Madrid, by which time the Spanish opposition had ceased to count as a factor in Britain's policy towards Spain.

Studies in English of the Spanish anti-Franco opposition of the 1940s are few. One notable exception is Paul Preston's *The Anti-Fascist Opposition: the Long March to Unity*, published in 1976, which provides a good account of the political organisation and guerrilla activities of the early republican opposition, both democratic and communist. More recently, in *The Politics of Revenge: Fascism and the Military in Twentieth Century*

Spain, Preston has turned to the military's monarchist opposition of the 1940s, and this theme, along with other aspects of the Spanish opposition, reappears in his authoritative biography, *Franco*. Richard Gillespie's detailed study of the Spanish Socialist Party includes its time in opposition to Franco, and Louis Stein, David Pike and Patricia Fagen's works on the post-Civil War republican diaspora provide further accounts, albeit more incidental, of the organised republican opposition. Juan Linz's 'Opposition in and under an authoritarian regime: the case of Spain' offers a conceptual framework within which to place the 'semi-opposition' of the monarchists.[16]

Still fewer are works in English on the relationship of the British government to the Spanish opposition. Denis Smyth and Glyn Stone have both analysed British reaction to the presence in London during World War II of Juan Negrín, the last prime minister of the Second Republic, and Smyth has also described British war-time efforts to bribe Franco's generals to curb their master's pro-Axis inclinations. Stone, too, has looked at Britain's wider commitment to the restoration of democracy to Spain from 1939 to 1946. In addition, a section of Qasim Ahmad's *Britain, Franco Spain and the Cold War, 1945–1950* considers the reaction of the anti-Franco opposition to Britain's policy of non-intervention.[17] Otherwise, the British government's attitude towards the Spanish opposition has been largely ignored by historians writing in English.[18]

It is, partly, to fill this historiographical lacuna that this study aims, first, to provide a fuller account than is at present available in English of the evolution of the democratic Spanish opposition in the 1940s. To this end, recourse has been had to the comparatively extensive literature in Spanish (Castilian) on the subject. The works consulted, including memoirs and published collections of primary material, are too numerous to be mentioned individually and are listed in the bibliography. Exception must be made, however, for Hartmut Heine's *La Oposición Política al Franquismo de 1939 a 1952*, whose exhaustive coverage of the opposition, republican and monarchist, in Spain and in exile, is as yet unsurpassed, and for Javier Tusell's *La Oposición Democrática al Franquismo (1939–1962)* and *Franco y los Católicos: La Política Interior Española entre 1945–57*. A, somewhat rancorous, commentary on recent monarchist historiography is to be found in Ricardo de la Cierva's *Don Juan de Borbón: Por Fin Toda la Verdad. Las Aportaciones Definitivas*.[19] In addition, contemporary reports on the Spanish opposition, received in the British Foreign Office from embassy and consular staff in Spain and now kept at the Public Record Office, Kew, have proved useful, as has the Spanish Socialist Party's archive in Madrid, the *Fundación Pablo Iglesias*, from whose holdings of party leaders' correspondence the course of the republican-monarchist negotiations of the late 1940s can be traced.[20]

Like its Anglo-Saxon counterpart, Spanish historiography has paid only incidental attention to Britain's relations with the anti-Franco opposition. Nor do Spanish archives yield a great deal more. The *Archivo de la II República Española en el Exilio, 1945–1977*, of the *Fundación Universitaria Española*, Madrid, contains, of course, an abundance of material on the republican opposition, but since, as this study will show, the British government took little interest in the successive republican governments-in-exile, its relations with them are of relatively little account. Tantalising evidence of British contacts with Franco's opponents inside Spain is found in the *Archivo General de la Administración*, in Alcalá de Henares, just outside Madrid, and in the *Archivo de la Presidencia del Gobierno, Fondos de la Jefatura del Estado*, Moncloa, Madrid. References to these contacts, and to the activities of the 'red hotheads' (*cabecillas rojas*) in Britain, are more frequent in the diplomatic correspondence of the *Archivo del Ministerio de Asuntos Exteriores* in Madrid, where copies of the Spanish government's numerous protests against British interference in Spain's internal affairs are also to be found. Judging from the material published so far by Luis Suárez Fernández, however, more abundant evidence of British dealings with the Spanish opposition, both in and outside Spain, is likely to be found in the archives of the *Fundación Nacional Francisco Franco*, in Madrid.[21] Despite protests, however, these remain closed to unauthorised historical researchers.[22]

Consequently, most reliance in this study has been placed on British archives, particularly those of the Public Record Office, in tracing Britain's relationship with the early anti-Franco opposition. As will be shown, British policy towards Spain in general, and the Spanish opposition in particular, remained fundamentally unchanged throughout the period in question. Furthermore, from its formulation in the last weeks of 1944 until its reappraisal in September 1950, Cabinet involvement in the making of policy towards Spain was minimal. There was, for example, no Cabinet committee on Spain and relations with the Spanish opposition remained very much the preserve of the Foreign Secretary and the Foreign Office.[23] Since, except for a brief period in 1947, Bevin stuck doggedly to a policy of non-intervention, debate on the Spanish opposition was usually instigated by his officials, often at junior level, in the Western Department of the Foreign Office, as policy was reassessed to take into account the evolution of both the anti-Franco opposition and its international context. It is this shaping of attitudes rather than specific changes in policy implementation that has been examined through British archival material.

1
Spanish Opposition before 1945

Republican opposition

The Spanish Second Republic succeeded the discredited monarchy of Alfonso XIII in 1931. There followed five troubled years, during which reforming and counter-reforming republican governments alternated, until a centre-left coalition – the *Frente Popular* – won a narrow electoral majority in February 1936. To an alarmed Spanish Right this victory seemed but the prelude to social revolution. Their response was the military rebellion of July 1936, which by October had come under the overall command of General Francisco Franco y Bahamonde, thenceforth Head of State of Nationalist Spain. It was, thus, in its defence of the Second Republic that republican opposition to Franco was born.[1] Nor was it extinguished by the military defeat of March 1939. For, far from seeking reconciliation with his former enemies, Franco in victory was determined to eliminate all vestiges of the Republic from his *New Spain*. Militant republicans therefore suffered persecution or fled into exile. And yet, from this collective disaster a new republican unity was not forged. In the five years following the defeat of 1939 the divisions of the *Frente Popular* lost none of their virulence, and the republicans failed to establish a credible focus for an anti-Franco opposition which could serve as a point of reference for Spaniards and foreign governments alike.

In explaining republican disunity, there is first the fact of defeat and its aftermath to be taken into account. The former *Frente Popular* bloc in Spain was left in disarray as most of its leadership fled the country, and its widespread dispersion compounded the difficulties of concerted action and consultation in exile.[2] After 1939, moreover, the unity and effectiveness of party organisations were seriously compromised by the replication of executive committees in and outside Spain. For those ordinary members of the Second Republic's organisations who did remain in Spain there was, too, the sheer struggle for survival in the face of daily repression on an unprecedented scale. On the other hand, many of those who sought refuge in France, or French territory, fared little better, surviving initial internment and forced labour only to suffer persecution under Vichy or the German Occupation.[3]

To these formidable geographic and physical obstacles were added political and ideological divisions inherited from the Civil War and before. Antagonism between the communists and the other *Frente Popular* parties was an immediate stumbling block.[4] An uncompromising anti-communist stance was adopted by the moderates of the *republican* parties, by the anarcho-syndicalist MLE and by a significant section of the PSOE. Yet, differences with the PCE did not automatically ensure cooperation between the non-communists. The desirability of collaboration with other political organisations was constantly debated within the libertarian movement, while the adamant refusal of many *republicans* to admit any alternative to the 1931 Constitution came up against the pragmatism of a section of the PSOE and, again, of the libertarians. Initially, though, tensions focused on the Second Republic's last prime minister, Juan Negrín López.[5]

The disruptive potential of the rivalry between *negrinistas* and anti-*negrinistas* was demonstrated even before the final collapse of the Second Republic. On 1 February 1939 the rump *Cortes* (Spain's legislative assembly) of the Second Republic met for the last time on Spanish soil in the castle of Figueras, a few miles from the French border. Five days later the surviving republican deputies dispersed in flight to France. With them went the President of the Republic, Manuel Azaña y Díaz, and the President of the *Cortes*, Diego Martínez Barrio, together with Negrín, who accompanied Azaña as far as the first French village before returning temporarily to Spain.[6] On 27 February, the day Britain and France recognised the Franco government, Azaña resigned as President of the Republic. Under the 1931 Constitution the President of the *Cortes* should then have assumed the temporary office of President of the Republic, but, at the first session in exile of the *Diputación Permanente de Cortes* (Standing Committee of the *Cortes*) in Paris on 3 March, Martínez Barrio refused to do this unless Negrín agreed to an immediate end to the Civil War. When this assurance was not given, the office of President of the Republic was left vacant.[7]

Leaving aside the constitutional challenge to Negrín's government arising out of Colonel Segismundo Casado López's anti-communist military *coup* in Madrid of 4 March, Negrín's opponents were quick to exploit the anomaly of a sitting government answerable to neither *Cortes* nor President of the Republic.[8] In the circumstances, they argued, the *Diputación Permanente* enjoyed constitutional precedence over the Council of Ministers, and this automatically entailed the resignation of Negrín's government. Not surprisingly, Negrín disagreed. At the end of March an uneasy compromise was reached, with Negrín's government recognised as the legitimate representative of republican legality in exile, though answerable to the *Diputación Permanente*. But, on 26 July 1939, the *Diputación Permanente* finally declared itself to be the 'sole indisputable institution remaining of our constitutional structure', and thus denied the Negrín government its constitutionality.[9] With good will, an amicable solution to the constitutional crisis might have been found. As it was, the situation had been exploited for political ad-vantage and signified, as the far from pro-*negrinista* Spanish historian, Salvador de Madariaga, later pointed out, the 'end of the Spanish Revolutionary Government as a juridical and political entity'.[10]

Prominent amongst Negrín's opponents was his fellow socialist, Indale-cio Prieto y Tuero.[11] Prieto had been appointed Minister of Defence in Negrín's government in May 1937 but the two men soon fell out over the prosecution of the Civil War. The consequent strained relations between them led Negrín to relieve Prieto of his post in April 1938. Although not at first an acrimonious separation, by the spring of 1939 the gap that opened up between them had become unbridgeable. In exile Negrín's determination to remain true to the institutions of the Second Republic was matched only by Prieto's determined search for alternatives. Early support for Prieto came from the moderate wings of the *republican* and Catalan nationalist parties, while Negrín's backers included left-wing *republicans* and Catalan nationalists, and – intermit-tently – the PCE. The libertarians and Basque nationalists tended to remain aloof.[12] It was, though, the relative strengths of the rival camps within the PSOE that mattered most, for, given the pivotal position of the PSOE within the former *Frente Popular* bloc, through its capacity for alliances to its left or right, the repercussions of this *prietista-negrinista* rivalry seriously affected the course of republican unity.

In exile in Mexico Prieto was able to strengthen his position by gaining control of a sizeable portion of the Second Republic's remain-ing assets, estimated at between $40 and $50 million, which had arrived at Vera Cruz in March 1939 in the hold of a yacht chartered by the Negrín government.[13] Bolstered by these funds, Prieto extended his influence over the local PSOE, until, by January 1940, a distinct *prietista* group had emerged. The *prietistas* were thus well placed to exploit the unexpected transfer of exiled republican political life to Mexico after the Fall of France in 1940. Indeed, in October they formed their own PSOE executive committee, which was then challenged by the *negrinistas* of the original executive committee in France. As a result two PSOE executive committees coexisted uneasily in Mexico during most of World War II.[14]

Apart from a short trip to New York, Negrín remained in France until forced to flee to Britain on 24 June 1940. There he founded the *Hogar Español* in October 1941 as a forum for all republican groups and later the *Instituto Español* and the *Fundación Luis Vives*. These politico-cultural initiatives notwithstanding, Negrín's scope for political activity was severely circumscribed by a British government wary of the propaganda value to Franco of his presence in London. Besides his physical distance from the main centre of exiled republican activity in Mexico, Negrín's political isolation also owed much to his insistence on the exclusive claim of his government to republican legality in exile. Given his determination not to weaken this constitutional position, Negrín was understandably reluctant to associate himself with any attempts to rebuild republican unity on an alternative basis.[15]

None the less, tentative steps were taken to re-establish republican unity in exile. In October 1940 a *republican* initiative led to the creation of *Acción Republicana Española* (ARE). Although it managed to achieve a degree of *republican*-socialist collaboration, its political base proved too narrow for it to serve as the nucleus of a broader republican front.[16] More successful, to begin with at least, was a bid by the exiled PCE to create a 'united front' of the Spanish Left. Having recognised Negrín's government as the sole legitimate executive power of the exiled Republic in August 1941, the PCE received the backing of *negrinista* socialists and *republicans* and formed the Mexican based *Unión Democrática Española* (UDE) in March 1942.[17] By September, however, fears of a Franco alliance with the Axis Powers had persuaded the PCE of the need for a broader Spanish government of national unity, which support for Negrín and the Second Republic was now seen as preventing. *Republicans* and *negrinistas* therefore withdrew from the UDE and it collapsed in January 1943. Having forfeited *negrinista* support, and with no hope of enticing the anti-communist *prietistas* to join them, the PCE was subsequently unable to gain any significant non-communist adherence to the UDE's successor in France – the *Unión Nacional Española* (UNE) – which the PCE had set up in November 1942 as an alternative basis for its projected government of national unity.[18]

Even so, the formation of the UNE alarmed the moderate democrats of the exiled republican opposition. As expectations of Axis defeat grew, after the allied landings in French North Africa in November 1942, they feared that any commitment by the Allies to the eventual overthrow of Franco could be compromised if the republican opposition were seen to be too closely identified with the communists. Consequently, in the autumn of 1943 a small group of exiled Catalan nationalists in Mexico initiated a round of inter-party negotiations. The collaboration of the *prietista* socialists proved decisive and on 25 November 1943, together with the Catalan parties, *Esquerra Republicana de Catalunya* and *Acció Catalana Republicana*, and the *republicans* of *Izquierda Republicana* and *Unión Republicana*, they signed a pact establishing the *Junta Española de Liberación* (JEL).[19] The JEL's founding manifesto of 23 December was clearly intended to advertise the democratic credentials of the republican opposition to the western democracies. It stressed adherence to the Atlantic Charter and to the cause of the United Nations and, by offering a 'moderate' democratic alternative to Negrín's discredited government, it sought to remove the communist stigma attached to the Second Republic as well as to pre-empt any move towards a monarchist restoration in Spain by the Allies.[20]

Even so, the JEL's apparent unity masked a serious *republican*-socialist division. Martínez Barrio, President of the JEL, and the *republicans* remained firmly committed to the 1931 Constitution. Against them, Prieto, the JEL's Secretary, held that this would achieve little except alienate the democracies and perpetuate the hatreds of the Civil War. As an alternative he proposed, in a speech in Havana, Cuba, on 11 July 1942, that a plebiscite should be held in Spain, supervised by the countries of Spanish America, to decide the future of the Spanish state.[21] By maintaining 'the most absolute fidelity' to the principles of the 1931 Constitution, until Spain, 'in the full exercise of her sovereign powers', decided to reform them, the JEL Christmas Manifesto attempted a compromise. But Prieto continued to press for his plebiscitary option, until it was finally accepted in September 1944 by all the JEL parties except *Izquierda Republicana*. Towards the end of the year, however, Martínez Barrio and the *republicans* were convinced that with German defeat now inevitable circumstances at last favoured the restoration of the Second Republic. *Prietista* obstructiveness, when the exiled republican *Cortes* was reconvened in January 1945 (see Chapter 3), brought things to a head and Martínez Barrio resigned from the presidency of the JEL on 1 February 1945.[22] With that the JEL lost whatever effectiveness it had had as a forum for republican unity and anti-Franco opposition.[23]

In the meantime, Prieto's authority, together with the JEL's, had been weakened by the resumption of Spanish republican political activity in 1944, first in liberated French North Africa and then in metropolitan France itself. This was signalled by the decision of the first PSOE Congress in exile in Toulouse of 24–25 September to rename itself the *Partido Socialista Obrero Español en Francia y su Imperio* (PSOE-in-France). The purpose of this change was to enhance the authority of the PSOE in Spain over *all* exiled PSOE organisations, and thereby weaken the *prietista* pretensions to PSOE leadership. The affirmation of Congress support for the Second Republic's 1931 Constitution further isolated the *prietistas*.[24]

Brief mention must be made of one other attempt towards the end of 1944 to unify the exiled anti-Franco opposition: by Miguel Maura, former leader of the *Partido Republicano Conservador* and Minister of the Interior in the Second Republic's first provisional government. Hoping to create an opposition front extending from republicans to monarchists, Maura had begun, very much on his own initiative, sounding out different political groups. What little interest his project might have received was forfeited, however, in December by his inept press statement claiming the support of almost the entire republican opposition. The subsequent flurry of *démentis* lost him all credibility and, although he persisted with his initiative well into 1945, it was not taken seriously by either the republican opposition or the British and French governments.[25]

During the German occupation of France a significant minority of the Spanish republican opposition had fought alongside the French Resistance.[26] With the gradual liberation of French territory in 1944 a force of some 12000–15000 Spanish guerrilla fighters, 5000 of whom were concentrated just north of the Pyrenees, thus became available for action against the Franco regime. So, in the third week of September, there began, largely under PCE direction, a number of small-scale incursions into Spanish territory until, on 18 October, an estimated 2500–3000 guerrilla fighters entered Spain in what became known as the 'invasion of the Val d'Arán'. Contrary to the guerrilla leaders' expectations, however, the local population did not rebel and vigorous counteraction by Franco's *Guardia Civil* halted the advance in two days. The 'invasion' thus amounted to little more than a quixotic skirmish, albeit at heavy human cost. In political terms, moreover, it proved an irrelevance and scarcely affected efforts elsewhere to establish a united anti-Franco opposition.[27]

In fact, although guerrilla action against the Franco regime was sustained over wide areas of Spain until the early 1950s, it did not, whatever its military impact, contribute significantly to the consolidation of a broad anti-Franco opposition front. The mainly communist-dominated guerrilla groups failed to achieve the political integration previously obtained by the French and Italian Resistance movements and so, unable to mobilise local populations, who lived in constant fear of reprisals from Franco's forces, the guerrilla fighters were gradually reduced to banditry. In the final analysis, though, it was the reluctance of the non-communist republican opposition leadership to sanction violence as a means of removing Franco that marginalised the guerrilla struggle and correspondingly enhanced the political alternative.[28]

For the republican political opposition in Spain itself the obstacles to establishing a united and effective political anti-Franco opposition were formidable and, not surprisingly, progress towards rebuilding party organisations was slow and hazardous. Once again, though, it was the PCE that attempted to lead the way with the formation of its *Junta Suprema de la Unión Nacional Española* (JSUNE) in Spain in September 1943. Most observers at the time, however, considered this to be little more than a phantom organisation, and it subsequently played no part in moves to establish republican unity.[29] Yet, the effect of the JSUNE's creation was to spur the CNT in Spain into seeking cooperation with the rest of the non-communist republican opposition. Accordingly, in the autumn of 1943, a libertarian, Juan José Luque Argente, was instructed to open talks with the PSOE. The *republicans* of the *Comité Nacional Republicano* were soon brought in and the tripartite negotiations culminated in June 1944 in the creation of the *Alianza Nacional de Fuerzas Democráticas* (ANFD). Luque was appointed the ANFD National Council's first General Secretary.[30]

The ANFD's founding manifesto of June 1944 – not published until October – stressed, like the JEL before it, its democratic credentials. Once a provisional government had re-established political freedoms in Spain, it would hold elections and submit the record of its time in office for approval by the *Cortes*. This body would then decide the future of the country, a secret clause in the ANFD agreement having declared the 1931 Constitution invalid. The manifesto ruled out a violent reversal of the regime by either *guerrilleros* or the Allies but, in a bid for the latter's support, it stressed the commitment of an eventual post-Franco government to the Atlantic Charter, good neighbourliness and the collective organisation of peace.[31]

Disappointingly, though, the support of the Allies was not forthcoming. This, and the failure to secure the adherence of the communists and of the Basque and Catalan nationalists, was an evident weakness, while the ANFD's pragmatic position on the 1931 Constitution promised conflict at some later date with the exiled *republicans* and *negrinistas*. Without wider support it was difficult to see how the ANFD could constitute an effective anti-Franco force and so, denied an opening to the left, it therefore looked to the right: to the monarchist opposition. Again the impetus came from the libertarians, a number of whom were disillusioned with republicanism, and contact was soon established with several members of the Spanish Right in Madrid, including two monarchist generals, Alfredo Kindelán y Duany and Antonio Aranda Mata, and with José María Gil-Robles y Quiñones in exile in Portugal. By mid-November 1944 ANFD libertarians and *republicans* had reached a fair measure of agreement with the monarchists on the need to exclude the communists from further negotiations, secure the cooperation of the socialists and encourage Anglo-American intervention; for the moment, though, the question of a monarchy or republic was left in abeyance. Unfortunately, as a result of the infiltration of the ANFD by a government agent, there were widespread arrests in December and the talks stalled.[32]

Taking into account the professed anti-monarchism of the December 1943 JEL manifesto and the anti-republican sentiments of the Pretender to the Spanish throne, the ANFD initiative was a bold step forward in the search for anti-Franco unity. Whether the monarchist response to the ANFD's overtures pointed to the existence of a monarchist anti-Franco opposition of any consequence is looked at next.

Monarchist opposition

The monarchy had been restored to Spain under the Constitution of 1876 essentially to preserve the gains of Spanish 19th century liberalism within an established conservative order. It was its subsequent inability to fulfil this function that led, almost half a century later, to its downfall. By 1923 social and regional discontent, exacerbated by the persistent failure of successive restoration governments to undertake any fundamental reform of Spain's archaic social and economic structures, had reached such a pitch that recourse to dictatorship seemed the only way of safeguarding Spain's social order. However, through his collusion in this violation of the 1876 Constitution, Alfonso XIII inevitably tied the fortunes of the Spanish monarchy to the personal success of General Miguel Primo de Rivera. When the latter's dictatorship collapsed in 1930, the ensuing crisis left the King isolated. Attacked from the left and undefended on the right, Alfonso unwisely chose to treat Spain's municipal elections of April 1931 as a plebiscite on the monarchy. When early voting returns confirmed the strength of anti-monarchist feeling in Spain's major towns and cities, he admitted defeat and fled the country.[33]

At a loss for a viable authoritarian alternative to the Republic, after the failure of Primo de Rivera's dictatorship, the traditional upholders of the monarchy could do little in 1931 but acquiesce in its temporary eclipse. As was to be expected, however, monarchist tolerance of the reforming governments of the Second Republic was short-lived. While only a minority – the 'insurrectionary Alfonsists' – actively conspired and propagandised against the Republic, such was the fear of social revolution engendered by the *Frente Popular* that monarchist support for the military rebellion of July 1936 was – regardless of dynastic allegiance – almost universal.[34]

Monarchist participation in the reactionary coalition of July 1936 arose, then, out of a confident expectation that the military insurrection would lead to the restoration of the monarchy. There was confidence, too, in Franco, whose elevation in September 1936 to *generalísimo* was due in part to the belief of at least two generals on the rebel *Junta de Defensa Nacional*, Kindelán and Luis Orgaz Yoldi, that he was firmly committed to the monarchy. Franco, though, was careful never to specify the time and nature of any monarchist restoration for his *New Spain*. During the Civil War he stalled by pointing to the pressures of command and, after victory, to the demands of establishing the new regime. Nevertheless, he could ill afford to alienate the monarchists, who constituted an important element in the balance of political forces supporting him, and so he temporised. His studied vagueness inevitably frustrated a number of monarchists who looked to a rapid restoration of the monarchy, and it was from this group that a monarchist opposition would eventually emerge both in Spain and in exile.

And yet, this monarchist opposition, even at its height, formed only a small and often ill-defined minority within the regime's larger monarchist 'family'. Clearly, the goal of restoring the monarchy to Spain was shared by all monarchists. However, the principal difference that arose between the monarchist opposition and the rest of the monarchist 'family' was over the role each side assigned Franco. For Franco's monarchist collaborators – the *franquista* monarchists – the restoration was to be effected 'neither without Franco, nor against him'.[35] They saw the monarchy as complementing and completing the Francoist system. For the monarchist opposition, on the other hand, the Spanish monarchy could not be identified with one side only – albeit the winning one – of the Civil War without abandoning its aspiration to reconcile the whole of the Spanish nation. For them the Spanish monarchy constituted an alternative to, and not a continuation of, the Franco regime. Thus, while the *franquista* monarchists saw Franco as the instrument of an eventual restoration, the monarchist opposition saw him as an obstacle to it.

Unlike the republican opposition, which was structured round the political organisations inherited from the Second Republic, the monarchist opposition consisted mostly of individuals and informal groups, often acting independently of each other. Nor was the composition of these groups necessarily homogeneous: the coexistence of opposition and *franquista* monarchists within the same groups was not uncommon. Numerically, moreover, the monarchist opposition was insignificant. Its handful of exiles hardly compared in number with the republican diaspora, while within Spain itself even the majority *franquista* monarchists were generally confined to a small social and political *élite*. But it was precisely its membership of this *élite* that enabled the monarchist opposition to exercise an influence out of all proportion to its size, for, unlike the republican opposition in whose rejection the Spanish Right closed ranks behind Franco, the monarchist opposition did have the potential to provide an ideological and constitutional alternative to the Franco regime which was acceptable to the Right.

The influence of this monarchist *élite* was felt particularly strongly in the Army, the mainstay of the Franco dictatorship.[36] But even here active monarchist opposition only ever came from a handful of senior officers. An early attempt to extend this opposition was made by

Eugenio Vegas Latapié, a founder member of the reactionary monarchist society, *Acción Española*.[37] At first a supporter of Franco, who appointed him General Secretary for Press and Propaganda in April 1937, Vegas had quickly resigned out of frustration with Franco's dilatoriness over the monarchy and, after the Civil War, began working against the new regime. Thus, in 1942 he tried to set up a number of secret pro-monarchist committees to win over sympathetic but uncommitted officers for a monarchist *coup* against Franco. His monarchist propagandising was cut short when his conspiring came to light and, in June 1942, he fled to Portugal and from there to Switzerland, where he was appointed head of Don Juan's Political Secretariat.[38]

Another member of *Acción Española*, the distinguished academic, Pedro Sainz Rodríguez, had been appointed Minister of Education in Franco's first Council of Ministers in January 1938. He, too, soon became disillusioned with Franco and was relieved of this post in April 1939 after describing him as a 'boarding-house Bonaparte'. Sainz Rodríguez shared Vegas' conviction that a restoration of the monarchy depended above all on winning over the Army and so, in the autumn of 1941, he began conspiring with a number of monarchist generals to remove Franco (see below). When, in June 1942, his subversive activities were discovered, he, too, was obliged to flee Spain and took up residence in Portugal.[39]

Sainz Rodríguez and Vegas' hopes of turning military discontent to the advantage of the monarchist cause had not been entirely misplaced, for criticism of Franco by his senior generals, especially in the first three years of World War II, was not uncommon. Until the autumn of 1942 there was considerable resentment at the extent of falangist influence in the new regime and alarm at Franco's pro-Axis foreign policy. Consequently, in October 1941, a group of senior generals, headed by the monarchists, Aranda and Kindelán, in conjunction with the civilians Vegas, Sainz Rodríguez and Gil-Robles, plotted for the replacement of Franco, in the event of a German invasion of Spain, by a joint military-civilian provisional *junta*; if the Germans went on to occupy the whole of Spain, it was planned that the generals on the *junta* would transfer to Spanish Morocco while the civilians would go to the Canaries, which Britain would then be invited to occupy. Within a few weeks, however, the monarchists substituted the plan for a *junta* with one for a regency of three generals, under whom it was envisaged that Aranda would form a military-civilian government. As the original anti-German thrust of the conspiracy became subordinated to an anti-Franco monarchist plot, it lost much of its earlier support from other senior officers. In any case, as a German invasion never occurred, the planned *coup* became redundant.[40]

After the replacement of Franco's brother-in-law, the pro-Axis Ramón Serrano Suñer, as Minister of Foreign Affairs by the monarchist sympathiser, General Francisco Gómez Jordana y Souza, in September 1942, military discontent with Franco abated, until the allied landings in French North Africa two months later. The Pretender to the Spanish throne, Don Juan, then called upon Franco to return to a policy of strict neutrality. General Kindelán followed this up with an outspoken speech criticising the immorality and 'profound discontent' of the Franco regime, after which he was removed from his post as Captain-General of Spain's IV Military Region.[41]

The following summer first General Orgaz, High Commissioner of Spanish Morocco, informed Sainz Rodríguez in Portugal of his readiness to rise against Franco, and then General Aranda, who had been replaced as Director of the Army's War School (*Escuela Superior*) by Kindelán in December 1942, proposed yet again a joint military-civilian government, but this time under a regency council along the lines of the Badoglio government recently formed in Italy. Franco's close adviser, Luis Carrero Blanco – appointed Under-Secretary of the Presidency in May 1941 – was sufficiently alarmed by all this to instruct the three Armed Forces Ministers to take the monarchist conspiracies seriously. His fears, though, proved groundless. In a letter to Gil-Robles in September, Orgaz himself had to admit that the bulk of the officer corps remained loyal to Franco and that support for his projected *coup* was not forthcoming.[42]

In fact, the furthest the monarchist generals were prepared to go in the autumn of 1943 was to send a collective letter to Franco on 15 September. This, though, amounted to no more than a mildly worded petition which respectfully asked him to consider whether the time had not yet come to grant Spain a monarchy. Franco easily dealt with the challenge, interviewing the generals individually and alternately cajoling and threatening them into submission.[43] In fact, the letter was the last serious monarchist challenge to Franco from his generals. As Germany's military defeat came closer, apprehension over Franco's pro-Axis sympathies was replaced by uncertainty over the Allies' plans for Spain and the alarming possibility of a republican restoration. Finally, the effect of the 'red invasion' of the Val d'Arán in October 1944 was to dissuade almost all Franco's senior generals from further serious moves to destabilise his regime, and they closed ranks behind their *Caudillo*.

The key figure of the exiled monarchist opposition after the death of Alfonso XIII in February 1941 was, of course, the exiled Pretender to the Spanish throne, Don Juan. The fourth of Alfonso XIII's five children and his third son, Don Juan was named heir to the Spanish throne in 1933 after his two elder brothers, Don Alfonso and Don Jaime, renounced their claims, the former following his morganatic marriage to a Cuban heiress and the latter because of a physical disability. Until 1946 Don Juan – who was also given the title of the Count of Barcelona – lived in a villa on the outskirts of Lausanne after moving from Italy to Switzerland in 1942.[44]

The Pretender's attitude towards the Franco regime was obviously crucial to the emergence of a credible monarchist opposition, and his advisers frequently pressed him to define his position in some form of public declaration or manifesto. However, Don Juan needed to move cautiously. A direct call for a monarchist *coup* against Franco, with its attendant risk of civil war, was out of the question. In the immediate post-Civil War period commitment in Spain to a *juanista* restoration was difficult to gauge and Franco's intentions were in any case obscure. In the early years of World War II, moreover, the British government, though warning Don Juan against accepting Axis support, made no move itself to assist in the restoration of the Spanish monarchy. So, it seemed to Don Juan at first that a policy of monarchist collaboration with Franco was the only feasible option.

Soon, however, the allied landings in French North Africa of November 1942 exposed the vulnerability of the Franco regime and improved Don Juan's bargaining position. In a series of letters and telegrams exchanged over the next fourteen months, the Pretender gradually distanced himself from Franco.[45] This move from collaboration to opposition was initiated on 11 November 1942 with a statement published in *Le Journal de Genève* – the so-called Geneva Manifesto – in which the Pretender disassociated himself completely from Franco's pro-Axis foreign policy and demanded instead a policy of 'absolute neutrality'.[46] It culminated in a long letter of 14 February 1944 to Don Alfonso de Orleans y Borbón, Don Juan's uncle and, since the previous June, his official representative in Spain, in which Don Juan argued that Franco's refusal to modify his foreign policy towards the Allies and to return to strict neutrality had left him no choice but to make his opposition to Franco public.[47]

It would be a mistake, however, to assume that under Don Juan's leadership the emergent monarchist opposition constituted, from its start, a *democratic* challenge to the Franco regime.[48] In his first political dec-

laration of 11 October 1935 the young Prince had unreservedly identified himself with *Acción Española*'s 'crusade' against the Second Republic and, in July 1936, while Alfonso XIII was appealing to Benito
Mussolini and Pope Pius XI on behalf of the rebels, Don Juan had had
himself smuggled into Spain to fight for the nationalist cause. Franco's
military successes in the Civil War prompted a series of congratulatory
telegrams from father and son alike. In October 1936 Don Juan condemned the Second Republic as the 'culmination of a process of nega-
tion of the Spanish spirit', and on the first anniversary of his father's
death, he spoke of opposing the 'red revolution, with a militant racial
policy, imbued with the Christian spirit'.[49]

Don Juan believed that the ideals of the *National Crusade* were embodied in the 'Traditional Catholic Monarchy', which, in spite of its glaring
illiberalism, he nevertheless held to be essentially moderate. In his view,
the Franco regime represented one extreme – totalitarianism – with
no greater claim to legitimacy than the other extreme – anarchism. It
followed that the monarchy, by holding true to the ideals which had
inspired the 1936 rebellion, occupied the middle ground between the
two! Against this Franco maintained that the monarchy Don Juan
represented was deeply flawed. For him the authentic traditional
monarchy was that of the medieval *reyes católicos*, and of Charles I and
Philip II. The Alfonsist monarchy, by contrast, had forfeited its traditional rights by turning 'liberal' and, as such, it had contributed in no
small measure to the spread of marxism in Spain. Spain's decadence, for
which the Alfonsist monarchy shared responsibility, could only be
remedied, Franco maintained, by the revolution he was then carrying
through.[50]

Yet, Franco never intended the total abolition of the monarchy. In his
scheme of things, it did have a role to play in his *New Spain* and was
intended to be the crowning piece on his work of national regenera-
tion, the completion of his 'national revolution'. In a statement to the
Argentinian newspaper, *La Prensa*, of 28 January 1944, however, Don
Juan insisted that the monarchy was *not* 'the crowning or final touch
to the structure created by the present regime'.[51] This, then, was the
issue that defined monarchist opposition to Franco and, on 25 January
1944, the Pretender unambiguously stated his position:

> The information which I have received from extensive and authen-
> tic national sources increases the divergence between our respective

visions of the international situation and over the repercussions which world events may have on our internal policies. Your Excellency is one of the very few Spaniards left who believe in the stability of the national-syndicalist regime and in the identification of the people with a regime, under which our still unreconciled Nation is supposed to find strength enough to resist the attacks of extremists at the end of the world war; all of which Your Excellency will supposedly achieve through adjustments and concessions to those Nations which may well feel ill disposed to the policy followed so far towards them.

This way of judging the present and the future is totally opposed to mine and, therefore, our attitudes cannot be reconciled. I am convinced that Your Excellency and the regime you embody cannot survive the end of the war, and that, if the Monarchy is not restored beforehand, you will be destroyed by the defeated of the Civil War, who will take advantage of the new international situation, which with every passing day comes out more strongly against the totalitarian regime which Your Excellency fashioned and established.[52]

Franco was unmoved, replying on 7 February that he would not relinquish power and that he placed full responsibility for any delay in restoring the traditional monarchy on Don Juan's shoulders alone. A week later, as already mentioned, Don Juan sent a long explanatory letter to Don Alfonso de Orleans, which was passed on to Franco: Don Juan could not, he said, 'commune' with the principles of the *Falange*.[53] There would be no further exchanges of political correspondence between Franco and Don Juan until after the Lausanne Manifesto of March 1945.

To an extent Don Juan's opposition to Franco was influenced by advice he received from José María Gil-Robles in exile in Portugal, whom he would appoint his official representative outside Spain in February 1944. This former leader of the right-wing clericalist *Confederación Española de Derechas Autónomas* (CEDA) had left Spain with his family in February 1936 and by the beginning of 1937 was living in Portugal.[54] In July 1942 he met the newly exiled Sainz Rodríguez in Lisbon and from October was joining him there in conversations with the British Ambassador to Spain, Sir Samuel Hoare. But although privately convinced by then of the need for a monarchist restoration, it was not until the following May that he declared to *La Prensa* that it was the 'sacred duty' of all those having some influence on public opinion in Spain to support the monarchy. This was followed by a letter to Aranda in December in which he formally declared himself a monarchist and pledged the 'mass of opinion which formerly supported my party to the service of the Monarchist cause . . .'[55]

Gil-Robles' vision of monarchy, though deeply conservative, avoided both the narrow traditionalism of *Acción Española* and the expedient *coup* strategy of the monarchist generals.[56] He persuaded Don Juan that the role of the monarchy was not simply to substitute Franco as protector of the Spanish Right. There was, instead, a need for a radical departure from the policies of reprisal pursued by the Dictator, since these would never bring peace to Spain, and only the monarchy could act as a force for reconciliation. In this way Gil-Robles held out the possibility of a change of regime and an end to the divisions of the Civil War, but without the threat of social revolution so feared by the Spanish Right.

Despite Gil-Robles' urging, however, the Pretender's break with Franco in January 1944 was not as final as first appeared. The simultaneous imposition of Anglo-American oil sanctions on Spain was an unfortunate coincidence obliging Don Juan to counter Franco-inspired stories that he was merely a tool of foreign interests. So, almost immediately after his statement to *La Prensa*, in a telegram of 3 February 1944, Don Juan confirmed his break with Franco but at the same time appealed for an agreement with him. In April he indicated to General Juan Vigón, Franco's Air Minister, his willingness to meet Franco, a call which he repeated in October. In March, moreover, he noticeably failed to support 50 Spanish university professors sanctioned by Franco for signing a letter, widely circulated in Madrid, expressing loyalty to the Pretender. Thus, for most of 1944, the monarchist cause seemed to flounder, causing Don Juan himself, in a letter of 23 September to Gil-Robles, to lament its 'basic lack of unity of direction, its permanent contradiction in aims and absolute sterility of action'.[57]

Conclusion

For the Spanish anti-Franco opposition, both monarchist and republican, doubts over German invincibility in the Second World War had been growing since the winter of 1942 until the Normandy Landings of June 1944 bore out their initial scepticism. During this period the opposition became convinced that in the post-war order there would be no place for Franco's anomalous regime. The Dictator would depart under allied pressure, so they thought, and from the ranks of the anti-Franco opposition, some would be called upon by the Allies to form the government of a new Spain. But the worrying question was – who?

Republicans and monarchists were both apprehensive that the other side could be chosen: hence their mutual eagerness to jettison whatever ideological baggage they believed compromised them in the eyes of the western democracies. A significant part of the non-communist republican opposition sought to erase the communist stigma attached to the Second Republic: hence the move to disqualify the Negrín government in February 1939 and then the formation of the JEL in Mexico and the ANFD in Spain as alternatives to the communist initiatives. In similar fashion, the Pretender to the Spanish throne tried to distance the monarchist cause from Franco, whose falangism he condemned as a fascist distortion of the original noble ideals of the National Rising.

And yet attempts to create a unified non-communist anti-Franco opposition had only limited success. By the end of 1944 it exhibited a bewildering complexity to the outside observer. On the republican side – a politically irrelevant guerrilla war within Spain and a recently defeated guerrilla force north of the Pyrenees; the leadership of the non-communist *Frente Popular* organisations scattered in France, Mexico and Britain, and the communist leadership in the USSR; reconstituted party organisations in France, Spain and North Africa, and sister, but rival, organisations in Mexico and Britain; three surviving 'united front' organisations – the communist UNE, the *prietista* socialist-*republican* JEL and the libertarian-socialist-*republican* ANFD. On the monarchist side, there was an exiled monarchist circle round the Pretender in Switzerland and another in Portugal, both by 1944 opposed to the Franco regime but not necessarily in full agreement with the small monarchist opposition inside Spain itself. With a few notable exceptions, the monarchist generals, who had plotted intermittently from 1941 to 1943, seemed reconciled to the Franco regime. Indeed, opposition to Franco from the majority of monarchists in Spain was either questionable or non-existent. It was, then, this broad array of opposition alternatives that presented itself to British foreign policy makers when in 1944 they turned to the 'problem of Spain'.

2
Britain and the Spanish Opposition until 1944

In August 1944 the German *Wehrmacht* began its withdrawal from the French Pyrenees. As its retreat gathered pace and the German military threat to the Iberian Peninsula receded, Spain's neutrality in World War II counted for correspondingly less in the Allies' strategic calculations.[1] The advantage in Anglo-Spanish relations, which hitherto had lain with General Franco, now passed to Britain, and the appropriateness of maintaining a conciliatory policy towards falangist Spain in post-war Europe could be reconsidered by the British government. The change in tone in Anglo-Spanish relations in 1940–44 and whether this change was matched by a similar modification in Britain's attitude towards the Spanish anti-Franco opposition are considered in this chapter.

Until the summer of 1944 the overriding aim of Britain's policy towards Spain had been the securing of Spanish neutrality in the World War.[2] In July 1941, Anthony Eden, the Foreign Secretary, reminded the War Cabinet of the basic reasons for this policy: Gibraltar's use as a naval base and as a staging point for the delivery of aircraft to the Middle East was wholly dependent on the maintenance of Spanish neutrality; any quarrel with Spain was likely to complicate Anglo-Portuguese relations and jeopardise Britain's air communications through Lisbon; Spain was an important supplier of essential foodstuffs and raw-materials – especially high grade iron-ore – and the short sea haul to Britain saved on shipping. Eden's conclusion, which held true until the Liberation of France in 1944, was that any deterioration in Anglo-Spanish relations, short of war, would benefit only Germany.[3]

It was, therefore, important for Britain to avoid unnecessary confrontation with Franco. Indeed, despite occasional diplomatic protests and financial and economic sanctions to curb the Dictator's pro-Axis sympathies, the tone of Anglo-Spanish relations, at least on the British side, was remarkably cordial for most of World War II. Even the oil embargo imposed on Spain, mainly at American insistence, from January to May 1944 to curtail deliveries of Spanish wolfram to Germany, left Anglo-Spanish relations relatively unscathed.[4] On 6 April, Eden, according to the Spanish Ambassador to London, Jacobo Stuart Fitzjames y Falcó, the Duke of Alba, assured him that Britain still looked forward to a policy of 'very friendly relations' with Spain. On 24 May, just three weeks after the resolution of the wolfram dispute, Winston Churchill, the Prime Minister, openly thanked Spain in the House of Commons for her services to the Allies and expressed the hope that she would be a strong influence for peace in the Mediterranean after the war. Thus, Alba could be excused for predicting, a few days later, that Anglo-Spanish relations were entering a period of 'sincere cordiality'.[5]

Yet, despite these effusions, it was only to be expected that after the Normandy Landings of June 1944 the mood should change. Almost immediately, in an interview on 12 June, Hoare impressed upon Franco that while the British government had no intention whatever of intervening in Spanish affairs, the fact remained that the close identification of falangism with Axis totalitarianism would inevitably prejudice Spanish relations in the eyes of the British public.[6] And it was Hoare – now Lord Templewood* – who, after four years of patient diplomacy keeping Anglo-Spanish relations on an even keel, initiated a reappraisal of Britain's policy towards Franco Spain. In a memorandum of 16 October he acknowledged that any political decisions on Spain still had to take into account the strategic importance of the Iberian Peninsula and past and future economic advantages. He also recognised, however, that public opinion would no longer tolerate the Spanish *status quo* and so some action by the British government was unavoidable. He therefore proposed a discreet 'warning' to Franco, which, he suggested, he could deliver before returning to England in December. This could point out that although it was not the business of the Allies to dictate the form of the Spanish government and that a country was free to have whatever government it liked, if Spain did not conform with the basic principles of the new order, she could not expect to be regarded as a member of the 'comity of European nations'.[7]

---

* Hoare was made Lord Templewood on 3 July 1944; in this chapter he will, however, still be referred to as 'Hoare'.

Nevertheless, Hoare stopped short of recommending the immediate imposition of economic sanctions, if Franco chose to ignore Britain's warning. Sir Alexander Cadogan, the Permanent Under-Secretary, thought, too, that the world economic situation would be sickly enough after the war 'without our indulging in the luxury of economic sanctions for ideological ends'.[8] By contrast, a more robust approach was suggested in a note of 4 November from Clement Attlee, the Deputy Prime Minister, a long-standing opponent of the Franco regime.[9] Arguing that Britain should aim for a government in Spain 'inclined to toleration and which would prepare the way for a development towards a democracy', he proposed cooperating with the USA and France over possible economic sanctions against Spain. Taking up Attlee's proposal, Eden, in a draft telegram for the British Ambassador in Washington, Lord Halifax, agreed that if Franco ignored the warning, new measures, including oil sanctions, would have to be considered.[10]

Eden's telegram, however, met with a critical response from the Prime Minister. The direct involvement of the USA, Churchill pointed out, would mean the adoption of a harder line towards Spain. This in turn could lead to the destabilisation of the Franco regime and to another 'bloodbath', which would harm British interests and benefit the communists. In a reference to the Spanish anti-Franco opposition, Churchill also made the point that any association with the Spanish Left would lose Britain all credibility with Spanish moderates and irremediably compromise the preferred British option of a democratic monarchist restoration for Spain. To these objections were added those of Lord Selborne, the Minister of Economic Warfare, who drew attention to the damage economic sanctions could do to British interests. Franco's atrocities, he also maintained, were 'fewer and less horrible than those that preceded them' and he could see no moral justification for attacks on a neutral country which had made no serious attacks upon Britain and for whose non-belligerency in 1940 Britain was much indebted.[11]

It was at this point that Franco himself inadvertently provided a pretext for the delivery of the 'warning'. Early in October 1944 he had been alerted to an imminent anti-Spanish campaign and so considered it crucial to take prompt action to safeguard Spain's position in postwar Europe.[12] Alba was accordingly instructed to communicate Franco's views on the future course of Anglo-Spanish relations to the British government. Besides emphasising the two countries' anti-Russian sentiments, Alba was to insist that of the three 'strongest and most virile' European nations left in a disintegrated continent – Britain, Germany and Spain – there remained only Spain to whom Britain could turn in 'mutual friendship'. On 9 November Alba gave Cadogan an indication of Franco's instructions, and although illness prevented the Ambassador from giving a full account for another twelve days, Eden had learnt sufficient by then to feel that they called for an early and unambiguous reply.[13]

In a memorandum of 18 November Eden set about redefining Britain's policy toward Spain. Balancing Attlee's denunciation of Franco's wartime conduct and regime against Churchill's, and Selborne's, concerns for Britain's strategic and economic interests, he proposed, as the only practical means of exerting pressure upon Spain to put her own house in order, a 'solemn warning', to be delivered to Franco without publicity, possibly supported by the USA, but not as a joint Anglo-American initiative. Churchill agreed to a 'rough' reply to Franco, 'to the evil features of whose regime he was only too fully alive', and, while unwilling to sanction any steps to encourage the overthrow of the Franco regime, recommended leaving Franco and his government to 'stew in their own juice'. For his part Attlee conceded that any measures harsher than a warning might provoke a nationalist reaction in Spain. After some discussion the Cabinet approved the sending of a letter to Franco, the contents of which were left to the Foreign Secretary and the Prime Minister to decide. Eden's first draft was rejected by Churchill as too severe but a watered-down version was finally approved by the War Cabinet on 18 December and sent to Spain two days later. As this was after Hoare's final interview with Franco, the British warning was not, in fact, delivered to the Spanish leader until 15 January 1945.[14]

Thus, by late 1944, as the Spanish historian, Florentino Portero, has pointed out, all the elements of Britain's post-war policy towards Spain were in place.[15] On the basis of Spain's pro-Axis wartime record and the consistently hostile attitude of the *Falange*, Britain declared herself unwilling to support Spain's participation in the post-war peace settlements or her entry into the future world organisation; Britain would certainly not join Spain in an anti-Soviet combination. This, however, was as far as the British government was prepared to go. Even though the survival of a fascist dictatorship in Europe lay upon Britain's liberal conscience, Spain's continuing strategic importance at the western entrance to the Mediterranean and Britain's commercial and financial links with Spain were sufficient reason for avoiding open confrontation with the Franco regime – whether through economic sanctions or the use of force. Admittedly, there had been a change in Anglo-Spanish relations, as cordiality gave way to coolness, but it was a change of tone rather than of substance and hardly amounted to a fundamental challenge to Franco, whose reply to Churchill of 20 February 1945 omitted all reference to the British warning.[16]

Whether this change, albeit slight, in Anglo-Spanish relations in late 1944 affected Britain's attitude towards the Spanish anti-Franco opposition can now be considered. It has already been emphasised that until the lifting of the German threat to the Iberian Peninsula in August 1944 British policy towards the Franco regime had been determined principally by the need to keep Spain out of the World War. During this period the British government was consequently wary of too obvious an association with the anti-Franco opposition for fear of compromising this policy. Moreover, what British interest there was in the Spanish opposition was reserved to that section of it which was perceived as 'moderate'. This, in its widest sense, meant for the Foreign Office almost the entirety of the non-communist opposition, providing it rejected the divisive legacy of the Second Republic: that is, not only Franco's falangism but also the Second Republic's Constitution of 1931. Spanish neutrality and opposition 'moderation' were, thus, the main criteria determining Britain's attitude towards the anti-Franco opposition during World War II.

For the British Right, whose prejudices extended into the Foreign Office, the majority of the Spanish republican opposition was not looked upon as 'moderate'. The Spanish Civil War had been seen as a conflict between two equally unpalatable extremisms – the insurgents' fascism and the Republic's revolutionary socialism – and subsequent republican insistence on the restoration of the 1931 constitution was criticised for perpetuating the divisions of the Second Republic.[17] Thus, for the four years of the German occupation of France, British cooperation with the 'Spanish Left' – as the Foreign Office indiscriminately dubbed the entire republican opposition – was out of the question. It would inevitably strengthen Franco's pro-Axis sympathies and so increase the likelihood of a German advance into the Iberian Peninsula. It was believed, moreover, that sympathy for the republicans would alienate the moderate anglophiles of the Spanish Right, including some of the generals. The attraction of the Iberian Peninsula into the Atlantic orbit of the British Empire and the USA, Hoare warned in December 1940, depended upon a stable regime within Spain, which only Franco could provide.[18]

Consequently, there could be no question of overt British association with the exiled republican opposition in Latin America. This was made clear on 17 March 1944 when Frank Roberts, Acting Head of the Foreign Office Central Department – where Spanish affairs were dealt with – told

Frederick Leggett, Minister of Labour, that Britain could not have any relations whatever with those who were in opposition to a government recognised by Britain. Not only the Foreign Office but all government departments, Roberts stipulated, were to maintain an attitude of 'complete aloofness' from Spanish refugee groups, whose activities, he insisted, were all directed in one way or another against the Spanish government.[19]

Ideological antipathies apart, the patent discord amongst the *émigrés* discouraged any British moves in their direction, even had the political will to do so existed. Given the prejudices of the Foreign Office, association with the communist controlled UDE and UNE was inconceivable, while the *republican*-socialist ARE's fidelity to the 1931 constitution was also unacceptable. When the JEL was formed in Mexico in November 1943, it seemed that a moderate republican opposition front had at last emerged worthy of British support. To counter this eventuality, however, Jordana, the Spanish Foreign Minister, immediately warned that any dealings with the JEL would be totally incompatible with good relations with Spain. Thus forewarned, the Foreign Office inclined towards caution and the JEL was kept at a distance. In any case, as was seen in Chapter 1, by the end of 1944 the JEL was a spent force and the British government was accordingly relieved of any obligation to develop relations with it.[20]

Yet, total indifference towards the exiled republican opposition during World War II could not be sustained indefinitely. The fact that one section of the opposition found itself in London during the war years forced the British government to declare its hand. In June 1940 it had been obliged on humanitarian grounds to grant Negrín a temporary visa to stay in Britain after his escape from France. However, for all but the Labour members of the coalition War Cabinet, the arrival of Negrín – the very personification of the 'red' Republic – threatened to prove a diplomatic embarrassment at a critical juncture in the war. Not surprisingly, therefore, barely a week after his visa was issued, the Cabinet agreed, on 2 July, that every inducement was to be given Negrín to leave the country. He was, though, subsequently refused political asylum in the USA and so, whether it liked it or not, the British government was forced to let him stay in England.[21]

As expected, the Spanish government was not slow to protest at Negrín's, and other republicans', presence in England.[22] Alba received assurances that the British government did not have the 'slightest contact, understanding or relationship of a political character with the Spanish refugees', but this was not enough to dispel the impression in Spain of continuing British contacts with them. In October, Hoare passed on a warning from the recently dismissed Spanish Foreign Minister, Juan Beigbeder Atienza, that the Spanish Army's determination to resist a German incursion would be jeopardised if the British government continued to back the 'reds'. If, Hoare advised, Britain wished to stimulate a movement of national resistance in the Spanish Army, it was 'essential' to get Negrín out of England. On 1 November the War Cabinet accordingly agreed that a second attempt had to be made to persuade Negrín to leave. However, when this became public knowledge, a number of Labour Members of Parliament threatened to turn the affair into a *cause célèbre*. According to the historian, Denis Smyth, Spain, in the person of Negrín, had become for the British Left the 'touchstone of Britain's claim to be espousing human liberation in opposition to Nazi enslavement'. With senior conservatives fearing for the stability of the wartime coalition, the War Cabinet therefore had no choice, on 28 November 1940, but to accept Negrín's permanent residence in England.[23]

For much of the war period there was no discernible change in the British government's relations with Negrín and the London based *émigré* opposition. Yet, in late 1944, as policy towards Franco Spain was reappraised, its attitude softened. In August Negrín had requested an exit permit to visit Mexico and the USA and this was granted. Then in October Negrín asked for permission to travel to Paris before his voyage to the USA. Eden now objected on the grounds that Negrín's presence in France would probably have a 'disturbing effect' on the Spanish element there, which in turn was likely to cause alarm in Spain and so strengthen Franco's position. He had previously not opposed Negrín's journey to Mexico and the USA, he explained, because this did not take him nearer to Spain nor disturb Anglo-Spanish relations. However, this time the Cabinet disagreed with Eden, and Negrín was granted his exit visa. Even so, the Foreign Office refused him permission to broadcast directly to a republican opposition meeting in Madison Square, New York, on 2 January 1945, on the pretext that he was still banned from political activities.[24]

In November 1944 an application was received from Dolores Ibárruri, General Secretary of the PCE since the previous May, for a transit visa through Britain on her way from the USSR to France. This prompted Isham Peter Garran, soon to be responsible for Spain and Portugal in the reorganised Foreign Office Western Department, to distinguish between support for the replacement of Franco's government by a moderate regime and British opposition to revolution. At the end of the month the British Embassy in Paris was duly informed that Britain was opposed to facilitating the journeys of exiled Spanish politicians and agitators to France on the grounds that their presence there could only disturb security and, through the fear they were likely to inspire of a new revolutionary outbreak, strengthen Franco's position in Spain.[25]

An indication of the British government's sensitivity over the Spanish republican opposition during World War II was also shown in its attitude towards coverage of Spain by the British Broadcasting Corporation (BBC). In the summer of 1943, Hoare began to draw the Foreign Office's attention to the harm being done to Anglo-Spanish relations by what he considered the excessive anti-Franco bias of the BBC's *La Voz de España*. His complaints were levelled in particular against Rafael Martínez Nadal, a republican exile who broadcast under the pseudonym of Antonio Torres. As a result of pressure from Hoare, Martínez was suspended in October 1943 until reinstated the following April. But Foreign Office insistence on keeping the restrictions on Martínez in place exasperated the Spaniard, who finally resigned on 14 June 1944 over an issue of censorship.[26]

Despite this, Spanish complaints against the BBC continued and were taken seriously by the Madrid Embassy.[27] Towards the end of December 1944 comments by Tom Burns, the Madrid Embassy Press Attaché, on a Foreign Office meeting called to discuss BBC broadcasts to Spain were endorsed by Hoare. Burns warned against shadow governments and political exiles who, he said, tended to be taken on their own valuation, 'if only for the reason that they have no other'. He therefore thought it important that no advertisement or support of them should go beyond 'what they earn or represent within the country itself'. An earlier memorandum on propaganda policy, 'A Stocktaking – November 1944', he recalled, had made a clear distinction between the *new* opposition to Franco and the *old* opposition of pre-Civil War days. British support for the latter, which, according to the memorandum, was to be found only among the *émigrés* and the 'incurably anarchic elements', would automatically alienate the 'solid opposition' in Spain. Therefore, British policy, Burns concluded, in a reaffirmation of the Foreign Office position, should be to deny the old Spanish republican opposition a voice and so avoid driving a wedge between the new opposition and its potential supporters.[28]

By the end of 1944 the impression in the Foreign Office of the exiled republican opposition was one of chronic disunity, and this was confirmed in a comprehensive review by the Foreign Office Research Department in January 1945. Its author, Garran, disputed the claims of the different exiled republican groups – namely, the 'Barrio-Prieto Committee' in Mexico (the JEL), the Negrín government in London and the communist JSUNE in Spain – to enjoy any substantial support inside Spain. Despite this, Garran still thought that a Spanish republican government-in-exile might conceivably be formed if Negrín came to a working agreement with the communist UNE in France and if the *negrinista* position on legitimacy were reconciled with the efforts then being made in Mexico towards reconstituting the Republic. Not surprisingly, though, this prospect of a republican government-in-exile of the Spanish Left, with Negrín responsible for bringing communists and *republicans* together, did not appeal to the Foreign Office and did nothing to soften its prejudice against the exiled Spanish republican opposition.[29]

From 1940 to 1944 the British government was also reluctant to be associated with opposition to Franco *inside* Spain. This reflected, of course, its concern over the strategic vulnerability of the Iberian Peninsula. Thus, a report prepared by British Military Intelligence in September 1940, whilst acknowledging that the internal republican opposition provided a potential nucleus for resistance against a German invasion, still cautioned against using it for fear of losing the support of influential elements in the Spanish government who were opposed to Spain's intervention in the war. This warning was repeated in February 1941, when Gladwyn Jebb, Chief Executive Officer of the Special Operations Executive (SOE), was told by the Chiefs of Staff that too obvious a use of republicans might offend Franco and provoke his entry into the enemy camp. Advice, too, from the Head of the Foreign Office Central Department, then Roger Makins, was that only in the event of an actual invasion should assistance be given to any groups or sections of the population who dared to resist. Otherwise, as his minute of 9 June 1941 made clear, he doubted whether it was worth compromising Britain's relations with the Spanish government by greatly increasing preparations for guerrilla warfare.[30]

It was Hoare's apprehension, in particular, over the consequences of dealings with the internal Spanish republican opposition that was responsible for the restrictions placed on the activities of Britain's three wartime secret service organisations in Spain: the SOE, the Secret Intelligence Service (SIS) and MI9.[31] Hoare, who as a former Head of Station in Russia in the First World War was no stranger to the secret services, was so alarmed at SIS contacts with the republican opposition that he insisted on all their activities coming under the direct supervision of Captain Alan Hillgarth, his Naval Attaché and SOE co-ordinator in Spain. Hillgarth was instructed to prevent any irregular British activity likely to justify complaints from the Spanish Interior Ministry.[32] Similarly, in June 1942, the SOE reached agreement with its American counterpart, the Office of Strategic Services (OSS), over their respective areas of responsibility in the Mediterranean sector: French North Africa and Spanish Morocco were allotted to the OSS, but it was specifically excluded from operating in Spain because of Foreign Office restrictions on secret service activity there.[33]

The British government's reluctance to support guerrilla activity in Spain was reinforced by the incidents along Spain's Pyrenean border in the autumn of 1944. The inability of the French authorities to discipline the Spanish guerrilla fighters massing there and their requests for an allied token force to help restore order pointed to a dangerous destabilisation of the whole region. Indeed, when the 'invasion of the Val d'Arán' took place in mid-October, the Foreign Office was thoroughly alarmed that a minor war in the Pyrenees would endanger the Allies' lines of communications through France.[34] As has been seen, rapid action by Spanish security forces quickly halted the invasion, but not before the whole episode had brought home to the Foreign Office Franco's determination, and his ability, to crush internal resistance. As it had always predicted, direct action against Franco had served only to buttress his position.[35]

If the British government felt little sympathy with those sections of the exiled and internal Spanish republican opposition it identified with the revolutionary Left, it was prepared to be more accommodating in its attitude to moderate republicans. In Spain these might have included the socialists, libertarians and *republicans* of the ANFD, since, as a coalition of moderates seeking a compromise solution to the problem of Franco's succession, the ANFD had much to commend it in British eyes. However, the opportunity for British support of the ANFD was temporarily lost at the end of 1944 after police arrests had incapacitated it.

Apart from the ANFD in Spain in late 1944 and the JEL in Mexico the year before, and until the exiled PSOE's conversion to the *prietista* thesis in mid-1947, there were few other moderate republican organisations or initiatives to which the British government could relate. In February

1940 the Foreign Office had received reports that exiled republicans and monarchists had formed a united Free Spaniards Committee, similar to Charles de Gaulle's *France Libre* movement, and the following August it considered the proposed creation by *émigré* moderates of a Committee for the Iberian Peninsula. Certainly the attitude of the Foreign Office towards these ephemeral organisations was less hostile than to the *negrinista* opposition. The Foreign Office Research Department, for example, advised that the government ought to encourage the Free Spaniards Committee in the hope that it would agree on a monarchist restoration after the war. Roberts, moreover, argued that since it was only Negrín, the 'black sheep of these democrats', who had promised to abstain from political activity while in England, the Foreign Office had no need to hamper the moderates of the Committee for the Iberian Peninsula in their contacts with each other and in Latin America, for the simple reason that Britain might need them some day.[36] In November 1944 negotiations between the exiled conservative *republican*, Miguel Maura, and Franco's representative to de Gaulle, José Antonio de Sangróniz, on a transitional government of national unity briefly raised hopes of a moderate alternative to the Franco regime. But, as has been seen, by the spring of 1945 nothing had come of Maura's initiative and British interest soon faded.[37]

Officially, the British government's attitude during World War II to the restoration of the monarchy to Spain was that it was an internal question for the Spanish people alone to decide. Privately, though, and in contrast to British indifference to the republican opposition, it was always recognised that there were some advantages to be gained from evincing a measure of sympathy for the monarchist cause. To an extent it served to counter the anglophobia of certain sections of the Spanish Right, inclined by German propaganda to suspect Britain of planning a *negrinista* communist regime in Spain after the allied victory. It was also the case that, although a monarchist *opposition* did not emerge until late 1944, the monarchists were seen by the Foreign Office as constituting an influential sector of Spain's governing *élite* whose loyalty to Franco was far from unconditional. As such, they tended therefore to be identified as 'moderates', with the potential to provide a non-revolutionary alternative to the Franco dictatorship and accordingly deserving of British support. It was also borne in mind that several senior generals were committed monarchists. The Madrid Embassy therefore kept in close contact with them, in particular with Beigbeder, Don Alfonso de

Orleans, Kindelán, Aranda and Orgaz, in the hope of using them to check Franco's pro-Axis inclinations and to stiffen Spanish resistance against a possible German advance into Spain.[38]

The significance of British cooperation with the monarchist generals, however, should not be exaggerated. In the autumn of 1941, for example, when Britain's military situation remained critical, the Madrid Embassy was authorised to give an undertaking to Sainz Rodríguez and his fellow conspirators that the British government would, if necessary, provide a warship to transport the civilian half of their proposed civilian-military provisional government to the Canaries, where it would receive British recognition (see Chapter 1). At the same time, though, the Embassy was instructed to refrain from too precise an undertaking, so as not to give Franco a pretext for accusing Britain of direct intervention in Spain's internal affairs. William Strang, a Foreign Office Assistant Under-Secretary, minuted that although British policy was to keep Spain out of the war and to stimulate resistance to a German advance into Spain, it was not necessarily to work 'actively' for the overthrow of the Franco regime or 'definitely' to promote the formation of an alternative military government.[39] Clearly, British interest in the military conspiracies of those years reflected more a preoccupation with Britain's wartime vulnerability than any genuine commitment to the monarchist cause. The fact that the generals involved were monarchist was, to a large extent, coincidental. Nor was Britain ever called upon to honour the pledges given in the autumn of 1942.

Foreign Office caution over supporting the Spanish monarchists was one of the few issues which led to differences between it and Britain's Ambassador to Spain. Hoare was an ardent monarchist, counting among his personal friends several members of the Spanish royal family, including the Duke of Alba, and was convinced that the Spanish monarchy represented a practical alternative to Franco and to falangism. This *parti pris* led him on occasions to forgo his customary diplomatic caution. Thus, in August 1941 he argued strongly for the immediate return to Spain of the Pretender to avoid his being exploited by the Germans for their own ends, and consequently gave his approval to plans for the small military *junta* headed by Orgaz which intended to replace Franco with a regency government. Against this the Foreign Office pointed out the obvious danger that without an assurance to the Germans from the *junta* that it would remain pro-Axis, German pressure would force it to resign. Any move to restore the monarchy to Spain was, in the opinion of the Foreign Office, more than likely to provoke a German invasion of the Peninsula.[40]

Still, in May 1942, Hoare wrote to Eden that he had told the monarchist Conde de Fontanar, one of his 'best friends' in Madrid, that in his opinion the King (*sic*) should announce his return to Spain at the earliest possible opportunity and thus fulfil his 'divine mission'; it was time, he had told Fontanar, for the generals to tell Franco to take the first steps towards a restoration. In his reply Eden was at pains to restate Britain's wartime policy towards Spain: if Germany invaded Spain, it was in Britain's interest to have a free Spanish movement and a movement for the restoration of the monarchy would have wide support; if Germany did not invade, Britain should also support any government willing and able to pursue a neutral policy. But, if a change of government occurred *before* the Germans had been weakened, any new government ran the risk of being overthrown. Therefore, Eden cautioned, 'we might be unwise to encourage or to precipitate changes, the result of which might well be, as things are at present, to substitute a positively hostile regime for the present relatively neutral one'.[41] Yet, Hoare persisted. At a dinner towards the end of June 1944 he recommended a monarchist restoration to Jordana as a way of avoiding a Soviet imposed government of the Left, and at a farewell banquet, held in his honour at the Portuguese Embassy in Madrid on 12 December, he said that Britain was anxious about Don Juan's inaction and that only a restoration of the monarchy could avoid another civil war in Spain.[42]

From the British government's point of view, from 1940 to 1944 there was, in fact, little tactical or strategic advantage to be gained from championing the monarchist cause. This was certainly the impression conveyed to the Pretender himself. From Sainz Rodríguez, for example, Don Juan learnt that though Churchill thought a restoration of the monarchy '*interesante*', it was not considered a serious option by the Foreign Office. In December 1943 Hillgarth passed on a similar comment from Churchill that the restoration of the monarchy was of no military interest at all to Britain.[43]

Strategic considerations apart, there were in any case considerable doubts in London over Don Juan's democratic convictions. As has been seen, despite his statement in *Le Journal de Genève* of 11 November 1942 distancing him from the falangist cause, it was not until January 1944 that Don Juan's break with Franco was made public. Even then it seemed far from definite, with reports reaching the Foreign Office of attempts throughout 1944 by Don Juan to meet Franco, and, in March, of his failure to give open support to a group of university professors sanctioned for circulating their pro-*juanista* letter. No wonder Cadogan felt some surprise when that same month the Madrid Assistant Press Attaché chose to describe Don Juan as a 'liberal prince'. In Cadogan's opinion, Don Juan was nothing more than a 'weather vane which has felt the direction of the wind'.[44] The weakness of the monarchist opposition, moreover, particularly after the Val d'Arán invasion of October 1944, did not escape the Foreign Office's notice.

A demonstration of the British government's attitude towards the Spanish Pretender was provided in late 1944 when the Foreign Office learnt of Don Juan's intention to come to London for the funeral of his grandmother, Princess Beatrice. Still fearing for Anglo-Spanish relations, Cadogan advised the Prime Minister on 27 October not to meet him, 'if only for the reason that it seems wiser to maintain our present policy of non-intervention in Spanish internal affairs and therefore to be able to show that Don Juan's visit to this country had no political significance'. As it was, higher forces stepped in, for, despite the fact that King George VI had sent a plane to Switzerland to fetch Don Juan, bad weather prevented his presence at the funeral at Windsor on 3 November. As for Don Juan's mother, Queen Victoria Eugenia, who did manage the journey to London, Roberts advised telling her that the question of a monarchy or a republic for Spain was 'entirely for the Spanish people to decide and that we really cannot take sides one way or the other'. On this occasion, however, it seems that Foreign Office advice did not prevent Doña Victoria from meeting several government ministers, including Churchill, which created an impression amongst the exiled London republicans that the British government did indeed favour a monarchist restoration. To some extent the balance was restored later that month, when a request from the French representative in Lisbon, Armand de Blanquet du Chayla, for British permission for the monarchist Gil-Robles to travel via London to Switzerland was dismissed on the familiar grounds that any help Britain gave him would amount to interference in Spain's internal affairs.[45]

It remains to consider whether Anglo-Spanish relations were at all affected by the little that Britain did do in connection with the Spanish opposition. That there were some contacts with the opposition groups in Spain was not denied. In July 1944, for example, Hoare admitted that a 'number of representatives of clandestine republican or other dissident organisations' were received at British consulates in Spain and although the advances of such dissident persons were in all cases discreetly repelled, it was probable that later they sometimes described the results of their interviews 'in glowing terms'. Hoare also believed that the 'rather less discreet interest' taken in Spanish republican activities by the Americans, together with reports of discoveries of American arms landed on the Spanish coast from North Africa, tended to heighten Spanish suspicion that Britain, like the Americans, was encouraging subversive elements.[46]

Surprisingly, too, in view of his vendetta against Martínez Nadal, Hoare was not himself entirely blameless for the impression given to the Spanish secret services during World War II of BBC solidarity with the republican opposition. Embassy and consular staff, Hoare admitted, did occasionally distribute BBC leaflets in a deliberate attempt to counter falangist propaganda, and as some of their most avid readers included opponents of the Franco regime, it was not surprising that when they were arrested and found with the leaflets in their possession, BBC links to the Spanish opposition appeared proven. It seems, too, that the Madrid Embassy gave some young PSOE activists a Roneo duplicating machine and 3 000 *pesetas* a month in return for producing wartime 'leaflets for freedom' and inserting British news about the war in their *Servicio de Información Socialista* bulletin. In addition, junior officials probably encouraged a number of libertarians, who came to Embassy film shows, to work for a non-communist opposition alliance, although this, according to Hartmut Heine, was without Hoare's knowledge and certainly did not point to any major British involvement in the formation of the ANFD.[47]

Franco's security services had been all too aware of British subversion in Spain during World War II.[48] But, as José María Doussinague, Director General of Foreign Policy in the Spanish Ministry of Foreign Affairs until June 1946, recalled in 1949, his ministry had generally looked upon British espionage with a *'criterio tolerante'*.[49] From time to time Franco, of course, had been happy to exploit it to British discomfiture. In January 1941, for example, he had, in the presence of the bemused Portuguese Ambassador, Pedro Theótonio Pereira, roundly berated Britain for 'filling the country with secret agents who were stirring up the Reds to make a revolution', and Hoare was obliged, on 8 February, to proffer a categorical denial that Britain had any agents or organisations of any kind engaged upon such intrigues. Similarly, three years later in March 1944, Hoare found himself having to deny that Britain had provided a plane to drop arms to 'red' rebels in the Sierra Morena, or that two British subjects arrested in Larache, in Spanish Morocco, were in fact spies. Even so, Jordana felt it necessary to remind Hoare that had it not been for the Spanish government's 'benevolence', energetic measures would otherwise have been taken against British agents.[50] It was significant, though, that when Franco finally drew attention in his letter of 18 October 1944 – in the midst of the British reappraisal of Anglo-Spanish relations – to Britain's wartime subversion, it was not so much to embarrass the British government as to illustrate Spain's past magnanimity. Although the activities of Britain's secret services had had a detrimental effect on Anglo-Spanish relations, Franco pointed out, and had 'created a hatred of foreign agents and a natural indignation amongst our own people', the Spanish State, 'with a clear vision of the future and of her traditional interests', had avoided as much as possible their publicity and the corresponding scandal.[51]

Conclusion

Britain's official policy towards Spain in 1944 was summed up by Eden in a meeting with René Massigli, the French Provisional Government's representative in London, on 28 August 1944:

> As regards the future, it would seem improbable that General Franco can maintain himself and the present Falange regime in power without modification in the Europe which emerges from this war. On the other hand, General Franco's opponents have hitherto shown little cohesion or skill and there is general desire throughout Spain to avoid further troubles and bloodshed [. . .] Our main desire is that order and peace should be maintained in Spain [. . .] Above all, we do not intend to interfere with Spanish internal affairs or to support any particular Party, whether that of the Monarchists or the Republican exiles. We are, however, constantly representing to the Spanish Government the importance in their own interests of putting their house in order and breaking with their unfortunate past, both as regards their German connections and Falangist malpractices at home.[52]

Until then Spanish neutrality had been essential for the success of the Allies in World War II. The British government had generally refrained from antagonising Franco, for fear of pushing him towards the Axis powers or destabilising Spain, which might have precipitated a preemptive move by the *Wehrmacht* into the Iberian Peninsula. For as long

as the German threat remained, therefore, there had been no open identification with the anti-Franco opposition. There was also the fact that
the republicans, as heirs to the ill-starred Second Republic, were severely
handicapped in the eyes of the Foreign Office by their disunity and their
partisan ideology which rendered them incapable of generating a viable
alternative to the Franco dictatorship.

In comparison, the monarchists, who in this period constituted more
an influential pressure group within the Franco regime than a clear
opposition to it, provided a useful means for influencing Franco's
foreign policy during the World War in Britain's favour. By August 1944,
however, this role had lost much of its importance, and the Spanish
monarchy had to be reassessed in terms of its potential for furnishing
a moderate – hence democratic – replacement for the Franco regime.
Yet, by late 1944 the British government was still far from sure whether
the monarchy, in the person of the young Pretender to the Spanish
throne, could fulfil that function. Furthermore, a restoration of the
Spanish monarchy by the Spanish Right for their own benefit carried
with it no more a guarantee of stability in the Iberian Peninsula than
an unmediated reversion to the Second Republic. The only solution for
Spain appeared to be some form of moderate compromise. This, during
the period in question, however, failed to emerge and a coalition of
moderate republicans and monarchists, sought by the ANFD, was too
short-lived to be of immediate consequence.

The assumed presence of 'moderates' in Spain further complicated
British policy towards the Spanish opposition. For, if the British government encouraged the republican opposition, the moderates' reaction
would be to move closer to Franco. Therefore, the British government
had to be seen to avoid giving any direct support to the Spanish Left,
and to Negrín above all. But this in turn risked giving the impression
that the British government was reconciled to the Franco regime, the
effect of which was equally to discourage the potential moderate opposition. Faced with this dilemma it was not surprising that the British
government kept to a policy of inaction. Thus, by the end of 1944,
Britain found itself, as it had been for most of World War II, avoiding
contact with the majority of the republican opposition, doubting the
viability of the monarchist cause and lacking a coalition of moderates
with whom to treat. Whether the evolution of the Spanish opposition
in 1945 would be sufficient to change this situation will be considered
next.

3
1945: Adjusting to Peace

The German surrender of May 1945 left the Franco regime exposed and all sectors of the Spanish anti-Franco opposition expecting the victorious Allies to move swiftly against 'fascist' Spain. Yet, republicans and anti-Franco monarchists were apprehensive over the eventual choice of regime to succeed Franco's. Each of the rival camps suspected the other of trying to steal a march on it and so both, in 1945, would take steps to ingratiate themselves with the Allies. In exile, the republicans revived the institutions of the Spanish Second Republic and the monarchists distanced themselves from the Franco regime. Inside Spain, the search for common ground between republicans and monarchists resumed. In contrast, the British government, which had no intention of forcibly removing Franco, kept to its *attentiste* policy despite the incipient internationalisation of the 'Spanish problem'.

The Spanish anti-Franco opposition

For many exiled republicans the revival of the institutions of the Spanish Second Republic – the *Cortes*, the Presidency of the Republic and the Government – was a moral and legal prerequisite for the restoration of the republican regime to Spain. Few were more convinced of this than Martínez Barrio, *republican* president of the JEL. It was mainly on his initiative that negotiations between the various *émigré* political associations in Mexico began in November 1944, as a result of which the first session of the reconvened *Cortes* took place on 10 January 1945 in the *Club Français* of Mexico City. Seventy-two deputies attended and another 49, who were unable to reach Mexico, sent messages of adherence. It was, though, a purely symbolic and commemorative occasion. The Secretary of the Chamber, Eduardo Frapolli, read out the names of the 127 deputies who had died since July 1939, and after a speech from Martínez Barrio the session closed.[1] A second session was planned for a week later; but this was reckoning without *prietista* objections.

In an article which appeared on 1 January 1945 in a *prietista* publication, *Adelante*, Prieto had argued that recalling the *Cortes* was a serious mistake. His position was that pragmatism, and not partisan dogmatism, over Spain's constitutional future would attract allied support for the republican cause, and so it was essential in his opinion that the JEL alone continued to represent the republican cause.[2] No doubt, too, Prieto's objection sprang from the misgivings he had over Negrín's capacity for mischief in any reconvened *Cortes*. The *prietistas* accordingly fell back on a constitutional quibble, protesting that the 72 deputies assembled fell short of the required quorum of 100 and that this automatically disqualified them from functioning as a legal parliament.[3] On the eve of the scheduled second session, the *prietista* deputies also threatened a boycott if communist deputies or their sympathisers attended. Martínez Barrio was thus left with no choice but to suspend the *Cortes* and, understandably piqued, resigned the presidency of the JEL on 1 February.[4]

Yet, *prietista* preference for the JEL could not be sustained indefinitely. At the UN founding Conference in San Francisco that spring, a JEL delegation – which included Prieto – successfully lobbied for a resolution effectively excluding Franco Spain from UN membership.[5] Apart from this, however, the JEL received no official recognition from the Conference since its claim to represent the entirety of the exiled Spanish republican opposition was demonstrably untrue. Prieto, moreover, could no longer ignore the adverse publicity republican squabbling was attracting at the very moment when Franco's departure seemed imminent and when Don Juan's Lausanne Manifesto (see below) signalled a rival monarchist bid for the Allies' favour. So, bowing to the inevitable, the JEL dissolved itself on 31 August 1945, four days after the formation of the new republican government-in-exile.[6]

Before then, unexpected backing for the *Cortes* had come from Negrín. At the start of the year he had still been insisting on his own government's exclusive claim to republican legitimacy.[7] But after the failure of the Val d'Arán invasion, even the PCE was calling for a plebiscite on Spain's constitutional future, and Negrín risked being isolated.[8] Possibly, too, Martínez Barrio had led Negrín to believe that he would head a new republican government. Whatever the case, in early August, soon after his arrival in Mexico City from San Francisco, he successfully persuaded the *émigré* republicans to reach agreement on a recall of the *Cortes*. Consequently, on 17 August, 96 deputies met in the Mexico City

Council Chamber, which was granted extra-territoriality for the occasion by the Mexican government. Martínez Barrio was acclaimed provisional President of the Republic, and, five days later, Negrín resigned as prime minister.[9]

Unrelenting *prietista* hostility, however, frustrated Negrín's ambition to be reappointed prime minister. For their part, communists and *negrinistas* were adamantly opposed to any but a government headed by Negrín. As a compromise Martínez Barrio therefore asked the *republican* José Giral y Pereira, *Frente Popular* prime minister in July 1936, to form the new government. Both Negrín and Prieto refused ministerial posts, and it was only after protracted negotiations that Giral managed to finalise his government on 26 August.[10] On 7 November he outlined his government's programme to the 140 deputies of the reassembled *Cortes*:

(a) The Government is founded upon the broadest base possible in present circumstances: parties not represented in it refused to join it;
(b) The Government are doing their best to secure recognition by democratic States and especially those that have never entered into official relations with General Franco;
(c) If and when the Government reaches Spanish soil, it will be one of national unity: apart from meting out just retribution to Franco's criminals, it will endeavour to create an atmosphere of harmony and tolerance;
(d) The Roman Catholic Church will be respected, but will not be permitted to engage in politics;
(e) The autonomy of the Basque, the Galician, and the Catalan 'regions' will be respected;
(f) The army will be reduced and expenditure on defence will depend on budgetary capacity;
(g) Great attention will be devoted to agriculture, education, labour legislation, and the raising of the standard of living;
(h) The Government would prefer that the overthrow of General Franco should be accomplished without bloodshed, but will not hesitate to use force if no other course is open.[11]

Despite communist opposition and reservations from Basque, Catalan and Galician nationalists, Giral's ministerial declaration was approved. But, in a speech to the *Cortes* the next day, Prieto accused the new government of lacking the moral and material strength to 'reconquer' Spain or to expect recognition or assistance from the Great Powers. His own support for Giral's government was emphatically conditional:

We will give our most enthusiastic support for the moment, but we do not commit the future to institutions that have no fixed date for their termination [. . .] I tell the Government and the Congress [. . .] that if ever these institutions lose their vitality and if, either in the international or national arena, there arises an alternative solution capable of restoring the Republic – and Spain accepts it – we will work for that solution. No one, after this declaration, could accuse us of disloyalty [. . .] We shall continue thus so long as there is no other path. But if the opportunity presents itself and is honourable, we shall make our choice in complete freedom.[12]

Thus, with his government hostage to the, mainly *prietista*, parliamentary PSOE, Giral's credibility was seriously damaged. Not surprisingly, a manifesto sent to British, American and Soviet diplomatic representatives shortly before the first session of the UN General Assembly in London in January 1946, calling for a break in diplomatic and economic relations with Spain, went unheeded. By the end of 1945, the Second Republic's first government-in-exile had been recognised by only a handful of Latin American countries: Mexico, Guatemala, Panama, Bolivia, Cuba and Venezuela.[13]

After his public break with Franco in January 1944, the Pretender to the Spanish throne, Don Juan, seemed at first to wait upon events, confident that the Franco regime's days were numbered. However, many of his advisors recognised the danger of surrendering the anti-Franco initiative to the republican opposition and pressed for a public declaration of *juanista* opposition to the Franco regime. Difficulties in communications between Switzerland and the Iberian Peninsula caused delays until finally, on 19 March 1945, Don Juan published his Lausanne Manifesto.[14] The Franco regime, this declared, had been inspired from the start by totalitarian systems and the Axis Powers, was 'contrary to the character and tradition' of the Spanish people and 'fundamentally incompatible' with the situation brought about by World War II. The answer, though, was not another republic, for, however moderate in its beginnings and intentions, this would inevitably lead to civil war. Instead, the manifesto stated:

Only the traditional Monarchy can be an instrument of peace and concord to reconcile Spaniards; it alone can obtain respect from abroad, by means of an effective state of law, and realise a harmonious synthesis of that order and freedom upon which is based the Christian concept of the State. Millions of Spaniards of the most varied ideologies, are convinced of this truth and see in the Monarchy the only saving Institution.[15]

This emphasis on the *traditional* monarchy reflected *juanista* concern not to alienate the *franquista* monarchists. Indeed, as already explained in a letter of 10 February to Kindelán, Don Juan was not abjuring the ideals of the nationalist 'Movement' but aiming rather to dissociate it from Franco's 'dictatorial fascist institutions'.[16] Nevertheless, the need to secure the backing of the allied democracies could not be ignored, and so the manifesto's programme also included provision for a constitutional plebiscite, recognition of human rights, political freedoms and regional diversity, and a wide political amnesty, as well as promising greater social justice and a fairer distribution of wealth.

Although the Lausanne Manifesto was not published in the Spanish press, it was widely circulated among the political *élite* in Spain. In April Don Juan followed it up with a call to Spain's monarchists to resign their positions in the Franco regime, and immediately the Spanish Ambassador to Britain, the Duke of Alba, tendered his resignation – even if for practical reasons it did not take effect until the following October. He was followed by Don Alfonso, who resigned his command of the Second Air Arm at Seville on 4 April and as a result was confined to his estate at Sanlúcar de Barrameda, near Cádiz.[17] Altogether, however, only eight monarchists in all heeded Don Juan's call and many *franquista* monarchists were dismissive. Antonio Goicoechea, former leader of the monarchist party, *Renovación Española*, but by then President of the Bank of Spain, spoke for them all when he declared in an open letter to the Pretender that he would be committing a crime of *lèse-patrie* and irreparably harming the monarchist cause, were he to adopt an attitude of open and hostile opposition (*disconformidad*) towards Franco's government. The Minister of Foreign Affairs, José Félix Lequerica, wrote to Don Juan in similar vein, and the *franquista* Marqués Villabrágima dwelt on the well-being and order he saw in Spain, where, despite the post-Civil War situation, he felt there was respect for the rights of citizens and only a moderate use of power![18] Thus, offering the *franquista* monarchists neither advantages nor guarantees, the Lausanne Manifesto clearly failed to precipitate the crisis of the Franco regime in the spring of 1945 that Don Juan expected.

The manifesto's effect was further blunted thanks to a steady procession of *franquista* monarchists journeying to Don Juan's villa in Lausanne during the rest of 1945. These intermediaries, often self-appointed, suited Franco's purpose well. An illusion of ongoing negotiations between the two men was created, which served to confuse observers in Spain and abroad as to the seriousness of Don Juan's break with the Franco regime. Above all, though, the visits enabled Franco to play for time in what, for his regime, were the critical first months of the post-war period.[19]

Yet, whatever Franco and his emissaries hoped, the visits did not improve relations with Don Juan. In August the Pretender made it clear to Miguel Matéu Pla, who was about to take up his post as Spain's diplomatic representative in Paris, that he would enter Spain as king, and by the *puerta grande*, or not at all. Again, in October he told a traditionalist monarchist, José María de Oriol y Urquijo, who had led him to believe a monarchist restoration under Franco was imminent, that he would return to Spain only on his own terms.[20] Any doubts over Don Juan's opposition to Franco were finally dispelled when, on 14 December, *La Gazette de Lausanne* published an interview in which the Pretender, with one eye evidently on the recently formed government-in-exile in Mexico, for the first time unequivocally stated his commitment to democracy. He fully pledged himself to the establishment of a democratic regime in Spain, modelled on the examples of Britain, the USA, Scandinavia and the Netherlands, and pledged himself to accept a decision by the nation even if it went against the restoration of the monarchy.[21]

To some extent Don Juan's stiffening opposition in 1945 can be explained by reports reaching him of renewed military plotting against Franco. Although the immediate effect of the Val d'Arán invasion in October 1944 had been to rally the generals behind Franco, by the following January a number of them were once again looking to a change of regime. The threat was certainly serious enough for Franco to order new military postings in March, the most significant of which were Orgaz's transfer from the High Commission in Spanish Morocco to the purely administrative post of Chief of the General Staff, and the appointment of Agustín Muñoz Grandes, former pro-Nazi commander of the Blue Division, to the key position of Captain-General of Madrid. Later in the month, at a meeting of the Army Supreme Council, and then at a Cabinet meeting in the first half of April, Franco took pains to stress his own monarchist commitment and announced the creation of a Council of the Realm to decide the succession on his death or retirement. As intended, these initiatives temporarily defused monarchist opposition until after the German surrender in May when the generals' fears for Spain's future resurfaced.[22]

But even then, a credible military opposition to Franco failed to emerge. In mid-August 1945 Kindelán met Don Alfonso in Sanlúcar de Barrameda, from where they requested Orgaz to sound out other senior generals on a joint move against Franco. Orgaz, however, proved uncooperative, and although a petition to Franco was drawn up, it was never presented. Meanwhile Kindelán's plotting had come to Franco's notice and on 25 August – one month after a blatantly monarchist speech to the *Escuela Superior del Ejército* – he was sacked from his post as its Director.[23] As for Aranda, he was simultaneously planning his own *coup*. On 16 August Gil-Robles learnt that he was pressing General Fidel Dávila Arrondo, the Army Minister, to deliver an ultimatum to Franco, after which – if Franco ignored it – Aranda intended to rise against the government using military garrisons loyal to him in Asturias. This plan, too, came to nothing.[24]

Indeed, Aranda's energies in 1945 appeared to be directed more against the monarchists of the rival 'Lisbon group' than against Franco himself. For, on the basis of his contacts with the ANFD in late 1944, he had reached the conclusion that of all the monarchists he was the one best placed to pursue negotiations with the republicans. In October 1945 he therefore wrote to Sainz Rodríguez and Gil-Robles proposing the creation of a centre party to support the government of a restored monarchy. As this party would need the cooperation of the Spanish Left, this ruled out, in Aranda's opinion, Gil-Robles' CEDA. Not surprisingly, Gil-Robles disagreed, but his subsequent attempt to bypass Aranda in favour of his own direct negotiations with the ANFD was equally unsuccessful.[25]

Despite the police action against it earlier in the year, by the summer of 1945 the ANFD had managed to reconstitute itself. When Aranda proposed resuming their interrupted negotiations, the ANFD at first refused, believing that after Japan's defeat allied action to restore the Spanish republic was imminent.[26] By late autumn, however, with the British Embassy in Madrid privately encouraging renewed republican-monarchist contacts, these hopes had faded.[27] By then both the ANFD and the monarchists were anxious to have an agreement ready for the first session of the UN General Assembly in January 1946, and so talks between them resumed in November 1945.[28]

At this point mention must be made of the issues at stake in all subsequent republican-monarchist negotiations. Whether a republic or a monarchy was to replace the Franco regime was, of course, the fundamental issue. Each side acknowledged, moreover, that a successful restoration of either regime against the will of the Spanish people was impossible. On the one hand, the republicans obviously lacked the means to restore the republic by force and were in any case committed to democratic procedures. On the other hand, a monarchist restoration by military *coup* – or indeed by Franco himself – would never receive international recognition. Therefore, both sides – albeit with serious reservations on the monarchists' part – recognised the need for a plebiscite, or national elections to a constituent assembly, to decide Spain's future regime. But this simply shifted the problem one step back – to the nature of the transitional regime, under which the electoral consultation was to take place, and to the exact timing of this consultation. Domination of an interim government by either republicans or monarchists during the transitional period would lend one side an unfair advantage and in all likelihood prejudice the outcome of any plebiscitary process. So, it was the nature of the transition – in particular, the *timing* of a plebiscite – rather than the final regime itself, that was to assume the greater importance in republican-monarchist negotiations over the next three years.[29]

By early November an ANFD-monarchist agreement was in sight. It had by then been agreed that a new state, based on the rule of law, would be established, civil freedoms legally guaranteed, and Spain comply with the international policy of the United Nations. It was accepted that the Army needed reassurance, but Franco, it was hoped, could be persuaded to make way for an interim government – a *Frente Nacional Democrático* – of moderate republicans and monarchists. According to contemporary reports from the British Embassy, it was also agreed that the next step would be to summon Don Juan back to Spain before a plebiscite, which both sides pledged themselves to respect, was held on the monarchy. Later accounts, on the other hand, state that the republicans did not agree to a plebiscite *a posteriori* but preferred both the republic and the monarchy to be suspended until a plebiscite *a priori* was held, and, in Don Juan's place, proposed the setting-up of an interim three-man regency.[30]

By the New Year of 1946 the draft republican-monarchist agreement was ready for ratification. However, at a joint meeting of the national executives of the PSOE-in-France and the UGT in Toulouse on 24–25 January, Giral's policy of unconditional commitment to the Second Republic was endorsed, and, as a consequence, the socialist representatives on the ANFD withdrew their support for the agreement with the monarchists. Added to this, a call from the PCE for a broad anti-Franco coalition of the Left – intended in part to sabotage the ANFD-monarchist agreement from which it was excluded – led to pressure from the PSOE-in-France on the interior socialists to admit communists to the ANFD.[31] Their subsequent entry in February 1946 proved unacceptable to the monarchists and brought the republican-monarchist negotiations to an end. A wave of police arrests in March and April completed the break-down.[32]

British reaction to the anti-Franco opposition

In February 1945 a memorandum from the Foreign Office Research Department to the Ministry of Information restated the British government's policy towards Spain:

(a) His Majesty's Government desire close and friendly relations with Spain. They also wish to develop good trade relations with Spain.

(b) British trade with Spain is in fact developing satisfactorily, but His Majesty's Government see no prospect of establishing really friendly relations with General Franco's Government in its present form. Moreover, the continuance of that regime in its present form after the defeat of Germany would be an anachronism, and there is a serious danger that if it is not modified there would be an outbreak of civil war or revolution later on which, in the opinion of His Majesty's Government, would be contrary to the interests of world peace and security.

(c) On the other hand, any attempt now by Spanish elements to overthrow the present regime by force would, in the opinion of His Majesty's Government, be equally undesirable. Recent events have shown that throughout Spain there is a profound desire to avoid a recurrence of civil war and any such attempt, which would be doomed to failure, would only result in strengthening the position of General Franco, who would pose as the champion of law and order.

(d) The ideal solution for Spain would be a peaceful transition to a moderate form of government, whether republican or monarchist. There would, however, appear to be little prospect of such a development in present circumstances, as all the information in the possession of His Majesty's Government points to the conclusion that the moderate elements are oppressed, apathetic and inactive.

(e) Indeed, the only practical possibility of an improvement in the political situation in Spain would appear to lie in the modification of the present regime by the elimination or suppression of its undesirable elements.[33]

Clearly, no mention was made of direct action by Britain – diplomatic, economic or military – to unseat Franco. Instead, the government looked to a 'moderate' Spanish opposition to bring about its 'ideal solution' of a constitutional monarchy or, possibly, a parliamentary republic. British support for this moderate opposition, moreover, would be offered only *after* its emergence, once it had become apparent that the 'great mass of Spanish opinion, inside the country as well as outside, was united in supporting a single opposition party against Franco'. The problem, however, was that at the beginning of 1945 such an opposition was conspicuously absent: in Mexico there was deadlock over the *Cortes*, from Switzerland Don Juan had yet to issue his manifesto, while in Spain republican-monarchist negotiations had been interrupted by police arrests, and the generals showed little sign of action. No wonder the British government fell back on the unlikely possibility of the Franco regime's reforming itself. Nevertheless, as has been seen, during 1945 the republican and monarchist opposition underwent significant changes. Whether these were sufficient for the British government to modify its opinion of the anti-Franco opposition will now be considered.

The major event in the history of the exiled republican opposition in 1945 – the formation of the Giral government – did not occur until August. For the first eight months of the year it was consequently Negrín, more than any other figure, who continued to test the British government's attitude towards the exiled republicans. Whether it was his self-promotion as republican leader, or simply his physical proximity to Whitehall, he remained – as he had, ever since 1940 – the *bête noire* of the Foreign Office. In March, for example, Eden was dissuaded from meeting Negrín, before the latter's departure for Mexico, as he was, in the Foreign Office's view, 'quite discredited' among Spaniards and had virtually no chance of ever returning to power in Spain.[34] In August, Robert Sloan of the Foreign Office Western Department, with responsibility, under Garran, for Spain and Portugal, advised that any public statements by the government or the Ambassador in Madrid should imply British determination not to 'foist' Negrín, along with Maura, Prieto, and others, on the Spaniards. A few days later a request from

Negrín to broadcast to Spain was accordingly ignored. Indeed, such was the 'constant denigration' of Negrín by the Madrid Embassy that on 28 August, a few weeks after coming into office, Clement Attlee, the new Prime Minister, felt compelled to ask the new Foreign Secretary, Ernest Bevin, for an explanation. Bevin's reply of 10 September reiterated the Madrid Embassy's view that Negrín's almost universal unpopularity in Spain was due first to the general belief that his return to Spain was certain to lead to civil war, and, secondly, that Negrín had taken the bulk of the Republic's funds with him into exile where he had lived in relative comfort ever since.[35] Only after Negrín's eclipse in Mexico did the Foreign Office finally soften its attitude. His application in August 1945 to return to Britain went unchallenged in the Foreign Office, even though it was still felt to be embarrassing, and – in a break with past practice – was not considered at Cabinet level.[36]

The formation of Giral's government-in-exile in August did not bring a change in the British government's attitude towards the exiled republican opposition. Prieto's attack on it in the second *Cortes* session, from which it was reported as emerging considerably weakened, did little to enhance its prestige in the Foreign Office's eyes. More seriously, however, was its signal failure to promise the ideal solution desired by the British government. Far from heralding a peaceful transition to a moderate form of government, it appeared to the Foreign Office more the harbinger of social strife. Officials were particularly alarmed by the eighth point in Giral's ministerial statement of 7 November which threatened the use of force to overthrow Franco, if no other course were open. Commenting on this '*solution of the Spanish deadlock if necessary by force*' [emphasised in the original], Sloan minuted that Giral's statement provided an ample explanation for the strong feelings in Spain against the return of any exiled republican government.[37]

It followed, in the Foreign Office's opinion, that there could be no British support for the republican government-in-exile for fear of alienating the moderates, republican and monarchist, in Spain itself. Indeed, a report received from the Madrid Embassy, soon after Bevin's appointment as Foreign Secretary, pointed to the anxiety already felt in many quarters in Spain that the new British government might attempt to impose upon Spain 'some of these discredited leaders'. The report stressed, too, that if the generals were faced with a demand to bring back an exiled republican government, they would prefer to keep Franco with all his disadvantages and in so doing they would have the backing of the 'great bulk of moderate opinion' in Spain. When the Papal Nuncio to Spain, Monsignor Gaetano Cicognani, saw Sir Victor Mallet,

British Ambassador to Spain, on 16 September, he confirmed the Ambassador's view that the 'inordinate amount' of publicity given to the formation of Giral's government by British and American press and radio had done more than anything else to strengthen Franco's position in Spain. The Ambassador also drew attention to the anti-communism of moderate Spaniards, who considered the Soviet regime just as dictatorial and repressive as Franco's and viewed with alarm the idea that 'Russia should spread into the western Mediterranean those tentacles which have already reached the Adriatic'.[38]

Fear of upsetting the moderates by appearing to support the exiled opposition lay behind the Foreign Office's ongoing battle with the BBC throughout 1945. In February, in an attempt to curb BBC criticism of the Franco regime which on occasions was felt to go 'beyond the policy of His Majesty's Government', Garran drew up a draft directive for broadcasts to Spain. In it the BBC was specifically asked to emphasise British respect for law and order and aversion to revolutionary methods, and, when preparing news bulletins for the Spanish Service, to treat news regarding the Spanish exiled politicians with reserve.[39] Despite this, the Madrid Embassy continued to complain of the pro-republican bias of the BBC. In June, for example, James Bowker, the Chargé d'Affaires, objected that coverage of the visit to France of Carles Pi i Sunyer, President of the Catalan National Council, was taken in Spain as implying British support for the exiled politicians and appeared to grant them official status. Again, in September, Mallet criticised the weekly feature, *Answers to Correspondents*, for conducting 'clandestine correspondence with increasingly subversive tone'. Consequently, the Foreign Office renewed its pressure on the BBC, and on 10 October Harman Grisewood, Acting Controller of BBC European Services, instructed the Spanish and Portuguese Services to discontinue their political commentaries. In reply to a letter of protest from Helen Grant, Assistant to the Spanish Programmes Organiser, Garran conceded that future broadcasts would perhaps have less appeal to extreme elements in Spain but thought, instead, that they might encourage the moderates to bring about a peaceful change of regime. Not surprisingly, Grant and her immediate superior, Henry Guyatt, Head of the BBC Spanish Section, were not satisfied with this explanation and were dismissed the following month for failing to cooperate.[40]

Thus, any official dealings with the republican government-in-exile, let alone its recognition, were out of the question. On 13 September, Manuel Irujo, Giral's Minister of Shipping and Commerce, acting on behalf of Fernando de los Ríos, Minister of Foreign Affairs, wrote to the Foreign Office requesting British recognition of the republican government-in-exile. Oliver Harvey, an Assistant Under-Secretary of State in the Foreign Office, minuted that so long as Britain recognised the Madrid government, the British government could not officially acknowledge the existence of a Spanish government in Mexico. Irujo's letter, and a second six days later asking the Foreign Secretary to advise His Majesty's Government of his appointment as Giral's representative in Britain, were therefore ignored. In October Irujo informed Bevin that during his forthcoming absence in Mexico he would be represented by José Ignacio de Lizaso of the Basque Delegation in London, but, on Foreign Office advice, this letter also went unacknowledged. When Lizaso in turn asked to meet Philip Noel-Baker, Parliamentary Under-Secretary of State for Foreign Affairs, his request was turned down on the grounds that Britain did not recognise the Spanish republican government.[41]

On 17 December Giral wrote to Bevin and the American Secretary of State, James Byrnes, who were in Moscow for tripartite talks on the post-war peace treaties. Giral insisted that the signatories of the Atlantic Charter could not ignore the legitimacy of his republican government, since it enjoyed the confidence of the President of the Spanish Republic and the *Cortes* and was recognised by all Spanish opposition parties. He drew attention to his pledge before the *Cortes* to hold general elections soon after the republicans' return to Spain and asked Bevin and the American President, Harry Truman, to translate their public repudiation of the Franco regime into a rupture of diplomatic and economic relations with Spain. The maintenance of the present situation in Spain by Britain and the USA, he warned, might 'lead our people, upon feeling themselves abandoned' to 'seek the realisation of their rights and aspirations through a desperate action, of the consequences it is impossible to foresee' (*sic*).[42] His letter concluded with a reference to the French proposal (see Chapter 4) for joint Anglo-American-French action against Franco, which Giral took as evident proof that 'the Franquist regime merits total rejection . . .'[43]

Neither Bevin nor Byrnes referred to Giral's request at the Moscow Foreign Ministers Conference. So, by the end of 1945 any hopes the Spanish *émigrés* had that the revival of republican institutions would win Britain's favour were disappointed. While the British government would not publicly condemn the republican institutions – and certainly not at Franco's bidding – the Foreign Office position, as restated by Garran that December, was unequivocal: the recognition of 'this so-called Government' by His Majesty's Government was not calculated to advance the cause of Spanish democracy.[44]

By contrast, one of the few republican exiles to escape British disapproval was Prieto. On 5 January – at the only Cabinet meeting of 1945 to have the Spanish opposition on its agenda – his request to attend an International Trades Union Conference in Britain raised no objections from the Foreign Secretary. Eden simply recommended that at the same time an entry permit should be granted to Gil-Robles, who would be in transit from Portugal to Switzerland, in order to keep a balance between Left and Right. Cabinet approval was therefore given.[45] The Foreign Office believed that, in contrast to Negrín and other republican exiles, Prieto did enjoy a measure of support within Spain, even within military circles. His *Cortes* speech of 8 November also gained Foreign Office approval, Sloan minuting that 'Prieto – more cautious and flexible in his outlook than his colleagues – alone would seem to have his finger on the pulse in Spain'. Still, although Sloan predicted that Prieto might have a major role to play in the future, by the end of 1945, as has been seen, Prieto's influence in the exiled opposition was much diminished.[46]

Although willing in 1945 to accept either a parliamentary republic or a constitutional monarchy in place of the Franco regime, British preference went on balance to the monarchy. This was indicated in a long minute written by Frederick Hoyer Millar, Head of the Foreign Office Western Department, on 27 August, which met with general Foreign Office approval, including Bevin's:

> It has often been suggested that in view of the conditions in present day Spain – the backwardness of most of the population, the high level of illiteracy, and the general lack of political sense among the inhabitants – a constitutional monarchy is the kind of government best suited to the country, and in view of the past history and tradition the kind of regime most likely to be acceptable to the majority of Spaniards. We have repeatedly been told that anything in the nature of a return to power by the exiled Republicans such as Dr. Negrín would arouse great opposition from all but the extreme Left elements in Spain, and would almost certainly end in civil war. On the assumption that this is really so, then the only alternative to continuing with Franco would seem to be some reasonably moderate centre government. This government could be either a constitutional monarchy or a Republic on the pre-war French lines. For historical reasons the bulk of Spaniards, and particularly the Army, who are still the most powerful element in the country, are much more likely to prefer the monarchy.[47]

Yet the unanswered question was whether the Pretender to the Spanish throne was capable of delivering the constitutional monarchy favoured by Britain. The Lausanne Manifesto in March certainly indicated a firmer *juanista* commitment to constitutionality than had previously been the case. But if this were the sole criterion of acceptability, then Giral's republican government-in-exile was more deserving of British support. As has been seen, though, the republican option was rejected because of the violent resistance it was expected to meet in Spain. What the Foreign Office had to decide was whether the *juanista* monarchy could be restored to Spain without provoking similar opposition. Here the Lausanne Manifesto provided a convenient test. If the monarchists in Spain, and especially the generals, approved Don Juan's stand against Franco and his manifesto's liberal constitutionalism, then a peaceful transition to a post-Franco regime was possible. On the other hand, if the manifesto attracted little or no support, the viability of the *juanista* alternative to Franco would remain open to question.

At this point, reference is made to a claim by Luis María Anson, at one time a member of Don Juan's Privy Council, that the British government was directly involved in the genesis of the Lausanne Manifesto. Anson argues that the manifesto formed part of a wider, Soviet inspired, plan for Spain which the Allies approved at the Yalta Conference of February 1945. According to this plan a Spanish guerrilla army was to be sent to the north of Spain; then, on the pretext of restoring order to the troubled region, the Allies were to enter the country, remove Franco and place the Pretender on the Spanish throne. Following the Yalta Conference Don Juan was accordingly informed by Allen Dulles, at that time chief of American counter-espionage in Europe and based in Berne, that the allied plan required a public declaration from him: hence the Lausanne Manifesto! Anson's claim would be discounted, had it not been given some credence in 1997 by two eminent Spanish historians, Ricardo de la Cierva and Luis Suárez Fernández.[48]

First reports reaching the Foreign Office indicated little monarchist support inside Spain for the Lausanne Manifesto. Five days after its publication Bowker wrote that it had come as rather a surprise to most monarchists; on 27 March he observed that it had left them, and the generals, 'in their usual state of doubt and dither', and that Franco's position had strengthened. Hoyer Millar wondered whether the Spanish people were prepared to risk another civil war 'just to re-establish such a very doubtful quantity as this monarchy', while Garran minuted that Don Juan seemed to have 'mishandled rather badly' the issuing of the manifesto; his supporters had not been warned in advance and the result was confusion. The lack of response to Don Juan's call for monarchist resignations led Hoyer Millar to conclude that the whole episode did not 'give one a very favourable impression of the political sense of the monarchist party'. Finally, on 6 April, Sir Orme Sargent, a Deputy Under-Secretary in the Foreign Office, simply commented: 'All very Spanish'![49]

In the months following the Lausanne Manifesto – as Franco had intended – conflicting signals from Spain made it difficult for the Foreign Office to formulate policy towards the *juanista* monarchy. In July the appointment of the committed monarchist, Alberto Martín Artajo, as Foreign Minister suggested a new pro-monarchist orientation to the Franco regime. But in September Martín Artajo's comment to Mallet that Franco was unlikely to restore the monarchy in under two years led the Foreign Office to assume that the exchanges between Franco and Don Juan that summer had proved abortive and that Franco was determined to retain power.[50] Accounts given the British Embassy by Oriol of his frequent visits to Lausanne during the year also added to Foreign Office uncertainty. In August, for example, Oriol told Mallet that he had been asked by Franco to convey a definite invitation to Don Juan to return to Spain to re-establish the monarchy. Within twenty-four hours, however, Mallet had to report that the initiative for the forthcoming visit to Don Juan had been Oriol's alone. In late November Oriol informed Mallet that he now doubted Franco's willingness to hand over power; yet a few days later he was insisting to Captain Mason Scott, the Embassy Naval Attaché, that Franco was indeed ready to make a 'straight transmission' to the King (*sic*) and retire with honour. The Foreign Office could only ponder, somewhat inconclusively, the relative strengths of Franco and Don Juan.[51]

The Foreign Office was aware, too, that the fate of the *juanista* cause depended ultimately on the monarchist generals. There was, as has been mentioned, occasional talk in military circles of moves against Franco to establish a constitutional monarchy. In January, for example, Generals Kindelán and Rafael García-Valiño, Chief of the Army General Staff, spoke to Brigadier Wyndham Torr, the Military Attaché at the Madrid Embassy, of plans for an interim *junta* of generals. But, as the arch-conspirator Aranda himself pointed out to Torr, Franco was removing the monarchist generals from key commands in the country, and, in any case, they were unlikely to shoot their fellow citizens just for the sake of Don Juan.[52] Furthermore, even if the generals did remove Franco, there was still the problem of the nature of their substitute regime, which, though monarchist, was hardly likely to advance Spain's democratisation. Certainly, the kind of authoritarian regime favoured, amongst others, by Kindelán, which Garran euphemistically termed 'democracy with limitations', would not have won general acceptance outside Spain.[53] The generals, in short, could not be relied upon in 1945 to provide an acceptable monarchist alternative to the Franco dictatorship.

The evident failure of the Lausanne Manifesto to consolidate the monarchist opposition in Spain explains Foreign Office warnings in 1945 against giving official British support, let alone recognition, to the *juanista* cause. In May Bowker reported a conversation between Harold Farquhar, the British Consul-General in Barcelona, and Matéu Pla, in which the latter asked for an Anglo-American declaration against Franco. Garran minuted that what Matéu really wanted was for Britain to support the monarchist cause, but there was no reason, he thought, 'why we should pull the Spanish Monarchist chestnuts out of the fire in this way'.[54] When, in October, Mallet sent the Foreign Office a list of names for a provisional government drawn up by the monarchist, Juan Ventosa y Calvell, a former Minister of Finance in Alfonso XIII's last government, the question of British support for such schemes arose again. Sloan minuted that the least the British government could do was to give an assurance that constructive efforts to remove Franco had Britain's support. Garran, on the other hand, was firmly against giving any encouragement to the monarchists, since that would have led straight to civil war, and preferred simply making it clear to the Spaniards that Britain wanted a peaceful change from the Franco regime. This line, Garran argued somewhat inconsistently, would give the necessary encouragement to moderate elements in Spain to pluck up courage and take steps to work out their own salvation. Hoyer Millar was against encouraging one group at the expense of another and advised that it would be better from Britain's point of view if Franco remained in power to face the food crisis expected that winter. The conclusion reached in the Foreign Office was that the British government should studiously avoid any direct encouragement to Ventosa, and Mallet was accordingly informed.[55]

Yet, in private the British attitude towards the monarchist opposition was often less intransigent than this official stance suggested. There was, for example, some sympathy for Gil-Robles. His support of the allied cause from September 1943 on was appreciated in the Foreign Office, where the Research Department held that Gil-Robles' catholic-clericalist party deserved to take its part, alongside liberals and socialists, 'in a parliamentary democracy on the pattern of Belgium'.[56] In January the Cabinet had raised no objections to Gil-Robles' proposed transit through London on his way to Switzerland. In the event, the

Portuguese authorities' refusal to issue a re-entry passport had prevented Gil-Robles from leaving Portugal and so the following November he was expected to re-apply to enter Britain. Apart from Garran, who now objected that Gil-Robles' sudden appearance in Britain would be interpreted as an indication of British government support, reaction in the Foreign Office was favourable, and Bevin, who declared himself puzzled by the extensive minuting the issue had generated, ruled that Gil-Robles could enter the country.[57]

Frequent and informal contacts were also maintained with prominent monarchists in Spain. Indeed, such was the stream of visitors to the British Embassy and Consulates there that at one point the Spanish Ministry of Foreign Affairs requested an explanation.[58] British views on the Spanish monarchy, though informally expressed, were consequently widely known in monarchist circles and beyond. On 29 November, for example, only two days after receiving Foreign Office instructions not to encourage Ventosa, Mallet told Oriol over lunch that His Majesty's Government would not withhold its recognition, were a constitutional monarchy to be restored to Spain. Nor, despite British insistence on its non-intervention in Spanish affairs, was the Ambassador slow to proffer his own advice, suggesting in late 1945, for example, that leading monarchists should make a common declaration for a restoration of the monarchy.[59]

By the end of 1945 the British government believed that neither the exiled republican opposition nor the *juanista* monarchy had individually the potential to inspire a broad, united opposition movement in Spain with sufficient moral suasion to bring about Franco's peaceful departure. But there remained the third option, a republican-monarchist coalition of 'moderates'. As already noted, ANFD-monarchist talks resumed in the late autumn of 1945 and an agreement on transitional arrangements for a new regime was predicted for the end of the year. Consequently, the Foreign Office had to consider the British government's attitude in the light of these developments.

At first the Foreign Office saw little reason to trust the ANFD. In October it received a highly critical report on it from Madrid. Mallet described the clandestine groups that made up the Alliance of Democratic Forces as 'for the most part, unorganised, without programme or prospects, and scattered throughout the country'. He doubted the readiness of centre and left-wing republicans to cooperate within the framework of a state headed by a constitutional monarchy, and, even if they were ready to cooperate, he questioned whether that amounted to anything more than the hope of idealistic and disillusioned republican leaders who did not represent the views of the masses. He pointed out that an 'abyss' existed between Left and Right, bridged only by a few far-sighted men, who until then had been effectively prevented by Franco's regime 'from riding common ground where their fellows may get together'.[60]

There were reservations, too, concerning the character of some of the monarchists expected to negotiate with the republicans. In July Bowker described Aranda as 'indiscreet and believed by many to be untrustworthy', and thought that this diminished the influence which his outstanding intelligence would otherwise have secured him. The *republican* Ramón Feced, whose opinions Tom Burns, the Embassy Press Attaché, valued highly, believed, moreover, that Aranda's efforts to enlist working class organisations into a new Christian-Democrat party were doomed to failure, as he was too implicated in the Civil War. Beigbeder, who had recently returned to Madrid from a two year military mission to Washington, was described by Bowker as dynamic but 'slightly irresponsible', and, while Orgaz's outstanding organisational ability was acknowledged, he was otherwise depicted as 'fat, agreeable to meet, strong-willed and unimaginative'. Kindelán in Spain, and Sainz Rodríguez and Gil-Robles in Portugal, were among the few who escaped criticism.[61]

None the less, by the late autumn of 1945 there were definite reports from Spain of a republican-monarchist *rapprochement*. It was already known that the ANFD libertarians were monarchist, and, on 10 October, Burns learnt from a delegation of the interior PSOE that Spanish socialism was by no means committed to a republican regime. To avoid reverting to the enmities of the Second Republic, it was prepared to recognise a non-political monarchy, provided it accepted genuine elections and a broad-based coalition government. Then, on 22 November, Mallet reported that verbal agreement had been reached between the ANFD and the monarchists.[62]

This news inevitably raised the question of British reaction to the agreement. On 4 December Sloan minuted that it constituted an 'important development' and, from the British and American point of view, seemed 'sound'. The important questions were when the agreement's plan would materialise and whether the British government should support it. As Britain's influence was an 'important factor', Sloan submitted, the British government should support the plan in its early stages, and, once the new regime consolidated itself, should give the *Frente Nacional Democrático* its full diplomatic support, especially as regards the UN. He advised economic assistance in the form of heavy material – such as dockyard equipment – to boost employment and, possibly, aviation fuel to help transport and palliate the effects of the drought then affecting Spain. As regards timing, Sloan thought that this was up to the Spaniards, but an increase in material help could be promised for two, four or six months' time. The Army, he believed, could be brought round by a British embargo on war material to Spain and also by British assurances of support for the republican-monarchist agreement, provided it did not lead to victimisation.

Garran, on the other hand, was against abandoning non-intervention since there was no guarantee the republican-monarchist initiative would succeed. 'If we were openly to support the movement and things went wrong we should be blamed for the whole fiasco and our prestige would suffer', he minuted. The 'movement' should be strong enough to stand on its own feet, and, as he remarked yet again, it was not for Britain 'to pull the Spanish chestnuts out of the fire'. Active British support for a monarchist restoration would be misunderstood in Britain and the USA and criticised by the USSR, and Britain would be accused of trying to restore the forces of reaction as in Greece. But the crux of the matter, as far as Garran was concerned, was the Army, which would not be influenced in the right direction by active British support for the republican-monarchist agreement since it was notoriously xenophobic and highly likely to resent foreign interference. Still, Garran accepted Sloan's suggestion that the American and British governments could let it be known that deliveries of military supplies to Franco would cease, and, as an additional measure, he proposed broadcasting BBC 'programmes of interest' to the Army!

For his part Hoyer Millar emphasised the communist threat. He feared that Anglo-American support for the monarchy could lead to Soviet intervention to strengthen the PCE, which in turn might bring about revolution. One of Britain's main objectives, he asserted, was to prevent Spain becoming a 'source of dissension' between the major European powers, and to achieve this it was necessary to stick closely to the policy of non-intervention. On 7 December Cadogan accepted Hoyer Millar's advice that there was no need to inform Mallet of any change of attitude by the British government.[63]

To an extent the Madrid Embassy inclined to Sloan's point of view. On 5 December Mallet wrote to Harvey that Britain could not leave the moderate opposition in 'mid air', and if a coalition came into being, it would have to be recognised. For Mallet, too, the military factor was paramount. The generals, and the Spanish Right, would never accept a republic and, therefore, the monarchy, which, he asserted, had not been a party to the Civil War, was the only solution. He admitted that any post-Franco military regime was likely to be too far to the right for foreign opinion – at least until elections were held – but in order to prevent a split in the Army, the Allies could not long delay recognition. Minuting on these views Sloan argued that unless the British government encouraged the Spanish opposition, it would appear to be departing from 'the main line' of its Spanish policy – the long-term development of political and economic relations with Spain. Encouragement of the opposition, moreover, avoided the risk of establishing a government solely 'on the strength of foreign opinion' and did stand a chance of consolidating opinion in Spain behind a new democratic regime. He did not, however, accept Mallet's proposal of British support for 'Right Wing administrators' while there was still the prospect of a moderate Left-Right coalition. Rather, British encouragement should go to all 'moderate and responsible elements'.

Once again Garran insisted that before receiving recognition any group or coalition wanting to replace Franco had to be strong enough to stand on its own feet. He felt, too, that in spite of complaints from various opposition leaders that the British government was leaving them suspended in mid-air, all the reports from Madrid indicated that they were making 'quite satisfactory progress' towards forming a broad coalition on which to base the new regime. For his part, Hoyer Millar advised against any precipitate action which might drive the Army into outright support of Franco. He accepted that at a later stage the British government would have to give the opposition some indication of British recognition, if they ousted Franco, but that moment had not yet arrived and would not until there was a reasonably strong opposition.[64]

On 11 December Harvey, who was on a 12-day visit to Tangier, reported a long conversation with Mallet on the Spanish opposition. Mallet predicted that because a 'sort of national group' had been formed, there would be a change of regime, possibly by the summer of 1946. When Harvey emphasised that, from the international point of view, this group should extend from left to right, Mallet assured him that as far as possible he was impressing this upon its leaders. As to who might figure in a government of national unity under Don Juan, Mallet mentioned Gil-Robles, Prieto, two generals or so and representatives from the socialist and trades union organisations. The forthcoming municipal elections, he told Harvey, might serve as an indication of 'how the wind was blowing', and if, as was believed, they were followed by elections to the *Cortes*, that could be the signal for the new national committee to take over. What was holding this group back, according to Mallet, was fear of civil war and therefore they needed the support of Britain and the USA, without which they might not be able to prevent the situation from 'slipping into an extreme communist and revolutionary government'.[65]

On 31 December 1945 Britain's position on the ANFD-monarchist agreement was made clear when William Perry George, a Counsellor of the American Embassy in London, visited Harvey at the Foreign Office. George was for recognising what he called the National Committee of Liberation the moment a satisfactory *coup d'état* had been carried out against Franco. Harvey agreed, though pointing to the universal concern to avoid civil war, but went on to explain that it was difficult for the British government to give the opposition a blank cheque in advance. The furthest they were prepared to go was for the British Ambassador in Madrid to say that, provided the opposition movement was widely representative of all classes and appeared to be supported by the country, recognition would no doubt be given.[66] Thus, as 1945 came to an end the prospective republican-monarchist coalition in Spain, though favourably looked upon, was no more successful in winning British recognition than Giral's government-in-exile or Don Juan's pretension to the throne of Spain. In the event, the collapse of the ANFD-monarchist agreement early in 1946 temporarily relieved the British government of any need to depart from its policy of inaction.

There was one commendable exception to Britain's policy of non-intervention in Spanish affairs. Motivated partly by humanitarian concern but mainly by pressure of public opinion at home, the British government occasionally interceded with the Spanish authorities on behalf of political prisoners, particularly those under sentence of death. The most publicised cases in 1945 were those of two communists, Santiago Alvarez Gómez and Sebastián Zapirain, who were arrested in August. The following month Mallet mentioned them twice to Martín Artajo and as a result both men were spared execution.[67]

Yet, the British government acted only when firmly convinced that it was dealing with genuine cases of political victimisation and remained, as ever, preoccupied with the danger of civil disorder in Spain. Thus, once it was assumed within the Foreign Office that Alvarez and Zapirain would not die, there was general agreement that enough had been done for them and that further pressure for their release would be open to the charge of promoting anarchy in Spain.[68] Mallet, in fact, frequently begrudged his interventions on behalf of political prisoners. On 4 October 1945 he wrote to Hoyer Millar that the whole story of Alvarez and Zapirain smelt of 'communist-planned agitation' and that he would not be surprised if the two men had been planted in Spain for the very purpose of trying to stir up bad blood between foreign governments and the Spanish Government.[69] On 15 November Philip Noel-Baker agreed with Garran in connection with another case – that of Ricardo Escrig Gonzalvo – that while Britain would welcome a change of regime in Spain, 'we do not want this to happen as a result of Civil War and consequently we clearly do not want to give any encouragement to subversive activity by extremist elements in Spain, which if successful can only have the result of provoking Civil War'. Garran thought, too, that, although Britain naturally wished to discourage the Franco regime from executing people on political charges, they should be careful not to undermine the influence which they could wield to that end by intervening in undeserving cases.[70]

The perceived shortcomings of the anti-Franco opposition went far to explain the reluctance of the two British governments of 1945 to give any part of it their official recognition. But this cautious policy was also influenced by the prevailing state of Anglo-Spanish relations, for, inevitably, any British accommodation of the Franco regime meant a corresponding reduction in support for his opponents.

Churchill's 'warning' at the beginning of the year had made it clear to Franco that his pro-Axis policies during World War II had gravely compromised Anglo-Spanish relations, and this message was repeated when Mallet presented his credentials as Britain's Ambassador to Spain on 27 July 1945. Again, the following month, Mallet left Martín Artajo in no doubt that unless the Franco regime were based on democratic principles it could not gain British approval.[71] At the end of 1945 Bevin, too, made no secret of his personal distaste for the Franco regime, bluntly declaring before the Commons on 5 December that he detested it and that it was 'one with which HMGs [*sic*] have no sympathy'.[72]

The British government was also aware of increasingly hostile international opposition to Franco. This, in the immediate post-war period, was given its first formal expression at the UN founding

Conference of San Francisco where, on 19 June, Spain, though not identified by name, was effectively excluded from UN membership. Thenceforth, whatever their private reservations, British governments were unable to adopt an exclusively bilateral approach to Anglo-Spanish relations or to contemplate a *rapprochement* to the Franco regime without damaging the infant world organisation and Britain's moral authority within it.

Yet, the credibility of the British governments' anti-Franco rhetoric of 1945 was undermined by their undisguised adherence to a policy of non-intervention in Spanish internal affairs. That Britain would not relax this policy at the end of the World War was made abundantly clear on 19 July, at the Third Plenary Session of the Potsdam Conference, when a proposal from the Soviet leader, Joseph Stalin, for breaking off diplomatic relations with Spain was roundly rejected by Churchill. A resolution, subsequently incorporated into the Conference's Final Declaration, stated the three signatory governments' opposition to Spain's membership of the UN, but its 'fairly anodyne' wording, as intended by the Foreign Office, had no effect upon Britain's policy of non-intervention.[73]

Towards the end of the Potsdam Conference, Attlee and Bevin had replaced Churchill and Eden as Prime Minister and Foreign Secretary respectively. Yet, while there was no doubting Attlee's personal commitment to democracy, the change of government made no difference at all to Britain's official policy on Franco Spain. On 20 August – just five days after the Japanese capitulation – during the Commons Debate on the Address, Bevin unequivocally reaffirmed British commitment to non-intervention in Spain:

> I will briefly quote HMG's view. It is that the question of Spain is one for the Spanish people to decide. I cannot go further than the declaration issued at the Berlin Conference, which makes it plain that while we have no desire permanently to penalise the Spanish people, we cannot admit Spain into the club, unless she accepts the basic principles of the club. These are the rights of people freely to choose their own form of government. On the other hand, I am satisfied that intervention by foreign Powers in the internal affairs of Spain would have the opposite effect to that desired, and would probably strengthen General Franco's position. It is obvious from what I have said that we shall take a favourable view if steps are taken by the Spanish people to change their regime, but HMG are not prepared to take any steps which would promote or encourage civil war in that

country. In this, I know, I am voicing the views not only of myself but of many ardent Republicans.[74]

Of course, the underlying reasons for Bevin's reluctance to take direct action against Spain were left unsaid. There were, first, Britain's continuing trade relations with Spain to be taken into account. Undoubtedly, Spain, amidst the economic dislocation of post-war Europe, remained an important supplier to Britain of minerals and essential foodstuffs, and in 1945–46 Britain had a purchasing programme of Spanish exports worth some £20 million. With her large sterling credits, moreover, Spain was well placed to assist in British plans for a Western European sterling bloc.[75] It was recognised, therefore, that direct action against Spain would have risked damaging retaliation from Franco. Furthermore, as the British Embassy in Lisbon reminded the Foreign Office in October 1945, any breakdown of order in Spain would also have had unfortunate repercussions in Portugal at a time when Britain was hoping to expand her exports there and, indeed, was on the verge of securing a £10 million order for hydro-electric power equipment.[76] While expressing his aversion to doing anything to strengthen Franco, at a Cabinet meeting of 23 October, Bevin had also to acknowledge that 'too strict a policy' over controlling exports to Spain would only result in diverting valuable export orders to the USA. Taking all this into account, it was therefore not surprising that in November the Foreign Office firmly advised against withdrawing Britain's Ambassador from Spain. For, despite the fact that this left Britain open to criticism, it was felt that in both the short and long term, Britain stood to gain from playing 'what will amount to a lone hand in Madrid' during so critical a period in Spanish affairs.[77]

This reluctance to act against Franco arose, too, out of Britain's continuing concern with imperial security. Spain and Spanish Morocco's strategic importance for Britain's lines of maritime communication had been amply demonstrated during World War II, and the ending of hostilities did not alter the situation. Indeed, on 1 June 1945 the Chiefs of Staff endorsed a Post-Hostilities Planning Sub-Committee paper which insisted that a friendly or neutral Spain was still essential for the security of Britain's vital Atlantic communications.[78] Of course, an alternative regime to Franco's could have been equally 'friendly or neutral', but until Franco's removal the British government had no choice but to work with the regime in place.

Nowhere was this more clearly illustrated, in the immediate post-war period, than over the International Zone of Tangier. Spain had occupied the Zone in June 1940, after the Fall of France, before taking over its administration five months later. At the end of the World War the problems facing the British government over Tangier were threefold. The first was how to end the Spanish occupation peacefully, since the logistical difficulties of mounting a successful military operation and of ensuring adequate food supplies to the Zone without Franco's cooperation were considerable.[79] There was, secondly, the problem of the Zone's new postwar adminstration, as a straight reversion to the *status quo ante* would have left the French in a position to dominate the whole of Morocco after the Spanish withdrawal.[80] Finally, after having to concede the USSR's right to participate in discussions over Tangier, the British government was concerned to keep Soviet influence in the Western Mediterranean to a minimum.[81]

Consequently, at the Tangier Conference in Paris of 10–31 August 1945 – involving Britain, France, the USA and the USSR – called to decide an interim statute for the Tangier Zone until an international conference of all the Algeciras Powers could agree a new one, the British found themselves cast in the role of Franco's defender. Thus, the British delegation took the lead in opposing a Soviet demand that Spain should not be included in the interim administration and any final conference on Tangier until democracy were restored in Spain.[82] In fact, the proposed international conference on Tangier never materialised. For Britain the indefinite prolongation of the interim Tangier administration delayed Soviet intrusion into the Western Mediterranean; France, too, was in no hurry to lose its advantages under the interim arrangements, and neither France nor the USSR was willing to contemplate a new statute as long as Franco remained in power. Largely through Britain's efforts, though, the real winner was Franco, who, after the evacuation of his troops from Tangier in October 1945, was rewarded with continuing Spanish participation in the administration of Tangier.

With Britain the apparent champion of Spanish interests in 1945, it was consequently not surprising that occasional expressions of British disapproval failed to dent Franco's confidence.[83] Officials in the Spanish Foreign Ministry were well aware of British fears of communist revolution in Spain and the need, therefore, for order and strong government there.[84] Acting on the advice of Carrero Blanco, Under-Secretary of the Presidency, Franco deliberately played up his regime's catholicism and anti-communism while looking forward to the inevitable conflict between the 'liberal powers' and the USSR, which, he believed, would bring his regime eventual recognition. Until that happened, though, Spain would adopt a policy of dignity and defiance with the watchwords of *orden, unidad y aguantar* (order, unity and endurance).[85] British non-intervention notwithstanding, Spain, as the newly arrived Spanish Ambassador, Domingo de las Bárcenas y López, impressed upon Cadogan at their first meeting in the Foreign Office on 11 December 1945, would brook no interference in her internal affairs.[86]

Conclusion

In 1945 the Spanish republican and monarchist anti-Franco oppositions assumed that Britain's policy towards Spain was motivated principally by a desire to see the restoration of democracy in Spain. After waging a world war against totalitarian fascism, Britain, they were convinced, would take the lead in a concerted move against Franco. All that was incumbent upon them was to present themselves as worthy democratic alternatives to the Franco regime. Yet what the majority of Franco's Spanish opponents failed to realise was that British policy towards Spain consistently awarded priority to Britain's economic and strategic interests. These required, above all, stability in the Iberian Peninsula and Western Mediterranean. Hence the total unacceptability, from the British point of view, of Giral's government, whose intransigent republicanism promised only renewed civil war and communist revolution. Don Juan's monarchy seemed equally incapable of uniting the Spanish nation behind it, since the Lausanne Manifesto had fallen at the first hurdle, unable to win the support of the Spanish Right, let alone that of the Left. Only the republican-monarchist coalition in Spain, negotiated in late 1945, appeared for a while to hold out any chance of providing the moderate alternative to Franco so favoured by Britain. But even here Britain was not prepared to risk retaliation from Franco by recognising a shadow government before it had established itself and secured the backing of the Army.

Without a credible opposition to hand and with important British interests at stake, Britain had little option but to accept continuing co-existence with the Franco regime. In October 1945 the case for inaction was put by Mallet:

> In general, I believe the nation now in gradual progress towards a somewhat more liberal system, and eventual change of the regime will take place quicker if left to itself for a while. Spain is suffering from being too much in the news, whereas compared with the vastly greater problems of the rest of Europe and Asia this comparatively prosperous country surely presents less urgent problems and can

safely be left over for later. It is not as if we were having any real difficulties with the Spanish Government over immediate questions.
For instance, over Tangier and Safehaven they are proving quite
amenable.

In other words the policy of non-intervention in Spanish affairs
which has been proclaimed both in Washington and London appears
fully justified. This, of course, does not mean that I should fail to
avail myself of any opportunity of rubbing in the extreme distaste
felt in Great Britain for Franco's regime, but it does mean avoidance
of nagging over minor matters in order not to antagonise friendly
officials whose assistance is useful to us. Franco's downfall is only a
matter of time, whether weeks, months or years, but what is essential is that when it comes there should be a peaceful transition to the
future regime, and that His Majesty's Government should not incur
the odium of having so forced the issue that bloodshed occurs.[87]

Mallet's analysis of the situation was fully endorsed by the Foreign
Office, although any hopes that Britain would be left to pursue its *attentiste* policy undisturbed were disappointed two months later. As 1945
drew to a close, the French government would react to increasing pressure at home by calling on the British and American governments to
join it in decisive action against the Franco regime. Much of 1946 would
subsequently be taken up by the need to meet the growing international
challenge to British policy on Spain.

4
1946: International Confrontation

In the winter of 1944–45 the British government had been able to formulate its post-war policy towards Franco Spain in relative isolation. Admittedly, there were, during the next twelve months, signs of mounting international disquiet over Spain but these had not been enough to force Britain's foreign policy makers to revise their self-styled 'policy of pin-pricks' – namely, criticism without intervention – towards the Franco regime. However, in late 1945 a marked deterioration in relations between the French and Spanish governments ushered in a period of international confrontation with the Spanish Dictator, from which the British government could not easily distance itself. Britain's policy towards the anti-Franco opposition in 1946 had, therefore, to take into account not only the evolution of the Spanish opposition itself but also, increasingly, *international* hostility towards the Franco regime.

The anti-Franco opposition

The ultimate goal of the Spanish republican government-in-exile was the replacement of the Franco regime by a democratic republic. Giral's exclusive reliance on diplomatic and economic sanctions to bring this about left republican ambitions very much dependent on international good will. Unfortunately for Giral, however, at the start of 1946 his four month old government had still to be formally acknowledged as a credible alternative to the Franco dictatorship by either France, Britain, the USA or the USSR. Admittedly, there was, in the new year, an upsurge in anti-Franco sentiment in France – and Giral certainly hoped to capitalise on this when he took up permanent residence there in February – but the French government was reluctant to add to its difficulties with Britain and the USA over Spain by unilaterally recognising the Spanish government-in-exile.[1] For their part, what residual sympathy the British and American governments might have felt towards Giral totally evaporated in March 1946 after the appointment of the communist Santiago Carrillo to his cabinet.[2] Furthermore, although Carrillo's appointment brought a flurry of recognitions for the Giral government from the East European bloc – which only reinforced Anglo-American prejudices – it was noticeable that the Soviet government's was not amongst them.[3] Having failed, therefore, to win over the major powers, Giral turned in 1946 to the UN in the hope that the new world organisation would put its moral authority at the service of his cause.

An opportunity to present the republican case to the UN soon arose when a Security Council sub-committee was set up in April to investigate the Spanish question. In May Giral submitted a comprehensive memorandum to the UN Secretary-General, Trygve Lie, which called upon member states of the UN to sever their diplomatic relations with Franco Spain. Failure to do this, it argued, would amount to retrospectively condoning Axis involvement in Spanish affairs, while the continuing existence of Franco's totalitarian system represented a real threat to international peace and security. Giral's memorandum also drew attention to the harsh repression of political dissent in Spain and in a final appeal claimed that the civilised world, through the UN and the Security Council, owed it to the Spanish Republic not to exempt Spain from the rules of justice, security and law, the 'sole guarantees of human coexistence', without which 'Spain and Western Europe would constitute a permanent danger to peace'.[4]

These arguments were repeated when Giral appeared in person before the Security Council sub-committee on 23 and 27 May and again in the autumn when he lobbied the UN General Assembly session in New York.[5] However, his bid for decisive UN action against Franco proved unsuccessful. Under the terms of the resolution finally adopted by the General Assembly on 12 December 1946, member states were not required to break off full diplomatic relations with Spain but only to withdraw their ambassadors and ministers plenipotentiary from Madrid. Not surprisingly, the limited scope of the resolution, and the absence from its text of any reference to the Spanish republican government-in-exile, undermined the confidence of the wider republican opposition in the Giral government. Consequently, at a joint meeting of the PSOE and UGT executive committees in Toulouse on 14–15 January 1947 – also attended by PSOE delegates from Mexico and Spain – the decision was taken to withdraw socialist support from the Giral government and on 27 January Giral's socialist, and libertarian, ministers resigned their posts. Without the support of the two major political organisations of the republican opposition, Giral's position was untenable and he resigned. Martínez Barrio's immediate choice of the moderate *republican* Augusto Barcia y Trelles, Giral's Minister of Finance, to lead the next government was also rejected by the PSOE, and it was not until 9 February that the second republican government-in-exile was formed by Rodolfo Llopis Ferrándiz, General Secretary of the PSOE.[6]

The PSOE's move against Giral in January 1947 was precipitated by the UN resolution, but it also reflected a more gradual shift in the party's position during much of 1946. This arose not so much from doubts over Giral's day-to-day political acumen – although Santiago Carrillo's ministerial appointment in March certainly caused the PSOE leadership serious misgivings – as from his intransigent republicanism. At a joint meeting of the PSOE-UGT executives in December 1945 and again at a PSOE plenary the following month, it had already been agreed that if the automatic restoration of the Spanish republic proved impossible, the PSOE should be free to recommend 'another formula', and this revised position was formally endorsed in a resolution carried at the Second Congress of the PSOE-in-France, held in Toulouse on 22–26 May 1946.[7]

Later that summer the exiled PSOE further modified its position when, in defiance of Giral, its executive committee advised the PSOE in Spain to accept the need for a plebiscite of the Spanish people. It also encouraged the interior PSOE to back an ANFD manifesto of 9 July 1946, which invited 'the rest of the anti-Franco forces' – namely, the monarchists – to join with it in overthrowing the Franco regime. Giral immediately condemned this call for a broad opposition front and reasserted his government-in-exile's exclusive claim to 'constitutional legitimacy and republican continuity', but he was not supported in this by his socialist and libertarian ministers.[8]

Not surprisingly, the growing tension between the PSOE and Giral worked to the advantage of the *prietista* faction of the PSOE. Towards the end of 1945 Prieto had already received unexpected support from the veteran socialist leader and former militant champion of the Spanish Republic, Francisco Largo Caballero. During his wartime internment in a German concentration camp, Largo Caballero had come to the conclusion that the Franco regime could only be replaced by a broad-based transitional regime committed to holding a plebiscite on the final form of the Spanish state. To this end he drew up an 11-point programme as a basis for negotiations between the main factions of the PSOE on the nature of this transitional regime, and in January

1946 made contact with several monarchists.[9] Although the initiative was brought to a premature halt by Largo Caballero's death two months later, it pointed to a new spirit of compromise, and at the PSOE Congress in May the rift between the rival factions of Mexico and France was officially healed. The party's new unity was further underlined by the Congress decision to change the name of the PSOE-*in-France* to the all-embracing PSOE-*in-exile*.[10]

Towards the end of 1945 Franco feared that the Foreign Ministers' Conference in Moscow in December might decide on direct action against Spain. He therefore began to seek – or, rather, to be seen to seek – agreement with the Spanish Pretender on a merger of the *juanista* monarchy with his own regime. Neither Britain nor the USA, Franco calculated, would overthrow a monarchist regime, whatever its *franquista* connections, for fear of provoking left-wing revolution in Spain. Accordingly, the Spanish leader intimated that he was prepared to accept a provisional government, with representation of all political parties, except the PCE, followed immediately by a monarchist restoration and spring elections to the *Cortes*.[11] Franco's intention at the time was to meet Don Juan. With the Pretender to the Spanish throne refusing to enter Spain except as king and the Dictator *persona non grata* north of the Pyrenees, the only practical venue was Portugal and so Don Juan was duly informed on Christmas Day 1945 that the veto on his move to Portugal had been lifted.[12]

In the event, the interview between the two men did not take place. The Moscow Conference ended on 26 December without any reference to Spain and, with the immediate threat to his regime lifted, Franco's habitual caution reasserted itself. Instead of a meeting with Don Juan, he now proposed informal talks between their respective representatives. Gil-Robles, however, warned Don Juan against any such meeting until Franco unequivocally recognised the Pretender's claim to the throne of Spain and had set a date for the handing over of power.[13] This was, of course, totally unacceptable to Franco, but, because of extensive foreign press and radio coverage of his supposed *rapprochement* with Don Juan, which he was reluctant to disavow, the Spanish leader was unable to reimpose his ban on the Pretender's move to Portugal.[14] Thus, on 2 February 1946, Don Juan and his wife, Doña María de las Mercedes de Borbón y Orleans, arrived at the airport of Portela de Sacavem, near Lisbon.[15] The royal party deliberately snubbed Nicolás Franco, brother of the Spanish Dictator and his Ambassador in Portugal, at the airport. A fortnight later, the breakdown in relations between Franco and Don Juan was confirmed when Nicolás Franco informed the

Pretender that his brother would never agree to a meeting on Don Juan's terms.[16]

The Spanish court's transfer to Portugal enabled Gil-Robles, by now acknowledged to be Don Juan's principal advisor in exile, to give a greater sense of direction to the monarchist opposition. As has already been noted, a prime concern of Gil-Robles was to secure the cooperation of the Spanish Right in the restoration of the *juanista* monarchy. He therefore thought it important to move quickly to neutralise the influence of the *juanistas'* main rival for the allegiance of the Spanish Right – the *Comunión Tradicionalista*. So, in less than a month after Don Juan's arrival in Estoril, Gil-Robles reached agreement with representatives of the *Comunión* on the constitutional bases of a restored Spanish monarchy (*Bases Institucionales para la Restauración de la Monarquía en España*).[17] According to these, all Spanish political life was to be predicated upon the Catholic religion, the 'sacred union' of Spain, and a 'representative' monarchy. There would be a unicameral *Cortes*, with one third of its members directly elected by universal suffrage, although ministers would not be answerable to it and the king would exercise his considerable executive and legislative powers only 'in collaboration' with it. Workers' representation was to be effected through corporative syndicates. All twelve *Bases* were subject to the nation's approval but, it was stated, without prejudice to the immediate implementation of those prerogatives 'inherent in the principle of legitimacy embodied in the person of the King'. There would, in other words, be no plebiscite *before* a monarchist restoration – a plebiscite *a priori* – and the monarchy would be submitted to popular approval only *after* it was in place – by a plebiscite *a posteriori*.[18]

Harking back to 19th century Spanish liberalism, the *Bases* were clearly intended to counter the effect of the democratic principles enunciated by Don Juan in *La Gazette de Lausanne* only two months earlier.[19] It was consequently not surprising that they were coldly received by the moderate monarchists within Spain while Aranda warned of probable opposition from the republicans. In a letter to Don Juan of 3 February, the ANFD had already pointed out that any solution of the Spanish political problem without its consent would be considered 'precarious and anti-democratic' and would meet with its 'unanimous disapproval and opposition'.[20] Not surprisingly, therefore, news of the *Bases* agreement temporarily destroyed all hopes of concluding an immediate ANFD-monarchist agreement.

Following this breakdown, the ANFD's organisation was severely disrupted by renewed police action, and it was not until the end of June that it succeeded once again in formally reconstituting itself. Fresh contacts with the monarchists began in August and the next month negotiations resumed. In anticipation, the ANFD had drawn up yet another manifesto in which it repeated its call for a provisional government of all anti-Franco political parties and trade union organisations, a plebiscite and elections to a constituent assembly within nine to twelve months, and a National Resistance Council to act as a consultative organ of the provisional government.[21] The manifesto served as a basis for the negotiations with the monarchists and a draft agreement was quickly reached. Under its terms, the ANFD was required to break with Giral, and the communists, and to support a provisional government – a *Gobierno de Reconciliación* – headed by a general, who would be responsible for appointing another 17 or 11 ministers, three of whom would also be generals with the remaining ministerial posts shared equally between republicans and monarchists. It was also agreed that there would be a plebiscite within a year.[22]

Gil-Robles feared that the effect of the draft ANFD-monarchist agreement would be to undermine his recent *Bases* agreement and so frighten off the Spanish Right. With Don Juan's official representative in Spain, Don Alfonso, confined to his Andalusian estate and Kindelán banished to Tenerife at the end of February for eight months, and after the death of General Orgaz in January, he was therefore determined to wrest the initiative from the principal *juanista* activist still at liberty in Spain – Aranda – and bring all future negotiations with the republicans firmly under Lisbon's control.

An opportunity for this arose at the end of September when the chief republican negotiator, Francisco Santamaría, CNT Political Secretary and, by then, General Secretary of the ANFD, went to Toulouse to represent the CNT and the ANFD at the Second Congress of the UGT-in-exile.[23] Returning to Paris after the Congress, he was persuaded by Julio López Oliván, a member of Don Juan's Political Secretariat acting on Gil-Robles' instructions, to discuss the draft ANFD-monarchist agreement with the Pretender and his advisors in Lisbon.[24]

Santamaría arrived in Lisbon on 15 October in the expectation that Don Juan would automatically approve the agreement. Instead, he found himself forced by Gil-Robles and Sainz Rodríguez to modify the draft he brought with him. The first four points of what was subsequently known as the Estoril Agreement incorporated relatively minor adjustments: they dealt with freedom of religion and the special position of the Catholic religion in Spain, the strict maintenance of law and order, the substitution of the right to strike by compulsory arbitration during an initial period of economic reconstruction, the guaranteed independence of the judiciary, and a commitment to review existing social legislation. The fifth point, however, considerably altered the original draft. Gil-Robles dismissed the idea of a National Resistance Council and the formation of a provisional government with equal representation for Left and Right and, although he agreed that there should be a plebiscite 'after a prudent and gradual restoration of legitimate public freedoms', introduced a significant qualification:

> However, if as a consequence of factors, which cannot today be foreseen, there came about a *de facto* situation in which the present Dictatorship regime were replaced by the Monarchy or the Republic, the supporters of the other form of government would accept the situation created, and could even collaborate with it, on condition that *a posteriori* its ratification or rectification were sought through the electoral body, and that in the meantime they were given the necessary guarantees for the defence of their ideals, within the limits of the Law.[25]

This, as the Lisbon monarchists fully intended, left open the possibility of a restoration of the monarchy through a military *coup* or even by Franco himself. If it accepted the fifth point, the ANFD consequently risked committing itself in advance to a right-wing regime, without republican representation, and with no real assurance of a subsequent electoral consultation. Therefore, on 13 November, the ANFD's official response to the Estoril Agreement made it clear that without definite guarantees for the transitional period there could be no agreement with the monarchists. As for Santamaría, once back in Madrid, he was severely reprimanded by the ANFD for exceeding his authority and replaced as General Secretary by Luque.[26]

Yet, despite ANFD hostility to the Estoril Agreement, republican-monarchist talks were not abandoned. In another draft agreement, forwarded to Lisbon at the beginning of December, the ANFD appeared more than ready to compromise: it now conceded equal representation for republicans, monarchists and the military in any future provisional government, thereby acquiescing in a minority role for the republican opposition.[27] Aranda pressed for Don Juan's acceptance of the concession to prevent the ANFD moving over to a revolutionary position. At the same time, he called on the Pretender to issue a manifesto ruling out a *juanista* restoration either at Franco's hands or through a military *coup* and making it clear that, if invited to return to Spain, Don Juan would accept a transitional government and a plebiscite.[28] Gil-Robles, however, suspected Aranda of simply exploiting the situation to keep control of the negotiations and refused to make any substantial changes to the Estoril Agreement. After a second appeal, this time from Luque, for a royal manifesto accepting a constitutional plebiscite, Don Juan's reply, received in Spain on 6 January 1947, chose to avoid the issue and emphasised instead the advantages for the ANFD of negotiating directly with the exiled monarchists in Lisbon.[29]

Once again, it was police action that interrupted negotiations when, in January 1947, 14 members of the ANFD were arrested. In addition, in the week before Christmas, Aranda unsuccessfully sought political asylum in the American Embassy in Madrid, from where he planned to form an anti-Franco government, and for this and his other monarchist activities he was also arrested and banished on 8 January to the Balearics for two months.[30] With both parties to the interior republican-monarchist talks temporarily out of action, it would be all the easier for the Lisbon monarchists to assume the direction of the republican-monarchist negotiations in 1947.

British reaction to the anti-Franco opposition

Towards the end of 1945 British policy towards Franco Spain was inevitably affected by the growing crisis in relations between France and Spain.

General Franco had broken off diplomatic relations with Vichy France in August 1944. At the end of October the Spanish government had then recognised the former Free French *Comité National de Libération* as France's Provisional Government, and diplomatic relations between the two countries were quickly regularised.[31] Even so, Spain was an emotive issue in liberated France. Among a population with recent and direct experience of German occupation there was widespread resentment towards a neighbouring regime which had identified itself with the Axis cause and still offered a haven to fugitive fascists. And yet the policy pursued by the French Provisional Government towards Spain, at least until the resignation of Charles de Gaulle in January 1946, was non-confrontational. It was acknowledged that without democracy in Spain, close Franco-Spanish relations were impossible, but, like the British, the French government could not disregard the commercial ties between the two countries. Consequently, no attempt was made to destabilise the Franco regime during de Gaulle's premiership.[32]

Not surprisingly, this cautious approach exasperated the French Left.

On 25 May 1945, at communist and socialist insistence, the Foreign Affairs Committee of the Provisional Consultative Assembly approved a resolution calling upon the French government to propose a joint allied initiative inviting Franco to abandon power immediately, or, if he refused to go, to break off diplomatic relations with Spain. This was followed, on 4 August, by a second resolution, which again urged the French government to break with Franco Spain, but this time also called on it to make every effort, together with Britain, the USA and the USSR, to support the exiled Spanish republican government then being formed. The French Foreign Ministry, however, hoped that by associating France with the Potsdam Declaration on Spain and by excluding her from the Paris Conference on Tangier that summer (see Chapter 3) it would sufficiently demonstrate its disapproval of the Franco regime. Georges Bidault, the French Foreign Minister, was also reluctant to jeopardise a Franco-Spanish commercial agreement then under negotiation, and so, with de Gaulle's support, he ignored the Foreign Affairs Committee's resolutions.[33]

The elections of October 1945 to the Constituent Assembly strengthened the position of the French Left and, on 5 December, the socialist and communist deputies of the Foreign Affairs Committee returned to the attack, criticising Bidault, the leader of the Christian-Democrat *Mouvement Républicain Populaire* (MRP), for ignoring the Committee's earlier resolutions on Spain. Fearing for the stability of the coalition government, but equally opposed to unilateral French action against Spain, Bidault attempted to deflect this attack by involving the British and American governments. Therefore, a week later, the French government addressed notes to Britain and the USA proposing that together with France they should reconsider their diplomatic and commercial ties to Franco Spain and emphasising that the severance of diplomatic relations 'would assume its full significance in the eyes of the Spanish people only if it formed the subject of a joint decision on the part of the American, British and French Governments'.[34]

In London some sympathy for the French position came from Philip Noel-Baker, Minister of State for Foreign Affairs. On 21 December he sent a note to Attlee, who was temporarily in charge of foreign affairs during Bevin's absence at the Moscow Conference of Foreign Ministers, saying that although he was not convinced that a rupture of diplomatic arrangements would lead to civil war in Spain, he agreed that they should not take the risk; and so he suggested, as a middle course, withdrawing Britain's ambassador from Madrid 'for consultations', as the Americans had done, and keeping him home on indefinite leave. He also proposed *de facto* contacts with some of the republican leaders, similar to those previously maintained by the British government with the Duke of Alba, Franco's representative in London, during the Spanish Civil War. This would not precipitate a crisis, Noel-Baker wrote, but could help prepare the way for Franco's disappearance and for free elections, in which, he insisted, the republicans, including the exiled republican leaders, should play a full part. Attlee, though, was sceptical of Spanish *émigré* support for the Giral government and believed the British reply, sent that day to the French, to be 'on the right lines'.[35]

In their note of 12 December, and in the previous resolutions of the Assembly and the Foreign Affairs Committee, the French had made no mention of a moderate Spanish opposition, favoured by the British, but identified the Giral government, which the British discounted, as the sole representative of Spanish republican legality. The French and British positions were thus diametrically opposed. Consequently, the British reply, delivered to the French Foreign Ministry on 24 December, attempted to redress the balance. In a reference to the ANFD-monarchist negotiations, which had resumed in Spain six weeks earlier, the reply drew attention to 'an increasing body of opinion' in Spain in favour of the early replacement of Franco by 'a broad coalition consisting of the parties of the Left, Centre and Moderate Right and moderate Monarchists'. It was this 'movement', the French were informed, that the British government hoped might provide a basis for an administration to replace the Franco regime, acceptable alike to Spanish opinion and to the British, French and American governments. It was therefore, the British reply concluded, in the best interests of Spain itself that the internal situation there should be allowed for the time being 'to develop spontaneously without external interference'.[36]

The British case for inaction did not satisfy the French Foreign Affairs Committee and on 28 December it referred the Spanish question to the Constituent Assembly. At the end of a three day debate a resolution was adopted on 17 January 1946, which while congratulating the French government for its approach to the British and American governments now invited it to prepare for breaking off relations with Franco Spain. The resolution also called on the French government to offer the right of asylum to exiled Spanish republicans and to make contact with their political leaders. Three days later de Gaulle resigned, and when Spain came up for discussion in the coalition cabinet of his successor, the socialist Félix Gouin, Bidault's voice was almost alone in opposing the Assembly's resolution, with Gouin himself speaking in favour of a break with the Franco regime. Again, however, Bidault stalled by asking for time for further consultations with other governments.[37]

On 1 February Bidault warned Bevin that it was becoming increasingly difficult to calm public opinion in France over Spain. He was under extreme pressure to take unilateral action and it was therefore important for Britain, France and the USA to adopt a common attitude, even if this differed from that originally suggested by his government. Bevin replied that the British government did not intend to shelve the Spanish problem but he was opposed to any action by the western democracies because Spain, he believed, was on the point of a change of regime. In fact, two days after this conversation Bevin admitted to Mallet that the Spanish situation was giving him cause for grave anxiety and that because of parliamentary pressure at home, Bidault's difficulties in France, and strengthening world opinion, the situation could not be held much longer.[38]

Consequently, the Foreign Office was obliged to review Britain's policy towards Spain. Although the resumption of the ANFD-monarchist talks in November 1945 had provided a convenient excuse for not acting upon the French note of 12 December, Foreign Office confidence in their success was in fact far less than the French had been led to believe. By mid-January Garran, for example, doubted whether the moderate and left-wing republicans would ever accept the monarchy and noted that the CNT had already threatened to withdraw from the ANFD if Franco met Don Juan. Mallet, too, after a secret meeting on 17 January with the ANFD's socialist representative and the – unidentified – chief monarchist negotiator, admitted that he was 'somewhat depressed' by the lack of precision in their ideas and had gained the impression that they 'were building too many castles in the air'.[39] Admittedly, the vague prospect of negotiations between Don Juan and Franco, with the possible participation of moderate republicans from Spain, temporarily raised the possibility of an alternative route to a moderate solution for Spain, especially after Bárcenas, the Spanish Ambassador in London, informed the Foreign Office on 24 January that Martín Artajo was planning to meet Gil-Robles to discuss the convening of a representative constituent assembly for April or May.[40] But, by the end of January the Don Juan-Franco negotiations had little to show for themselves, and, with the ANFD-monarchist talks also stalled, it was observed in the Western Department that the Spanish sky had 'clouded over'.[41]

Even so, the possibility of a meeting between Don Juan and Franco had brought the question of British support for the *juanista* monarchy once more to the fore. On 7 January Mallet wondered whether, with Franco 'really wobbling', a clear statement from the British government that it would be prepared to recognise a constitutional monarchy, based on democratic principles and early elections, 'might just turn the scale'.

Against this, Garran pointed out that such a statement would constitute direct intervention in Spanish internal affairs, although, he added, Spaniards ought to have had sufficient confidence in the British government by then to know that it would look 'favourably' on any democratically based Spanish government. While Bevin did not disagree with this, he declined to commit himself at that stage and merely observed that the Foreign Office had no real idea of the attitude of the ordinary Spanish people. Mallet was accordingly informed that there could be no question of prior British recognition of a constitutional monarchy, and within 24 hours of Don Juan's arrival in Portugal the British Ambassador in Lisbon, Sir Owen O'Malley, was instructed to avoid all official contact or relations with the Pretender. The next day, 4 February, Bevin reminded the Cabinet that it was important that the British government 'should not appear to favour either of the alternatives which confronted the Spanish people'.[42]

In the Western Department, however, Harvey continued to take a more vigorous line arguing that if pressure on Franco were not stepped up, he would cling on, his opponents in Spain would go on 'funking a *coup d'état*', and Don Juan's conversations would drag on until, possibly, he compromised himself by contacts with Franco or his brother. It was unlikely, Harvey insisted, that the British government could continue to resist political pressure at home, or from France and the USA, to withdraw Britain's Ambassador from Spain or break off diplomatic relations. He therefore favoured more active intervention in support of an alternative regime, which, as the republican government-in-exile had no backing in Spain, inevitably meant the monarchy. Mallet should therefore be instructed to urge the opposition in Madrid to take immediate action to depose Franco and invite Don Juan to return. Sir Orme Sargent, appointed Cadogan's successor as Permanent Under-Secretary in February 1946, thought there was much to be said for adopting Harvey's course.[43]

On 15 February Mallet reported that an agreement between Franco and Don Juan was now thought imminent in Spain, following which Franco would step down in favour of a provisional government, made up mainly of generals, who would then summon Don Juan back to Madrid. Until that happened, however, Mallet warned against diplomatic or economic sanctions. His argument for doing nothing was supported by Hoyer Millar, who pointed out that Britain's material interests would not be prejudiced by 'a short continuation of the present state of affairs', while it really seemed the 'height of folly', when there were so many other major problems and Britain was under so much pressure in other directions, for the government to do anything which might precipitate trouble in Spain and lead to a situation 'from which only the Russians would benefit'. Hoyer Millar's caution was shared by Bevin, when he again discussed Spain with Harvey and Hoyer Millar on 18 February prior to a meeting with Bidault. He showed less enthusiasm for the monarchist option than either Harvey or Sargent, suspecting Don Juan of having had close relations with the Germans during the war, and he doubted whether Britain would gain from his return to Spain. He saw no advantage either in withdrawing Britain's Ambassador from Madrid and made this clear to Bidault later that day.[44]

On 21 February seven Spanish republicans, including Cristino García Granda, a former commander of the French Resistance, were executed in Madrid for anti-Franco activities. There had already been 14 executions in January, bringing anti-Franco feeling in France to a new pitch, and the next day the French Constituent Assembly adopted a resolution recalling its earlier one of 17 January and again inviting the government to break off diplomatic relations with Franco's government.[45] This time, though, the resolution was backed by industrial action from postal and railway workers and a call from the communist-dominated *Confédération Générale du Travail* for an immediate severance of diplomatic relations with Spain. The French Cabinet was forced to act and on 26 February it decided, first, to propose to the British and American governments that the UN Security Council should consider the dangers to international security arising out of the situation, and, secondly, that the French border with Spain should be closed from midnight of 1 March.[46]

Despite Attlee's feeling that the execution was 'an excuse for political murder', there was considerably less sympathy in the Foreign Office for the executed García than in France, and a formal British protest was not sent to the Spanish government. Instead, Attlee, in Bevin's absence, informed the Cabinet on 25 February that he was instituting a review of Britain's policy towards Spain in the light of the executions to consider whether further steps ought to be taken to expedite a change in the Franco regime.[47] Two days later, however, the French Foreign Ministry sent notes to the British, American and Soviet Embassies in Paris, and the Foreign Office was informed that since 12 December 1945 the Spanish situation had worsened to the point that it now, in the French government's view, endangered international peace and security; the British government was therefore asked whether it would join France in laying the matter before the UN Security Council.[48]

The arrival of the second French note coincided with an inter-departmental meeting at the Foreign Office, chaired by Harvey, to consider the possible consequences of a rupture of relations with Spain. A substantial case against economic sanctions was put by representatives of the Treasury and the Ministries of Food and Supply. Even if universally applied, it was argued, there was no guarantee that sanctions would bring Franco down; indeed, they could provoke the very civil war that Britain was so anxious to avoid. Franco, it was estimated, could survive at least four months of an oil embargo and it would take eight months to bring about the complete collapse of the Spanish economy. Sanctions, moreover, would prejudice Europe's general economic recovery and harm Britain's financial and commercial interests. In addition to importing Spanish fruit and vegetables, wine and iron ore, Britain depended on Spain for two-thirds of its supplies of potash. Indeed, the closure of the Franco-Spanish border already seemed likely to deprive British agriculture of Spanish super-phosphates. Further anti-Franco measures could also have unfavourable repercussions for Gibraltar. The conclusion reached at the meeting was that Britain would obviously suffer 'very materially' if economic sanctions were imposed.[49]

With this in mind, it was not surprising that Bevin described the French proposal to refer Spain to the UN Security Council as 'most ill-advised'.[50] Yet, despite these objections the French note could not be ignored. Bidault's position in Gouin's coalition government was precarious and a diplomatic rebuff from Britain and the USA risked discrediting not only his foreign policy but also his party, the moderate MRP, both in the country at large and in the Constituent Assembly. A stable France, in Britain's calculations, was essential to European security, and with the French electorate about to vote on a new constitution, the Foreign Office recognised the danger of giving the French communists an undue electoral advantage. On the other hand, there was no sympathy for the French proposal to involve the Security Council. How then was the Foreign Office to reply to the French note? In December it had argued the need not to jeopardise an imminent republican-monarchist agreement, but at the end of February this excuse no longer held. The only way out of the dilemma, as Bevin acknowledged on 2 March, was for Britain and the USA to join France in a joint declaration against Franco Spain in return for a French agreement not to bring the Spanish question before the Security Council.[51] For this compromise solution Bevin was indebted, though, not so much to his own officials at the Foreign Office as to a proposal that had originated in the American State Department.

Towards the end of World War II there had been little to distinguish American policy towards Franco Spain from Britain's. By the autumn of 1945, however, the USA's attitude towards Franco had become noticeably more hostile than Britain's.[52] The American Ambassador, Norman Armour, was not replaced after he left Spain in December and American interests were represented by Philip Bonsal, the Chargé d'Affaires. So, soon after the French note of 12 December 1945 was received in Washington, the Spanish Ambassador to the USA, Juan Francisco de Cárdenas, was told by 'his old friend', James Clement Dunn, Assistant Secretary of State, that the USA intended to support the French call for a break of diplomatic relations with Spain. On 22 December, Dean Acheson, who was Acting Secretary of State during James Byrnes' absence at the Foreign Ministers Conference in Moscow, accepted the French proposal for tripartite talks.[53]

Acheson's move alarmed the Foreign Office, especially after it learnt that Bidault himself had confided in the Americans his hope that the British and American governments would in fact reject his call to break with Spain! Bevin wondered where it was all leading to: 'we shall be landed into intervention', he complained, 'and I am against it[;] is not all this the slippery slope?' He was therefore unwilling to agree to a tripartite meeting, since it would 'savour too much of intervention in Spanish affairs', and preferred keeping in touch through normal diplomatic channels.[54] Two weeks later, however, John Balfour, British Minister at the Washington Embassy, was told by Acheson that although the USA did not disagree with Britain's policy towards Franco Spain, in view of the behaviour of the French Constituent Assembly some 'new positive movement' was needed to prevent the French government from being isolated and vulnerable to communist influence. Acheson therefore proposed a joint declaration to 'give heart to those elements in Spain which hesitated to dissociate themselves from Franco for fear of what might then befall their country'. It would manifest their common dislike of the Franco regime, their aspiration to see Spaniards governed according to their wishes, and their determination not to maintain existing diplomatic relations indefinitely. The declaration could be made, Acheson suggested, by the Foreign Ministers of Britain, France and the USA at the forthcoming UN General Assembly in London.[55]

This suggestion, too, was coolly received in London. As reaction in Spain to the French Assembly's resolution of 17 January 1946 had already confirmed, the Foreign Office told Balfour on 26 January, it was questionable whether a tripartite declaration would serve Britain's main objective of 'getting the Spaniards to combine together to get rid of Franco'; moreover, if the USSR participated in the declaration, the Spanish moderates would be alienated even further. Consequently, the Foreign Office thought it premature to make any declaration until the results of Don Juan's visit to Portugal were known.[56] Just as the ANFD–monarchist talks had provided an excuse to counter the French note of 12 December 1945, so now the prospect of a Don Juan-Franco *rapprochement* was used to fend off the American initiative. Still, Acheson bowed to British pressure and agreed to wait.[57] However, the crisis in Franco-Spanish relations at the end of February 1946 placed the USA, like Britain, once more in a dilemma. The 'Mexico City' government, in the State Department's view, had no chance 'of coming to anything', but nor by then had either of the moderate alternatives recently promoted by the British Foreign Office.[58] In the circumstances Acheson decided to resurrect his idea of a tripartite declaration.

A draft text was sent to London on 25 February. Two days later, as has been seen, the French government sent out its second note, and the Americans responded by proposing their joint declaration to them. This was immediately accepted by the French, following which, as Bevin admitted to Attlee, it was difficult for Britain to refuse to cooperate with the USA and France. So, at the beginning of March the Foreign Office informed Washington that it, too, accepted the text of the declaration, subject to a few amendments, and, at a meeting of the Cabinet on 4 March, Bevin recommended it as 'expedient'. That evening, following Cabinet approval, it was sent to Spain.[59]

The Tripartite Declaration warned the Spanish people that their 'full and cordial association' with the victors of the Second World War was impossible as long as Franco remained in power and, while rejecting direct intervention in Spain's internal affairs, it none the less expressed the hope that:

> [. . .] leading patriotic and liberal-minded Spaniards may soon find means to bring about a peaceful withdrawal of Franco, the abolition of the Falange, and the establishment of an interim or caretaker government under which the Spanish people may have an opportunity freely to determine the type of government they wish to have and to choose their leaders. Political amnesty, return of exiled Spaniards, freedom of assembly and political association and provision for free public elections are essential. An interim government, which would be and would remain dedicated to these ends should receive the recognition and support of all freedom-loving peoples.

Such recognition would include full diplomatic relations and the taking of such practical measures to assist in the solution of Spain's economic problems as may be practicable in the circumstances prevailing. Such measures are not now possible. The question of the maintenance or termination by the Governments of France, the United Kingdom, and the United States of diplomatic relations with the present Spanish regime is a matter to be decided in the light of events and after taking into account the efforts of the Spanish people to achieve their own freedom.[60]

Thus, the Tripartite Declaration had the merit, in the eyes of the British and American governments, of appearing to promote a moderate solution to the Spanish problem, even though a united moderate opposition did not exist in Spain. It also enabled the two governments to dissociate themselves from the original French intention of laying the Spanish question before the UN Security Council while offering the French Foreign Ministry a demonstration of apparent international solidarity with its position. Nevertheless, by making explicit the preconditions for recognising and assisting a provisional Spanish government, Britain, together with France and the USA, had, despite itself, made a formal commitment to the anti-Franco opposition the implications of which would be felt later.

Immediate hopes that the Tripartite Declaration would resolve the three month crisis over Spain were disappointed. Bidault doubted whether it gave effective support to the moderate Spanish opposition and told Alfred Duff Cooper, the British Ambassador in Paris, on 12 March that his government still intended to bring the Spanish question before the Security Council.[61] Although Bidault's doubts were borne out by reports from the British Embassy in Madrid, the British government remained firmly opposed to any form of direct action against Spain, and efforts to persuade the French to abandon their proposal continued into April. Hoyer Millar even warned of a serious strain on Anglo-French relations if the French persisted in their Spanish policy and, on 19 March, Bevin told the French Ambassador, René Massigli, that the French were making a 'great mistake', especially at a moment when there was a reasonable chance of ending the Franco regime.[62]

Nevertheless, Bidault persisted, proposing amongst other measures, in a note of 22 March, tripartite consultations with 'qualified representatives of the Spanish opposition'. This proposal also proved unacceptable, but Bevin, who was anxious not to give the French a 'flatly negative reply', offered private talks in London between the Foreign Office and the French and American Embassies, where, he hoped,

Britain's objections to increasing pressure on Spain could be explained. Bevin's offer was accepted by the French on 12 April but, four days later, with the UN Security Council about to debate Spain, the French accepted the British view that they should not appear to be going behind the back of the Security Council – and of the Council of Foreign Ministers due to meet in Paris on 25 April – by holding tripartite discussions, and they were cancelled.[63]

Spain had been the subject of debate at the first session of the UN General Assembly in London in February 1946, when a mildly worded resolution inviting member states to act in accordance with the San Francisco and Potsdam Declarations in their relations with Spain was, almost unanimously, adopted. Next, at Polish initiative, Spain was placed on the agenda of the UN Security Council when it met in New York in April.[64]

On 17 April the case against Spain was put by Poland's representative on the Security Council, Oskar Lange. The existence of the Franco regime, Lange argued, could not be regarded as simply an internal affair. Because it had been brought to power with the support of Fascist Italy and Nazi Germany and had been an active partner in World War II against the United Nations, it was of concern to all UN members. The regime had caused international friction by compelling France to close its border with Spain, along which Spanish troops were then massing. Franco, moreover, had allowed Spain to become a refuge for German assets, personnel, and scientists, who were engaged in pursuits dangerous for the peace of mankind, and for a large number of war criminals, nazi leaders and agents, who were using Spain as an operations base for their activities and plans of reconquest. Considering the Franco regime, therefore, to be a danger to international peace and security, the Polish resolution called upon members of the UN to sever their diplomatic links with Spain immediately.[65]

Lange's arguments were opposed the next day by Sir Alexander Cadogan, Britain's permanent representative at the UN. According to Cadogan, before undertaking any collective action, the Security Council had to be sure it was not intervening in affairs which came under Spain's internal jurisdiction. There was no proof, he maintained, that Spain constituted a threat to peace or was capable of acts of aggression sufficient to warrant breaking off relations. Furthermore, UN action against Spain would set a dangerous precedent and itself constitute a threat to peace, leading possibly to Spain's destabilisation and civil war. Cadogan reiterated the British view that Spaniards alone should decide the government they wanted. A long UN debate would frustrate the transition to democracy, strengthen nationalist support for Franco, and place before the democracies the option of either accepting Franco or armed intervention.[66]

Behind the British case, of course, lay deeper anxieties. The fact that the Polish resolution received, and would continue to receive, strong support in the ensuing Security Council debate from the USSR was taken by the Foreign Office as clear evidence of Soviet wishes to meddle in Spanish affairs. Two months earlier the State Department had sent the Foreign Office a copy of a telegram from George Kennan, the USA's Chargé d'Affaires in Moscow. The USSR, the telegram read, regarded Spain as a 'key territory', since it occupied an important flanking position to France and Italy, where the Russians hoped to achieve a dominant political position, and provided an entry to Morocco and a direct channel of influence to Latin America; Spain also controlled the western entrance to the Mediterranean, a sea to which the USSR was 'close to being a littoral power'. Kennan's assumptions were corroborated in a report of 1 March by the British Joint Intelligence Sub-Committee, which similarly foresaw a policy of opportunism by the USSR to extend its influence. Bevin was consequently in no doubt that the Russians were 'only too anxious to make trouble' over Spain and would welcome any opportunity, including civil war, for reviving direct intervention there.[67]

The Polish resolution was not carried in the Security Council and, in an attempt to resolve the consequent deadlock, a five man sub-committee was set up. This found – its Polish delegate dissenting – that although the Franco regime did not threaten international peace and security at the time, it nevertheless represented a *potential* threat. The sub-committee therefore recommended, first, that the Security Council should endorse the recent Anglo-French-American Tripartite Declaration on Spain and, secondly, that, unless the conditions set out in the Tripartite Declaration, including the removal of the Franco regime, were fully satisfied, the UN General Assembly should adopt a resolution requiring every member to break off diplomatic relations with Spain immediately.[68]

The Security Council began considering its sub-committee's report on 13 June but again, mainly because of Soviet objections, was unable to agree a resolution. A three-man drafting committee, consisting of Cadogan and Lange with the Australian Herbert Evatt as chairman, also failed to agree. After further protracted wrangling, a resolution was finally adopted by the Security Council on 26 June – with Poland and the USSR again opposing – according to which Spain was to remain on the Security Council's agenda and leaving its members free to bring the Spanish question up for reconsideration at any time.[69]

The two month Security Council debate occasioned yet another Foreign Office examination of policy towards Spain. Both Garran and Mallet now spoke in terms of an *evolution* rather than a *termination* of the Franco regime. In a long memorandum, written on 7 June after his return from a visit to Spain, Garran warned that the policy embarked upon by the UN would lead inevitably from diplomatic to economic sanctions, and these in turn would result in either the perpetuation of the Franco regime or the establishment, in conditions of economic chaos, of an extreme left-wing government 'almost certainly under the influence of Soviet Russia'. A moderate regime was still possible under a monarchist restoration, but, in view of his present strong position, this could be effected only with Franco's concurrence. Garran therefore advised diplomatic pressure, possibly with the assistance of the Portuguese Dictator, António de Oliveira Salazar, or of the Vatican, to bring Don Juan and Franco together.[70]

Mallet observed that the sole effect of the Polish appeal to the Security Council – along with the closure of the Franco-Spanish border and the Giral government's return to France – had been for Franco to abandon his earlier plans for a monarchist restoration. So, the choice now facing the British government, Mallet believed, was between leaving Franco quiet, in the hope that he would himself accelerate his regime's evolution towards a monarchy, or attempting to push him in that direction. As there was no republican opposition group capable of assuming power, the alternative to Franco was a *juanista* restoration, which could only be brought about by Franco himself 'preparing the machinery and ordering his generals to assist him in carrying forward his plan'. It was therefore necessary, Mallet advised, to cease 'public pressure' and, instead, apply 'great secret diplomatic pressure' on Franco, and the British government should give an assurance of full diplomatic recognition once the monarchy were restored.[71]

Sargent disagreed, arguing that as long as Franco remained in power, the evolution of his regime was not a viable solution. Franco would never be persuaded to restore the monarchy peaceably and legally, and Don Juan, Sargent thought, was wise enough to see that accepting power from Franco, whether directly or through the intermediary of a foreign government, would be fatal for his cause. If the Spanish problem was to cease poisoning the politics of the world, Franco had, therefore, to be driven from power, 'in a manner which would strike the imagination of all concerned', or else passions had to cool before a peaceable change of regime could take place without attracting worldwide attention.[72]

As for Bevin, he still saw no reason to change British policy on the Spanish monarchy, and, at a meeting with Mallet on 25 July, also attended by Philip Noel-Baker and Harvey, he reaffirmed Britain's commitment to strict non-intervention. Admittedly Giral's government stood very little chance of coming to anything, but Bevin still had 'considerable doubts' about Don Juan and was not prepared to take any action to encourage him:

> We should go on as we are in the hopes that things will gradually improve in Spain, and that we should not take any drastic steps to encourage the opposition elements; that we should continue to deprecate anything in the nature of the breaking off of diplomatic relations or the imposition of economic sanctions, and that we should be guided accordingly if and when the Spanish question comes up at UNO.[73]

It was precisely this last eventuality that Sloan considered towards the end of August. He noted that contacts by then had been resumed between the reconstituted ANFD and the monarchists and that, in Spanish official circles, there was talk of Franco taking an important step in October or November towards liberalising his regime. Foreign pressure, Sloan thought, of a 'discreet nature' and at the right '*psychological moment*' [emphasised in the original] could ease the way to favourable developments in Spain. Therefore, Britain should use such powers as she had, including the veto, to prevent Spain being openly discussed at the UN or rather, if the Foreign Secretary thought otherwise, to have the matter 'thrashed out' by the Assembly before it came before the Security Council again. Whatever happened, Sloan minuted, the British government should minimise the adverse effects that a renewed UN debate would produce in Spain by stating at the outset that Britain did not regard Spain as a threat to international peace, and would discuss the matter in the UN solely in order to discover whether the UN was actually empowered to handle a case of that kind.[74]

As anticipated, on 24 October Trygve Lie proposed that the General Assembly should discuss Spain, and one week later the Assembly's General Committee referred the question to its First Committee (Political and Security).[75] The British position remained that no action of any kind should be taken against Spain. Encouraged, albeit mistakenly, by the recent signing of the republican-monarchist Estoril Agreement, the Foreign Office preferred to believe that a solution to the Spanish problem would only be achieved by a reconciliation between the Spanish opposition parties, and between 'the parties on the Right, in the Centre and on the Left'; it was, moreover, no use trying to bring this reconciliation about by pressure from outside, 'for the moment this force was removed the different parties would fall apart again'. None the less, the Foreign Office soon realised that this view was unlikely to win support in the First Committee, and so the British delegation was instructed to leave the initiative to the Americans.[76]

Thus, when debate began on 2 December there were three draft resolutions before the First Committee: one American and two Polish. The American, and the first of the two Polish resolutions, called for the Franco government to be barred from membership of the UN and from participation in any of its organisations and agencies. But the second Polish resolution repeated the call for members of the UN to terminate diplomatic relations with the Franco regime immediately. A compromise resolution, drawn up by a sub-committee of 18, was rejected by the First Committee, and the deadlock was resolved only when a Belgian amendment to the American resolution was adopted. The First Committee's draft resolution was then approved, on 12 December, at the 57th Plenary Session of the UN General Assembly by 34 votes, including Britain's, to 6 against, with 13 abstentions.[77] The resolution confirmed that until a new and acceptable government was formed, Spain was debarred from membership of 'international agencies established or brought into relationship with the United Nations, and from participation in conferences or other activities which may be arranged by the United Nations or by these agencies'. The resolution further recommended that

> [. . .] if within a reasonable time there is not established a government which derives its authority from the consent of the governed, committed to respect freedom of speech, religion and assembly, and to the prompt holding of an election in which the Spanish people, free from force and intimidation and regardless of party, may express their will, the Security Council [should] consider the adequate measures to be taken in order to remedy the situation.[78]

As has been noted already, the December resolution did not require member states to sever their diplomatic relations with Spain completely but recommended only that their ambassadors and ministers plenipotentiary accredited there should be immediately recalled. Mallet accordingly left Madrid on Christmas Day and Domingo de las Bárcenas, the Spanish Ambassador in London, returned to Spain on 15 January 1947.

If international opposition to the Franco regime was a determining factor in the formulation of British policy towards Spain in 1946, the Foreign Office could not ignore anti-Franco sentiment in Britain itself. Public protests, though not frequent, were a reminder of Franco Spain's continuing capacity to rouse emotion.[79] On 19 September 1945, for example, after a demonstration in Hyde Park against the arrests of Sebastián Zapirain and Santiago Alvarez, 200 protesters marched to the Spanish Embassy in London. The arrest of Cristino García on 15 October 1945 and his execution the following February also provoked a public outcry.[80] For the Labour government of July 1945, however, occasional public protest was generally less embarrassing than the opposition it faced from a small minority within the Labour movement itself.

On 20 August 1945, in the Commons Debate on the Address, the new Foreign Secretary, Ernest Bevin, had made it clear that the advent of a Labour government did not signify a radical change in Britain's policy towards Spain. The government, Bevin stated, would take a favourable view if steps were taken by the Spanish people themselves to change their regime, but since intervention by foreign powers in the internal affairs of Spain would probably strengthen Franco's position, it was not prepared to take any steps which would promote or encourage civil war in that country.[81] Bevin was criticised by Harold Laski, Ehairman of the Labour Party National Executive Committee, in a speech delivered later that month in France at a conference of the French socialist party. In October, 21 Labour Members of Parliament (MPs) then wrote to Attlee expressing their disquiet at the trend of his government's foreign policy, which in dealing with countries such as Spain, Greece and Germany, seemed to be affected by an 'anti-Red virus'; in particular, in Spain, and Greece, they protested, Britain should have been setting a moral example to strengthen democratic socialist resolve.[82] Two months after that, in the House of Commons, Ian Mikardo, Labour MP for Reading, referred to the trial of 22 Spanish republicans in Spain and asked how Franco had so regained confidence as 'to thumb his nose in this way' at the British government. Bevin's reaction was uncharacteristically forceful and he told the Commons that '. . . we detest the regime [. . .] the whole regime is one with which HMGs have no sympathy'. He restated this position to the Commons on 23 January 1946, although this time adding that the government declined to indulge in 'diversionary tactics of any kind', by following, for example, other countries in not recognising Franco.[83]

The execution of García a month later placed Bevin under further pressure. Walter Citrine, Secretary-General of the Trades Union Congress, informed him of the General Council's endorsement of the World Federation of Trades Unions' resolution calling for a breach of diplomatic relations with Franco's Spain.[84] As a result the Commons was informed on 4 March that Britain's Ambassador in Madrid would be impressing upon the Spanish Foreign Minister the 'deep resentment' felt in Britain at the execution and that the sentences passed on 37 socialists were 'utterly repugnant' and would 'inevitably have a most serious effect upon Anglo-Spanish relations'.[85] On 5 June 1946, the government's thinking on Spain policy was further explained by the Prime Minister during the course of a foreign affairs debate:

> [. . .] but the real question which faces all of us, is how best we are going to enable the Spanish people to decide for themselves, and get a decent Government. The latter is a very long-term aspiration as far as Spain is concerned, because they have had, I think, a succession of very bad Governments for very many years. It is a fact that the Spanish people react very strongly against foreign intervention, and I am sure that we will have to take action which will be best calculated to make the Spaniards get rid of their present Government, and also get a decent Government in its place. Because you get rid of one Government, it does not necessarily follow that you get a better one, or that you even get one at all in some countries. We are watching, therefore, the proceedings of the UN organisation.[86]

Five days later the Labour Party's first post-war conference opened in Bournemouth and Bevin had yet again to defend his non-interventionism. A resolution highly critical of his foreign policy was moved by J.W. Kagan, the Democratic Labour Party (DLP) delegate from Hendon, calling for a return to a policy of support for socialist and anti-imperialist forces throughout the world. Although Kagan withdrew his resolution when Bevin took it as a censure motion, a second resolution was immediately moved by Henry Solomons, the DLP delegate from South Hammersmith, urging the government to break off relations with

Franco and to appoint a representative to the republican government-in-exile. This challenge failed, and Bevin's policy was endorsed by the Conference.[87]

None the less, on 14 October 1946, the government was once more on the defensive. Opening a Commons debate on Spain, Francis Noel-Baker, Labour MP for Middlesex, Brentford and Chiswick, warned against Britain's inactivity over Spain and spoke of the need to bring the Resistance (*sic*), the exiled republican opposition and political and military elements in Spain together. At the forthcoming session of the UN General Assembly, Britain, he urged, should take the initiative in proposing action, the simplest form of which was economic sanctions. In his reply, the new Minister of State for Foreign Affairs, Hector McNeil, recalled the Security Council sub-committee's finding that Franco Spain was not a threat to international peace and security. The Franco government, moreover, was not inconvenienced by partial foreign diplomatic representation in Madrid and it was difficult to see how economic sanctions could be imposed. McNeil also doubted whether there was an alternative government available to Spain 'just now'. Later in the debate Ernest Davies, Labour MP for Enfield, argued that failure to take action had harmed the cause of social-democracy and called for recognition of the Giral government. Attlee maintained, however, that all the evidence at his disposal pointed in the opposite conclusion: that external intervention would only strengthen Franco, which would, he said, be 'a very deplorable result'.[88]

A week later the TUC Conference in Brighton adopted a resolution instructing its General Council to draw the government's attention to the desire of the Trades Union Movement to 'sever all economic and diplomatic relations with Franco'.[89] But left-wing dissatisfaction with Bevin's overall foreign policy was given its clearest demonstration on 12 November 1946, when Richard Crossman, MP for East Coventry, and Michael Foot, MP for Devonport, Plymouth, moved an Amendment to the King's Speech calling for closer cooperation with nations 'striving to secure full socialist planning and control of the world's resources ...' It was eventually signed by 58 MPs, and, although withdrawn by Crossman and Foot, was pressed to a division by John McGovern and Campbell Stephens, both Independent Labour Party MPs. In the event, none of the rebels voted against the government and the amendment was defeated 353–0; but 130 Labour MPs abstained. Although Bevin's position was secure, the challenge had served to remind him of the limits to which his accommodation of the Franco regime could safely go.[90]

Although the British government continued to apply its policy of 'pin-pricks' towards the Franco regime, Anglo-Spanish relations were, in 1946, not unduly hostile. Bevin's opposition to the Giral government and his general anti-communism were appreciated in Spain, so much so that when reports of Bevin's health problems circulated in July, Bárcenas, the Spanish Ambassador to London, expressed alarm at the prospect of his having to resign from the Foreign Office![91]

Nevertheless, British contacts with the anti-Franco opposition remained a source of Anglo-Spanish friction. On 20 October 1945 a Madrid police report drew attention to the fact that after the arrest of the CNT National Committee in March 1945, a certain Antonio Barranco Haglin had escaped to the British Embassy where he had been given employment in the food-store. It was alleged that Barranco, appointed CNT Treasurer in July, used this food-store as an operations centre for the CNT, particularly for members arriving from abroad. César Broto Villegas, appointed the CNT's General Secretary in July, had also hidden in the Embassy, as had other anarcho-syndicalists. Members of the new National Committee had meetings in the Embassy and, in addition, the CNT's funds, archives, duplicators, type-writers and propaganda, as well as two pistols owned by Broto Villegas, were stored there.[92]

The following year a second police report described how Juan Costa Reboredo, *alias* José García Durán, the CNT National Committee's Political Secretary and its representative on the ANFD, was shot during a police raid and, after escaping from hospital, had also taken refuge in the British Embassy. According to the police, the Embassy staff were well aware of García's presence and had even arranged an interview for him with either the *Daily Telegraph* or the *Daily Express*. García sheltered in the Embassy until he was re-arrested on 24 May 1946, during one of his periodic sorties from the Embassy, and it was his subsequent confessions that provided the Spanish authorities with their information about the CNT's presence in the Embassy.[93]

On 7 June 1946 Martín Artajo wrote a letter of protest to his 'dear Ambassador and Friend', and Mallet replied a week later assuring his 'dear Minister and Friend' that García had never lodged in the Embassy or in any other Embassy building. Mallet went on to say that it would have been impossible for García to have remained hidden in the food-store without the knowledge of the official in charge, who had been there some 26 years. Admittedly, Barranco had been in the employment of the Embassy for nearly three years, his mother having been a British subject before her marriage, but Mallet had been unable to trace any

CNT archives in the store, and when he heard that Barranco was associating with certain political elements, he had immediately sacked him.[94]

Spanish allegations about Barranco had been specifically denied, but the British government made no secret of its contacts with the wider anti-Franco opposition. On 1 July 1946, for example, McNeil informed the Commons that 'not only His Majesty's Ambassador in Paris, but several members of his staff have seen prominent Spanish Republican exiles in recent months'.[95] Again, in a draft letter, of 3 August, to Sir Henry Ashley Clarke of the Paris Embassy, Hoyer Millar mentioned that the Madrid Embassy maintained contact with the CNT, 'as with other opposition groups in Spain'.[96]

At the end of 1946, however, the Foreign Office learnt to its alarm of reports in the American press that the British Embassy in Madrid was actively involved in the organisation of internal opposition to Franco. Not surprisingly, the Spanish Ministry of Foreign Affairs sent Mallet a *note verbale* on 21 December strongly protesting against the British government's political contacts with 'persons attempting to overthrow the present regime'. The Spanish government, the note insisted, had always wished to disbelieve these reports but, after previous British denials, was profoundly surprised at the news from London that British diplomats in Madrid had been meeting heads of Spanish political parties of the Right, Centre and Left in order to explore the possibility of forming a provisional government to replace Franco. This, the note stated, had been confirmed by Morgan Phillips, Secretary to the Labour Party, when addressing members of the Labour Party, and commented on in the international press. The American State Department, it was pointed out, had immediately denied any involvement on its part, and the Spanish government now hoped the British government could do the same.[97]

From its investigation the Foreign Office discovered that the 'statement' objected to by the Spanish government arose out of a passage in a letter sent by Phillips to the Spennithorne branch of the Labour Party. To the charge that Bevin 'supported a reactionary Fascist Government in Spain', Phillips had replied that 'the Socialist Movement was actively working to overthrow the Franco Government both outside and *inside* Spain'. Later, at a press conference, a non-committal comment on the matter by Francis Williams, Attlee's press advisor, had convinced the Associated Press and United Press correspondents of British intentions to form an interim government in Spain in cooperation with the Spanish opposition. In the Foreign Office William Hogg, who had since replaced Garran as Acting First Secretary in the Western Department with responsibility for Spain and Portugal, expressed dismay at the effects of the reports on Anglo-Spanish relations and at the possible danger to Embassy lives, and Washington was immediately informed that the reports were in no way authoritative nor issued with Foreign Office approval.[98]

The British Embassy replied to the Spanish *note verbale* on 27 December. It regretted that the Spanish government should have paid so much attention to certain newspaper reports, which were based on a complete misunderstanding of the position, and insisted there was 'no truth whatsoever' that any member of the Embassy had exceeded his proper role, although the British Ambassador and members of his staff had 'in the normal course of their duties and in the exercise of their proper functions' met representatives of all sections of Spanish opinion, many of whom were opposed to the existing regime in Spain. The suggestion, moreover, that the British Embassy had been actively conspiring to set up an alternative Spanish government would have been entirely contrary to the publicly stated policy of the British government that it was up to Spaniards themselves to decide on their form of government and regime.[99]

Conclusion

1946 began, as it ended, with reports to the British Foreign Office of a possible republican-monarchist agreement negotiated by the moderate opposition in Spain. ANFD suspicion in early 1946, however, that the Pretender's imminent move to Portugal was but the preliminary to a reconciliation between himself and Franco, in which the ANFD would play no part, contributed to the breakdown of the first round of negotiations. The determination of the monarchists in Lisbon, led by Gil-Robles, to keep concessions to the ANFD to a minimum ended the second round at the end of the year, and the situation was further aggravated by the action of the Spanish police. Thus, since it consistently refused to treat with the one organised sector of the anti-Franco opposition – Giral's government-in-exile – the British government looked in vain, for most of 1946, for a credible alternative to the Franco regime.

This was, of course, a powerful reason for doing nothing and for simply leaving it to the Spaniards to remove Franco by themselves. But the French call for stronger measures against Spain, which initially attracted some sympathy from the USA and provided the USSR with an opportunity for involvement in Spanish affairs, placed the British government's policy of inaction under strain. Consequently, the chances of a successful ANFD-monarchist agreement were deliberately exaggerated by the Foreign Office in order to counter the first French note of December 1945, and a possible *rapprochement* between Don Juan and Franco was similarly exploited to reject the USA's proposal for a tripartite declaration the following month. But, with the republican-monarchist negotiations in Spain deadlocked, the second French note in February 1946 forced the British government to accept the American proposal for a joint declaration. Poland's referral of the Spanish question to the UN Security Council, with Soviet connivance, placed the British government once more in a difficult position. Either it abandoned its policy of *attentisme* or it risked appearing as Franco's defender before the new world organisation and the Labour movement at home. The tactic reluctantly adopted by Britain, first in the Security Council and then in the UN General Assembly, was therefore to acquiesce in any resolution against Spain short of a complete severance of diplomatic or economic relations.

To some extent this tactic was justified by the limited scope of the General Assembly's resolution of December 1946. Yet, the resolution offered only a breathing space, for unless there were some evidence of progress towards the Franco regime's democratisation, the Spanish question would in all probability soon come before the UN again. Faced with the alarming prospect of a decision for harsher sanctions against Spain, the British government would have to consider in 1947 whether the time had not finally come for a more interventionist role in Spanish affairs.

5
1947: British Intervention

The Tripartite Declaration on Spain and the UN resolution of 1946 called for a government in Madrid committed to democratic freedoms. The assumption that such a government would automatically receive international recognition gave the Spanish opposition in 1947 an added incentive for working towards an anti-Franco coalition. However, the UN resolution also required the restoration of democratic government to Spain 'within a reasonable time', after which the Security Council was to consider further 'adequate' measures to remedy the situation. This time-limit, interpreted as extending probably at most until the next session of the UN General Assembly in the autumn of 1947, alarmed the British government.[1] It therefore took a more direct interest than hitherto in the Spanish opposition's attempts to establish a democratic alternative to the Franco regime, which, it hoped, could then be used to counter possible UN demands for harsher sanctions against Spain.[2]

The anti-Franco opposition

The principle of republican legitimacy had worked against the emergence of a broad anti-Franco front, but after the fall of Giral's government in January 1947, Llopis, the new Prime Minister, appeared to adopt a more flexible approach. His government's programme, announced on 14 February, certainly reaffirmed his commitment to the re-establishment of the Spanish Republic, but, as he told a member of the British Embassy in Paris four days later, the final form of any new regime would be decided by a general election. However, before attempting a *rapprochement* with the monarchists, Llopis was more concerned with uniting the republican opposition. He therefore planned to cooperate with the interior republican opposition over the formation of a new National Resistance Council, which would be represented in, and answerable to, his own government. This, he believed, would put him in a strong position to argue that the Spanish republican government-in-exile met the requirements of the UN resolution of December 1946 and was consequently entitled to international recognition.[3]

Unfortunately, the principal organisation of the interior opposition, the ANFD, with which Llopis opened talks in March 1947, considered the National Resistance Council as envisaged by Llopis to be a direct threat to its own authority and so withheld its cooperation.[4] Yet, even with the ANFD's support, Llopis' government would have stood little chance of UN recognition. Growing tension between the western democracies and the USSR in 1947 meant that the appointment of a communist, Vicente Uribe Galdeano, as Minister of Economy in the Llopis cabinet reinforced Anglo-American prejudice against it. The appointment also made cooperation between the Spanish monarchists and the republican government-in-exile over the formation of a broad anti-Franco coalition, a *sine qua non* of UN recognition, even more improbable than before. It was, though, the decision of a PSOE Assembly of Regional Delegates in Toulouse in July 1947 to back Prieto's strategy for a republican-monarchist *rapprochement* (see below) that did most to undermine Llopis and he resigned as Prime Minister on 6 August 1947.[5]

Three weeks later, the *republican* Alvaro de Albornoz y Limiana, who had succeeded Martínez Barrio as President of the JEL in Mexico and was later Minister of Justice in Giral's first government-in-exile, formed the third Spanish government-in-exile. Composed solely of *republicans* it marked a return to Giral's uncompromising republicanism.[6] In an attempt to enhance the international standing of republican institutions, Albornoz proposed holding a session of the *Cortes* in a French *château* at Blois to coincide with the autumn session of the UN General Assembly. The French government's unwillingness at the time to jeopardise negotiations with Spain over the Franco-Spanish border, however, forced Albornoz to abandon the idea. He travelled, instead, to New York, where he addressed a large meeting in Madison Square, presented the President of the UN General Assembly with a memorandum calling for sanctions against the Franco regime, and addressed notes to Britain, France, the USA and the USSR asking for their support for Spanish republicanism.[7] For all his lobbying, though, Albornoz was unable to influence the UN General Assembly's debate on Spain, and the resolution adopted on 17 November 1947 did not impose the extra sanctions on Franco Spain he wanted. Albornoz would remain as Prime Minister until August 1951, but after Llopis' resignation the exiled Spanish government, as Hartmut Heine has pointed out, had ceased to be 'a factor of any importance' in the Spanish anti-Franco opposition.[8]

In Spain itself, despite police action against the ANFD and Aranda's two month confinement in the Balearics, contacts between the ANFD and the interior monarchist opposition resumed in January 1947. Luque, the ANFD General Secretary, had avoided arrest and Beigbeder stood in for Aranda during his absence. There was, though, little room for negotiation as it became increasingly apparent that the draft republican-monarchist agreement forwarded to Lisbon in December 1946 would never receive Don Juan's approval, while the Estoril Agreement, forced upon Santamaría the previous October, remained equally unacceptable to the ANFD. At the end of February, moreover, Don Juan instructed Beigbeder to call off his negotiations with the ANFD, which from then on were to be conducted from Lisbon.[9]

It was in anticipation of this latest development that that same month Gil-Robles created the *Confederación Española de Fuerzas Monárquicas* (CEFM). Intended to serve as a monarchist front in any negotiations with the republican opposition, the CEFM brought together three right-wing political groupings dating from the Second Republic – Gil-Robles' *Acción Popular* and *CEDA*, Sainz Rodríguez's *Renovación Española* and *Bloque Nacional*, and the Conde de Rodezno's *Comunión Tradicionalista*.[10] The interior monarchists reacted by setting up their own organisation in Spain, the *Nuevo Orden Monárquico*, renamed, after Aranda's return to Madrid in March, the *Comunidad de Organizaciones Monárquicas de España* (COME). The purpose of these two, largely phantom, organisations, Aranda admitted, was similarly to provide the interior monarchists with the necessary authority to pursue their own negotiations with the ANFD now that they were no longer permitted to do so in Don Juan's name.[11]

Aranda thus felt empowered to sign the December 1946 agreement with the ANFD on behalf of the COME without prior royal authorisation. A *fait accompli*, he no doubt calculated, would have left Don Juan no choice but to give his subsequent assent to the agreement or otherwise accept responsibility for the final breakdown of the republican-monarchist negotiations. Within the ANFD itself there was disagreement over signing the agreement, but all discussion was brought to an abrupt end on 8 April when Beigbeder, in his capacity as the COME President, told libertarian and *republican* ANFD representatives that without Don Juan's signature any agreement reached between them would be invalid.[12] Clearly, the interior monarchists had been unable to force Don Juan's hand and had, therefore, to admit defeat.

At this the ANFD was left with no choice but to throw in its lot with the exiled monarchists and so, on 19 April, Luque left for Paris, intending to travel from there *via* London to Lisbon. The British government, however, doubted whether without PSOE participation the Luque mission was sufficiently representative of the republican opposition to warrant its involvement and so refused to issue a transit visa. By now Gil-Robles, too, had changed his mind over the advisability of receiving Luque – whom he suspected, in any case, of being a police informer! With the *juanistas* coming under heavy attack in the Spanish press following Don Juan's stand against Franco's proposed Law of Succession (see below), a meeting between the Pretender and a prominent anarcho-syndicalist, Gil-Robles feared, would only have added grist to the General's mill. Even if Luque had reached Lisbon, in all probability Gil-Robles would simply have tried to force the Estoril Agreement upon him, much as he had done with Santamaría in October. Not surprisingly, therefore, nothing came of the Luque mission and at the end of May the ANFD General Secretary departed empty-handed for Madrid.[13]

During Luque's absence, his own organisation, the CNT, had fallen victim yet again to police action. This so weakened the ANFD that, for the rest of 1947, it ceased to play any real part in republican-monarchist negotiations. In October it briefly showed signs of life when it signalled its backing for Prieto's plan for a coalition government, but, a month later, the police arrested almost the entire national committee of the ANFD together with a majority of its regional delegates then in Madrid for a plenary meeting. Yet, even before this final onslaught, with the ANFD in disarray and the interior monarchist group around Aranda all but disowned by Don Juan, it had become apparent that the locus of republican-monarchist negotiations had shifted from Spain to the exiled opposition – specifically, to the PSOE-in-exile and the Lisbon monarchists.[14]

In 1947 Prieto was to regain his former influence within the PSOE-in-exile. He believed that the Tripartite Declaration and UN resolution of 1946 had vindicated his long held conviction that only a government of the 'broadest possible combination of anti-Franco elements', committed to holding a plebiscite, could realistically expect international recognition and support, and that, if Franco were ever to be removed, absolute priority had to be given by the anti-Franco opposition to the creation of this broad coalition. Prieto therefore saw his task in 1947 as threefold: to win over his party, the PSOE, to his views, to obtain the backing of the British government, and to persuade the exiled monarchists to engage in dialogue with the republican opposition.[15]

In July 1947 Prieto travelled from Mexico to France to attend a special four-day Assembly of PSOE Regional Delegates (*Asamblea de Grupos Departamentales del PSOE*) in Toulouse beginning on 25 July. After stressing how little time the PSOE had in which to find an acceptable solution to the Spanish problem before the UN General Assembly in the autumn, he secured a mandate from the delegates to work for an agreement with the monarchists. The Assembly then approved the formation of a three-man Special Committee whose purpose was to investigate the possibility of forming an opposition coalition government which met the requirements of the Tripartite Declaration.[16]

The Special Committee comprised, initially, Prieto, Trifón Gómez San José, Vice-President of the PSOE executive committee and, at the time, Llopis' Minister of Emigration, and Luis Jiménez de Asúa, a former minister of the Second Republic and Ambassador to Czechoslovakia, who was then living in Argentina. In September it published an appeal calling on all anti-Francoists to agree on a government acceptable to the UN, pledging the PSOE's respect for any regime freely chosen by the Spanish people and challenging the monarchists to match the socialists' new readiness to compromise.[17] According to a report from the British Embassy in Madrid, the appeal was 'warmly welcomed' by the majority of the republican opposition in Spain, Aranda's monarchist group, and many non-committed intellectuals, older politicians, churchmen, economists, industrialists and agriculturalists.[18]

To secure British backing for his initiative, Prieto next went, on 26 September, with Luis Araquistain Quevedo, a former republican Ambassador to Paris then living in London, to present his case directly to Bevin at the Foreign Office. Using Araquistain as his interpreter, he described how, at his instigation, the PSOE had abandoned the principle of republican legitimacy in order to work for a coalition of all anti-Franco opposition elements in the hope that this could lead to a provisional government which met the requirements of the Tripartite Declaration. The next step, Prieto said, was for the monarchists to come half way to meet the socialists. But this they were reluctant to do, because they still hoped for a restoration of the monarchy through Franco or a military *coup*, following which they expected Anglo-American recognition. Prieto therefore asked Bevin to put pressure on the monarchists by means of a second Tripartite Declaration making it clear that the British, French and American governments would not recognise a monarchy restored against the will of the people. He suggested that the appeal to 'patriotic and liberal-minded Spaniards' in the original Tripartite Declaration should be widened to include all those who wished to replace the Franco regime without civil war and should state that the three governments concerned desired to see a coalition of all these opponents and would back it once it was formed. Prieto assured Bevin that the republicans would respect the monarchy, if it was wanted by the people, but they would fight against a restoration imposed by military *coup* or Franco. In a passing reference to the incipient Cold War, Prieto also warned that if his attempt to form a provisional government failed, the Spanish masses would inevitably go over to communism. On the other hand, were the coalition government he desired to come to power, the whole of Spain would come within the orbit of the Western Powers.[19]

In a BBC interview after his meeting with Bevin, which he said he had left 'satisfied and happy', Prieto called once again for an opposition coalition.[20] Hopes for this coalition depended, of course, on the attitude of the Lisbon monarchists. Prieto had contacted them early in 1947 through Félix Vejarano, a member of Don Juan's Political Secretariat, and a meeting with Gil-Robles had been arranged for August in Paris. Unfortunately, Gil-Robles had been prevented from attending because of illness in his family, but, three weeks after Prieto's interview with Bevin, the two men finally met in London.[21]

The fact that the October meeting took place at all signalled a clear change in the exiled monarchists' attitude to the republican opposition. At the beginning of 1947 the Lisbon group was still persuaded that a *juanista* restoration could be effected through the Spanish Right, or even Franco himself, independently of the republicans. If there were to be negotiations with them, then, as Don Juan's newly created Privy Council made clear at its first meeting of 10–15 March, any concessions to the republican opposition would not go beyond the limited democratic provisions of Spain's 1876 Constitution.[22] Within three weeks, however, this position would be undermined by the action of Franco himself.

The Spanish leader, no less than his opponents, was fully alive to the possibility of UN sanctions against his country in the autumn of 1947. Although resolutely opposed to the democratisation of his regime, he therefore thought it prudent to make some 'democratic' gesture and, to this end, presented the text of a proposed new law – the Law of Succession – to his Council of Ministers on 28 March. This defined Spain as a kingdom, although, according to its second article, Franco remained Head of State. Only in the event of his death or incapacity would a Council of the Realm, together with the government, designate his successor or a regent. While he lived, Franco reserved to himself alone the right to nominate the next king of Spain. Thus, the proposed Law of Succession confirmed Franco as the final arbiter of an elective monarchy under which Don Juan forfeited his right to be king through dynastic succession to become but one of several candidates for the Spanish throne.[23]

Not surprisingly, when Carrero Blanco, Franco's Under-Secretary to the Presidency, visited the Bourbon Pretender in Estoril three days later to inform him of the proposed Law of Succession, he was left in no doubt as to *juanista* hostility. At their second interview Don Juan handed him a note rejecting the Law as an unacceptable infringement of the principle of hereditary succession.[24] This was followed, on 7 April, by what became known as the Estoril Manifesto – not to be confused with the Estoril Agreement of October 1946 – published in the Spanish and world press two days later. The proposal to alter the nature of the monarchy without consulting either the king (*sic*) or a truly representative *Cortes* was denounced as illegal, and Franco was accused of seeking dictatorship for life and of 'disguising beneath the glorious mantle of the monarchy a regime of purely arbitrary government'. Don Juan was therefore duty-bound to make a 'public and solemn declaration of the supreme principle of legitimacy' which he embodied and of the 'imprescriptible rights of sovereignty' placed in his person by the Providence of God.[25]

On 13 April an article appeared – without Don Juan's permission – in *The Observer* detailing an interview which the Pretender had given its correspondent, Rafael Martínez Nadal (*alias* Antonio Torres of the BBC), the previous September. In it Don Juan was reported as ruling out the possibility of any agreement with Franco except for one covering arrangements for the unconditional transfer of power to the monarchy. He called for a plebiscite on the monarchy in Spain and foreign intervention against Franco, promised legal protection to the UGT, the CNT and other organisations of the Second Republic, approved of negotiations with the republican opposition, and committed himself to an 'administrative separation' of Church and state, an unconditional political amnesty and respect for regional differences. Although he concluded by defending his original support for the nationalists in the Civil War, he added that he was glad he had not fought in it![26]

The combined effect of the Estoril Manifesto and the *Observer* article, however, was to spark off an intense campaign by the Spanish press against the Pretender and his advisors. Consequently, Don Juan, depicted as an irresponsible and unpatriotic democrat, lost the sympathies of almost the whole of the Spanish Right. Under pressure from Franco, the Portuguese Dictator, António de Oliveira Salazar, warned Don Juan and Gil-Robles to abstain from further political activity in Portugal, and Gil-Robles, Sainz Rodríguez, Vejarano and Vegas Latapié were placed under *résidence surveillée* some distance from Lisbon.[27] In Spain the Law of Succession was approved in a national referendum on 6 July 1947 by 92.9 per cent of the votes cast. Even allowing for extensive ballot rigging and intimidation, the result was an undeniable triumph for Franco, leaving Gil-Robles' insurance policy of retaining the loyalty of the Spanish Right gravely compromised.

Five days after the referendum Gil-Robles left Portugal for an extended tour of England, France, Switzerland and Italy. In London he took advantage of a private visit to him on 12 July from William Horsfall Carter of the Foreign Office Research Department to argue the case for British support for the Spanish opposition. What was wanted, Gil-Robles said, was a programme which could command the support of the Spanish Right and yet orientated towards the Left. This meant significant compromises by leaders of both Right and Left, who, if they were to carry their followers with them, had to be sure of external backing before signing any firm compact. Without effective Anglo-American support, Horsfall Carter was warned, the opposition of the Right would lose patience and 'knuckle under to Franco', while the Left would be 'thrown into the arms of communism'. Therefore, Gil-Robles wanted Britain, whose policy so far had been 'words not deeds', to put secret pressure on Franco to depart, together with some concerted announcement blessing an interim caretaker government with a rider that it should exclude all dealings with the communists.[28]

Tentative arrangements were made for Gil-Robles to meet McNeil, the Minister of State for Foreign Affairs, but when Reuters reported that the interview was to be at the Spaniard's request, Gil-Robles feared complications in Spain and Portugal and cancelled it.[29] Four days later, on 23 July, he left for Switzerland and from there travelled on to Italy. At Castel Gandolfo he handed Pope Pius XII a letter from Don Juan intended to undo the harm caused by his *Observer* interview and explaining, in particular, that it had never been Don Juan's intention to call for a complete separation of Church and state in Spain. When Gil-Robles went on to inquire of Pius XII's attitude towards the monarchist opposition, the Pope diplomatically observed that it was a matter on which each citizen could be guided exclusively by his political preferences. In interviews with other cardinals and prelates, notably Cardinal Federico Tedeschini, a former Papal Nuncio to Spain, and Monsignor Domenico Tardini, Vatican Pro-Secretary of State, Gil-Robles emphasised the Church's need to distance itself from the Franco regime.[30]

Back in Switzerland Gil-Robles told the pro-monarchist socialist Amado Granell that he was now prepared to meet Prieto, but after receiving news of family illness on 20 August, he immediately returned to Portugal. Once there Gil-Robles was reluctant to leave his family again for fear that he would be compromised by any talks with the republicans and refused permission to re-enter Portugal. By now, however, the British Foreign Office was actively involved. On 23 September, three days before Bevin's meeting with Prieto, an official from the Embassy in Lisbon assured Gil-Robles that Bevin and the British government put themselves fully at Don Juan or his representatives' service in order to facilitate a meeting with the republicans. Foreign Office pressure was also brought to bear on the Portuguese authorities, as a result of which Gil-Robles was issued with a three month exit and return visa on 11 October. Three days later he left for London.[31]

The talks between Gil-Robles and Prieto were held in a flat near Piccadilly Circus, the two men meeting, according to Prieto, on four occasions between 15 and 18 October.[32] As intended, discussion centred on arrangements for the transitional period following Franco's departure. Gil-Robles' position is known to us from an interview which he had with Bevin half way through the talks, on 17 October, and from a memorandum which he drew up for the Foreign Office the next day. Prieto had already made his position clear to Bevin on 26 September but he, too, gave the Foreign Office a memorandum on 19 October outlining his responses to the monarchists' demands, which Gil-Robles had summarised for him verbally at their last session together.

What Gil-Robles wanted was the restoration of the *juanista* monarchy *immediately* after Franco's departure with a plebiscite to determine the final form of the Spanish state some time later. He was opposed to the establishment of an alternative provisional regime first and a plebiscite *before* a monarchist restoration. Gil-Robles, in short, wanted a plebiscite *a posteriori* on the monarchy and not *a priori*. Therefore, in his interview with Bevin on 17 October, Gil-Robles made it clear that he totally rejected Prieto's reliance on the Tripartite Declaration of March 1946 to justify a plebiscite *a priori*. He argued that if a plebiscite were held before the complete restoration of civil liberties to Spain, it would have to be policed by foreign powers and would be as 'bogus' as Franco's referendum on the Law of Succession. Alternatively, if full civil liberties were restored at once, Gil-Robles predicted anarchy and civil war, of benefit to the communists alone, while the middle classes, the Army and the Church would rally to Franco. Plebiscites in Italy and Greece had required the presence of foreign armies but in Spain it would be the Spanish Army who held the ring. The Army, however, would never consent to a plebiscite that might result in electoral victory for the defeated of the Civil War. Furthermore, Gil-Robles asked, if through unforeseen circumstances, such as death, Franco did relinquish power to Don Juan, would the Pretender be obliged to refuse it because of some previous commitment to a plebiscite?

No, the way forward, according to Gil-Robles, was, first, to avoid any further UN action, secondly, to relinquish the formula of the Tripartite Declaration, and, thirdly, to seek some form of intervention which would not alienate the people of Spain by offending their national pride. Monsignor Tardini, he said, had recently shown 'great interest' in his proposal that the Vatican should take the initiative over Franco's departure. He therefore proposed that the three signatories to the Tripartite Declaration should agree a 'formula' with the Vatican for the removal of Franco. He concluded with a declaration of the principles that would guide Don Juan if he came to the throne:

(1) The iniquitous features of the present régime should be abolished, without violence and without giving scope for private vengeance.
(2) The influence of communism should as far as possible be eliminated.
(3) Measures of social reform should be introduced in agreement with the workers' organisations.
(4) The rule of law should be reintroduced at once.
(5) Negotiations should be opened for a Concordat to regulate the functions of Church and State.
(6) Political liberties should be reintroduced gradually and as cir-

cumstances permitted and should be at least as extensive as those provided for in the Constitution of 1876.

(7) Finally, the régime should be regarded as provisional until it had been confirmed either by a plebiscite or by a popularly elected Constituent Assembly.[33]

If force of circumstances were to lead to the emergence of a republic, Gil-Robles added, the monarchists would work with that regime, provided it bound itself by the same principles.

Gil-Robles' memorandum of 18 October went over much the same ground, drawing attention again to the dangers of a plebiscite *a priori*. It placed, though, greater emphasis on the practical difficulties of removing Franco if the Tripartite Declaration were invoked. Franco would exploit it to frighten the Spanish people with the result that his supporters and the whole neutral mass of Spaniards would simply close ranks, forcing the Powers to go to extreme lengths – including coastal blockades and the closure of the Portuguese frontier – to overcome their resistance. This was neither feasible nor was it acceptable to Gil-Robles as a Spaniard. The solution was, he repeated, an approach from the Vatican, the effect of which would be to calm down the feelings of those who might otherwise be alarmed, while it would not in any way be prejudicial to national dignity, since it would be 'a question of a spiritual power intervening in a state of affairs that concerns Western civilisation itself'.[34]

Prieto's memorandum, of 19 October, took the form of responses to seven points, similar to, but not identical with, the seven principles which Gil-Robles had outlined to Bevin. Prieto was in broad agreement with five of the points. He agreed 'absolutely' that the elimination of the abuses of the Franco regime was to be undertaken without vengeance or reprisals. He raised no objection to the second point that maintenance of public order was a priority. He accepted, too, the special position of the Catholic Church, emphasised in Gil-Robles' third point, although he felt that a Concordat was not the responsibility of a *provisional* government and that all that was needed initially was a guarantee of religious freedom. He was in complete agreement with the fourth point covering social legislation and was also satisfied with the assurance, under the fifth point, that basic human rights should be legally guaranteed from the very start, even if the re-establishment of political freedoms took longer.

As was to be expected, however, substantial differences arose over Gil-Robles' sixth point, which argued that as the problem of how 'to get decent political life functioning in Spain' was the fundamental one, the question of 'what processes circumstances will permit for bringing that about may be regarded as a secondary matter'.[35] For Prieto, however, the question of procedure was far from being a secondary matter. It was, on the contrary, central to the normalisation of Spanish political life. There was, in his view, no alternative to the procedure specified in the Tripartite Declaration and UN resolution. The choice of regime and its head of state could not be left to Franco, since this would imply recognition of the legality of his regime and of his Law of Succession, while a restoration of the monarchy by military *coup* was equally unacceptable. In short, Prieto wanted the complete opposite to Gil-Robles: first the establishment of a provisional coalition government, followed by the restoration of civil liberties, and then a constitutional plebiscite, prior to a possible monarchist restoration – a plebiscite *a priori* and not *a posteriori*. Otherwise, he noted, there was always the danger of restoring an institution only to have to dismantle it afterwards, with all the problems that might ensue.

As for Gil-Robles' seventh point, which reiterated his proposal for a formula concerted by the signatories of the Tripartite Declaration and the Vatican, Prieto declared himself ready to accept any means of bringing Franco down and, after the Church's identification with the nationalist cause during the Civil War, welcomed any attempt by the Holy See to make it clear that Franco could no longer hide behind the Church. For all that, Prieto remained firmly convinced that the procedure laid down by the Tripartite Declaration was the best, adding, for the benefit of the Foreign Office, that, once a provisional government had been established, Spain would apply for admission to the UN and for participation in the European Recovery Programme.[36]

Gil-Robles left London on 20 October and after a short stay in Paris arrived back in Portugal two days later.[37] There he was greeted by the scandal he had anticipated. The Lisbon and Madrid press accused him of making a revolutionary pact with Prieto and, mischievously, claimed that he had been disowned by Don Juan.[38] A thoroughly alarmed Gil-Robles immediately requested Prieto to deny all reports of their London meetings and, on 24 October, Prieto obliged with a *démenti* in *France Presse* and *Radiodiffusion*.[39] Even so, the Spanish government pressed Salazar to deport Gil-Robles and it was not until 12 November that he learnt to his relief that he would after all be permitted to remain in Portugal.[40]

Prieto left London, the day after Gil-Robles, and also stayed briefly in Paris. While there, he was reported in the French press as claiming British Labour Party approval for his insistence on the Tripartite Declaration and a plebiscite *a priori*, and, to Foreign Office alarm, that

Britain, France and the USA had given an assurance that they would 'in God's good time' take positive steps to oust Franco. This, he added, could be achieved only through the economic asphyxiation of Spain.[41] From France Prieto returned to Mexico where his son, Luis, was terminally ill.

The London talks had confirmed important differences between Prieto and Gil-Robles. Prieto's hopes of having a PSOE-CEFM agreement ready for the UN General Assembly autumn session had been disappointed and both men had been forced to issue statements denying they had even met. None the less, Gil-Robles could not ignore the improvement in Franco's position as east-west tension mounted, and Prieto, who had staked his political reputation on a *rapprochement* with the monarchists, needed to report some progress at the Third PSOE Congress scheduled for February 1948.[42] So, on 27 November, Gil-Robles wrote to Vejarano, who had accompanied him to London for the talks, that he was interested in renewing conversations with Prieto. Vejarano, who had been invited to Washington to meet Norman Armour, now US Under-Secretary of State, passed on Gil-Robles' message to Fernando de los Ríos, formerly Giral's Foreign Minister, in New York, who conveyed it to Prieto. In his reply of 13 December Prieto said that he, too, was ready to resume negotiations.[43] Since Gil-Robles could not leave, nor Prieto enter, Portugal, Prieto decided in the spring of 1948 to go to France and from there negotiate with Lisbon by letter and through emissaries.

British reaction to the anti-Franco opposition

The UN resolution of December 1946 had placed the British government in a dilemma. On the one hand stood its commitment to the UN, perceived as indispensable to the security of the British Empire, and the recognition that failure on Britain's part to implement resolutions on Spain could dangerously undermine the new world organisation. On the other hand, as Bevin acknowledged in January 1947, the recommendation for further Security Council action had landed the government once more 'on the slippery slope'. The UN, he regretted, had successfully asserted its right to take action to bring about change in the internal regime of a foreign country. Consequently, if the Spanish question reappeared before the Security Council or General Assembly, the precedent set the previous December would make it difficult for the British delegation to argue against more drastic measures.[44]

There was, too, continuing apprehension that UN sanctions would destabilise the western Mediterranean, where the Russians, Bevin had earlier observed, were only waiting to move in.[45] Indeed, Gibraltar's 'vital' strategic importance was reaffirmed by the Oversea Defence Committee in April 1947, and, the following month, the Chiefs of Staff warned against any measures prejudicing access to Spanish, or French, North African colonies in time of war.[46]

Nor, in the straitened domestic circumstances of 1947 could Britain's commercial and financial links with Spain be lightly dismissed.[47] Where British priorities lay was demonstrated in March 1947 with the signing of a Monetary Agreement to replace the Anglo-Spanish Clearing Agreement of March 1940.[48] It was admitted in the Foreign Office that a conflict existed between 'our political attitude towards Spain and our essential economic advantage', but William Hogg, Acting First Secretary in the Western Department with responsibility for Spain and Portugal, emphatically denied that the agreement would keep Franco in power for a single day, if the Spanish opposition elements were united against him, adding, for good measure, that if its effect were indeed to deter the opposition from uniting, then they were 'as frivolous as Franco says they are and incapable of any serious political activity'.[49]

Despite this, the Foreign Office continued to see in the Spanish opposition a convenient means of fending off UN calls for sanctions against Spain. If it could be shown that progress was being made towards the formation of a credible anti-Franco coalition, then, it believed, the British government would be in a good position to argue that a precondition of democratic government in Spain had been met and that UN sanctions were consequently unnecessary. In early 1947, however, it was still unclear from which sector of the Spanish opposition such a coalition might emerge.[50]

The Foreign Office placed little faith in the republican government-in-exile. In February Duff Cooper, Britain's Ambassador to France, reported that a future Llopis government would seek some basis of agreement with the monarchists. But, against this, Douglas Howard, the British Chargé d'Affaires in Madrid, observed that no genuine representative of the Spanish Right would ever seek a *rapprochement* with the government-in-exile, and this was confirmed in March when López Oliván told Hoyer Millar that negotiations with Llopis would be tantamount to monarchist recognition of the republican government-in-exile.[51] Consequently, when Llopis asked to be received by Bevin at the end of February, the Foreign Office advised against it. He met, instead, Hector

McNeil, the Minister of State for Foreign Affairs, who deliberately avoided making any promises, and Llopis returned to Paris four days later having achieved nothing.[52]

If little was expected of the Llopis government, still less was of its successor. When news of its formation reached the Foreign Office in September, Hogg described Albornoz's government as 'a very colourless affair', destined to disappear once a more active coalition of the Spanish opposition were formed.[53] After this the Spanish republican government-in-exile excited no further interest in the Foreign Office and by the autumn of 1947 it had ceased to count in British policy towards Franco Spain.

Foreign Office hopes for the ANFD-monarchist agreement of December 1946 also dwindled as it became clear in the first quarter of 1947 that it would not be ratified in Lisbon. Possibly because of their personal contacts with him, the Embassy staff in Madrid retained their confidence in Aranda longer than most, but Howard's belief that he provided the only chance of a way out of the *impasse* in republican–monarchist negotiations was considered exaggerated in London.[54] Instead, the Foreign Office recognised that the key to republican-monarchist negotiations was held by the Lisbon monarchists. Yet what pressure, if any, the British government might put on them was debatable.

At the beginning of February a moral case for intervention was advanced by Horsfall Carter. Spanish socialists and libertarians, he argued, had taken a big risk in withdrawing support from the Giral government and throwing away the notion of 'republican legality' in favour of an *entente* with the monarchists. They had done this, first, in the belief that they had more chance of maintaining their position within a constitutional monarchy than under a restored republic where they saw themselves swamped by communists, but, secondly, because they felt that this 'broad entente of anti-Franco elements' based on the ANFD was the one solution for Spain which had the backing of the British government: hence, as they saw it, Britain's 'moral responsibility'. Since, though, the Lisbon monarchists were not responding to the republicans' advances, the British government, Horsfall Carter advised, was obliged to 'find some means of applying the spur' to them.[55]

At Mallet's suggestion, Hoyer Millar did tell López Oliván that it would facilitate matters greatly if the Lisbon monarchists were 'to be rather more energetic' in their attempts to reach agreement with the other opposition groups.[56] But this mild prompting was as far as the British government would go. At the end of March 1947 its policy towards the Spanish opposition remained almost totally passive.

It was at this point that McNeil intervened. In a minute of 1 April he drew attention yet again to the possibility of the Spanish question coming before the UN Security Council in June, or even earlier at the General Assembly's special session on Palestine scheduled to begin on 28 April. If in the meantime, he pointed out, no further progress had been made in Spain towards Franco's removal, there was a serious risk that Britain would be pressed further towards economic sanctions or 'some other noxious course'. McNeil, therefore, proposed a joint approach by Britain, France and the USA – not specifically to the organised Spanish opposition but, more widely, to Spanish catholics, monarchists, republicans and the Army, pointing out the urgency of the situation and explaining that the three governments' obligations towards the UN might involve them in action which, despite seriously injuring their own interests, would also hit Spain hard. McNeil's hope was that this would inspire the Spanish groups he mentioned to take rapid action by, at the very least, forming a 'shadow government'. Once this was in place, the three governments would then advise Franco to go, with a warning that UN pressure might otherwise lead to action with very serious consequences for Spain.[57]

McNeil's proposal met with reservations from the Western Department and there the matter might have rested, had it not coincided with a similar initiative from the American State Department.[58] By the spring of 1947 Soviet-American relations were fast deteriorating and as American attitudes hardened, so did apprehension in the State Department that, by doing nothing to hasten Franco's departure, Anglo-American *attentisme* over Spain was playing into the communists' hands. So, encouraged – albeit misleadingly – by reports from Philip Bonsal, the USA's Chargé d'Affaires in Madrid, to believe that prospects for an anti-Franco coalition in Spain were 'promising', Acheson, the Acting Secretary of State, decided in March 1947 to resume the interventionist policy that had inspired his original call for an anti-Franco declaration in January 1946.[59]

On 10 April his new policy was officially communicated to the Foreign Office by Lewis Douglas, the American Ambassador in London. Anticipating the Marshall Plan, announced later in the summer, it was a plan for combating communism by promising financial and economic aid to any freely elected government replacing Franco. As long as the Dictator remained in power, it was argued, the Spanish situation was dangerous, since it blocked the USA, and Britain, from assisting Spanish economic reconstruction as 'an effective barrier to civil strife and communist domination'. It also gave the USSR a propaganda advantage, with the western powers cast in the role of defenders of fascism and reaction. Since there was nothing to suggest that Franco's Law of Succession would prevent UN action against Spain, but there was evidence of increased activity by non-communist Spanish opposition groups, Acheson proposed that the USA and Britain should agree a 'positive policy' to induce a change of government in Spain. This would enable both countries to assist in creating healthy economic and political conditions in Spain and, at the same time, help the UN attain its objectives.

Acheson suggested that a precise indication of the support which a regime based on democratic principles could expect from the USA and Britain would go far towards giving confidence to all Spaniards desiring change, particularly in the Army. He envisaged that relations with a post-Franco regime would fall into two stages: during the first, interim, stage the USA and Britain would enter into friendlier political relations with the Spanish government and at once lift all economic restrictions on Spanish trade, in the expectation that other UN member states would follow suit. In the second stage, following constitutional elections, consideration would be given to greater economic and political support, including backing for Spain's admission to the UN and increased aid for economic and industrial development. The point was then made – in support of elections *a priori* and not *a posteriori* – that the additional aid envisaged would be compromised if Franco's departure were followed by an *immediate* restoration of the monarchy. Only if elections showed it to be the 'clearly expressed choice of the Spanish people', could the monarchy expect political and economic aid from the USA.[60]

Acheson's proposals were immediately discussed by Sargent, Mallet and Hoyer Millar. Mallet, in particular, argued that if foreign pressure were resumed, Franco would not budge. It would be difficult making secret approaches in Spain because of the multiplicity of political parties and the difficulties of contacting their leaders, and Army leaders would have to be reassured that the move was not in any way inspired by Moscow. He recommended instead waiting for about six weeks until reaction in Spain to Franco's Law of Succession and Don Juan's Estoril Manifesto could be assessed. Although McNeil was against any delay, arguing that Franco was then 'off balance', that the Spanish opposition groups might in time quarrel and that it was not known when the Spanish question might come before the UN again, he none the less agreed to wait for an appreciation of the situation from the Madrid Embassy before further discussion.[61]

In Madrid Howard thought the Estoril Manifesto unlikely to shake the allegiance of Franco's supporters while Don Juan's declaration in *The*

Observer that he would return to Spain *before* a plebiscite could alienate the Left. The Army, moreover, was fundamentally loyal to Franco, and it was too soon to comment on republican-monarchist negotiations. Howard did not rule out the possibility of Franco's going under certain conditions but thought the possibility 'extremely remote'. He objected, moreover, that the proposed Anglo-American action amounted to intervention, which might involve more and more extreme forms in violation of the UN Charter. It could split the moderates in Spain, leading to a situation of ultra-violence and anarchy. If, on the other hand, the USA and Britain stood by the UN Charter and refused to tolerate outside intervention, there were, he believed, 'at least good prospects that under the stress of circumstances Franco's moderate opponents on the Left and Right will finally come together'.[62]

At a meeting with Sargent on 17 April Mallet endorsed Howard's report. Franco, he thought, could go either through 'voluntary' resignation or a military *coup* and either solution could in theory be hastened by foreign pressure or economic sanctions, and, if these failed, by military intervention. But if the effect of economic sanctions were long delayed, there was a risk of Spaniards rallying to Franco against foreign dictation, certainly in the event of armed intervention, and the consequent danger of civil war would be very great. For Mallet, the key to the situation was, as always, the generals, but how were the captains-general of Spain's eight military regions to be approached? Furthermore, as a military *coup* could only be effected in favour of the monarchy, if the British and American governments were not prepared to give it a 'direct stimulus', then, Mallet advised, they should keep quiet and let the Spaniards work out their own solution. As for approaching Franco, he did not see how a chargé d'affaires could gain access to him or, if he did, how much weight he would carry in a country where rank counted for so much. Mallet's not unexpected conclusion was to leave things as they were.[63]

Bevin, who was in Moscow until 29 April for a meeting of the Council of Foreign Ministers, agreed. He described Acheson's scheme as 'ill-considered and based on wishful thinking rather than a realistic assessment of the facts'. As Franco Spain was not of itself a danger to international peace, intervention would constitute a breach of the UN Charter and set a very grave precedent. On 25 April, therefore, he instructed that policy towards Spain should remain unchanged, and one week later the American Ambassador was accordingly informed.[64]

The State Department, however, felt that its proposals had been misunderstood. On 13 May Acheson told Lord Inverchapel, the British

Ambassador in Washington, that he had not envisaged threats but rather an 'objective explanation of our views' to Franco, the generals, the opposition and all other interested Spaniards. In this way, they would be shown the gains accruing from a change of regime rather than the penalities from their doing nothing. Shortly before this, in conversation with a British Embassy official, Samuel Reber, Chief of the Western European Division of the State Department, had drawn attention to the fact that the State Department regarded its proposals as a means of strengthening its hand to stave off UN demands for economic sanctions, rather than as a step towards them. It was concerned that silence and inaction on Spanish affairs might be taken as acquiescence and even as tacit approval of the Franco regime as a bulwark against communism. Furthermore, it was strongly believed in the State Department that the trend of events in Spain was likely to increase the communists' chances of making mischief and, ultimately, of damaging the USA's strategic position. Reber hoped, therefore, that their discussions could continue, although, he added, not yet with the French.[65]

The Foreign Secretary's instructions notwithstanding, the American proposal continued to receive Foreign Office attention until Bevin finally called a meeting on 12 June to review the whole situation. The seriousness of the matter was indicated by the unprecedented number attending: McNeil, Harvey, Hoyer Millar and Hogg, together with Christopher Mayhew, Parliamentary Under-Secretary for Foreign Affairs, Nevile Butler and Gladwyn Jebb, Assistant Under-Secretaries, and Paul Gore-Booth, Head of the United Nations (Economic and Social) Department. Bevin stressed to them all the disastrous economic consequences for Britain if there were a break with Spain and this made it 'impossible to contemplate' the application of economic sanctions to Spain at that time. He preferred, instead, a joint Anglo-American initiative to persuade other UN members that intervention in a country's domestic affairs was ruled out by the UN Charter. If American cooperation over this proved impossible, then Britain, according to Bevin, might have to approach UN members alone.[66]

Bevin intended putting these views to the American Ambassador without delay but, in the event, his preoccupation with the Marshall Plan talks in Paris left him no time to meet with Douglas. It was therefore only after another meeting, on 3 July, between Harvey and John Hickerson, Deputy Director of the Office of European Affairs in the State Department, who pressed the case once more for joint action over Spain, that the decision was finally taken to inform Washington on 26 July that the Acheson plan was being turned down.[67] After six months British policy in 1947 thus remained as Sloan had defined it in March: 'non-intervention tempered by passive encouragement of the responsible opposition to Franco'.[68]

In the meantime the probability of UN action against Spain had not diminished. In his Annual Report of 4 July, Trygve Lie, UN Secretary General, pointedly observed that the problem of Franco Spain had not been 'satisfactorily resolved in the spirit of the resolution passed by the General Assembly'.[69] So, having just rejected the Acheson plan, the Foreign Office looked for some 'nucleus' round which a provisional Spanish government could form. Reliance on the republican government-in-exile was obviously out of the question while reports from the Madrid Embassy continued to discount any agreement between the ANFD and the interior monarchists.[70] This left the Lisbon monarchists, more open to compromise since the Law of Succession and the referendum of 6 July, and the PSOE-in-exile, converted to *prietismo* three weeks later. It left, in other words, Gil-Robles and Prieto as the potential arbiters of a republican-monarchist agreement.

At the beginning of August the Foreign Office learnt that Prieto wished to discuss his plans for a republican-monarchist 'fusion' with Attlee or Bevin. Although he did not wish to refuse this request, Ponsonby Crosthwaite, Head of the Western Department since June, was wary of creating the impression of an 'international socialist line-up' since this would arouse misgivings among the non-socialist opposition parties in Spain, and so Prieto was informed that he could meet Mayhew instead. Prieto did not respond to this invitation and by the end of the month Mayhew was in any case no longer available. By now, however, with the next session of the UN General Assembly fast approaching, Sargent thought it might be useful if Bevin did see Prieto after all, particularly in order to impress upon him how 'foolish' it would be to raise the Spanish question there, and an interview was arranged for Friday 26 September.[71]

Bevin was well briefed for the meeting, Prieto having earlier expounded his views to Guy Millard of the Paris Embassy and Denis Healey, the Labour Party's International Secretary.[72] Thus, it was known in the Foreign Office that he would ask for a second Tripartite Declaration by Britain, France and the USA making it clear that a restoration of the monarchy would not be recognised unless sanctioned by the will of the people (see above). Bevin was able to tell Prieto that he warmly welcomed his efforts to reach agreement with other forces opposed to Franco and that that there was no truth in the rumour that the British and American governments, or their general staffs, were in any way relying on the Spanish Dictator. He assured him that the British government would take much the same view of a regime installed by military *coup* as it took of Franco's. Although Britain had made its position clear in the original Tripartite Declaration and elsewhere, Bevin none the less said that he would study the question of a fresh declaration and, if his Cabinet colleagues approved, would take the matter up with the American and French governments. He agreed that it was essential that the Spanish people should be consulted about their future form of government but emphasised again that the form in which the question was put to them and the stage at which such consultation was to take place had to be a matter for agreement between the opposition parties. He would, though, consider privately advising the monarchists to be accommodating, just as he had done earlier to 'the parties of the Left' through Trifón Gómez.[73] Bevin also told Prieto that he was most anxious for a government to come into being in Spain with which Britain could do business in the interests of the economy of Europe, but he did not think it desirable at the time to make any further statement about the possibility of such a government benefiting from the outcome of the recent talks in Paris on the Marshall Plan. Finally – in an undisguised attempt to promote republican-monarchist negotiations – he told Prieto that the British government would be letting the Portuguese know of its hope that Gil-Robles would be allowed to return to Portugal after visiting England.[74]

On 17 October, half-way through the talks between Prieto and Gil-Robles, Bevin was told by Gil-Robles that he rejected the Tripartite Declaration and proposed that the signatories to the Declaration should agree a formula for the removal of Franco with the Vatican. Bevin made very much the same points as he had to Prieto three weeks earlier. The British government's policy was that political freedom should be reintroduced into Spain without violence and by agreement among the parties opposed to Franco, and so he hoped Prieto and Gil-Robles would reach agreement. Britain was also anxious to recognise and support any government which proved to have the confidence of the Spanish people. For that reason it had refrained until then from any intervention calculated to produce disorder. Gil-Robles and Prieto, Bevin then pointed out, attached too much importance to the actual wording of the Tripartite Declaration, which had not been intended as a rigid programme but only to indicate the views of the three powers on the Spanish question. Whatever regime succeeded Franco, monarchy or republic, it had to rest on the consent of the governed, and, in a restatement of his policy of non-intervention, Bevin insisted that the exact method of bringing about a change of regime could only be agreed upon by the Spanish opposition.[75]

Having brought the two Spaniards together, the Foreign Office was obliged to consider the implications of a possible republican-monarchist agreement. In a lengthy memorandum of 31 October, John Curle, who had been transferred in February 1947 from the British Embassy in Lisbon to the Western Department as Second Secretary, wrote that the Spanish Army, as the victors of the Civil War, would never stomach a plebiscite on the lines Prieto suggested. Therefore, Curle argued, Prieto's plan was hopeless. There were, however, grounds for supposing that the Vatican might cooperate with Gil-Robles' proposal, which, if backed by the PSOE and CNT, could prove acceptable to 'the generals, the Church, bankers and industrialists wanting a share in the Marshall Plan, and all those who do not like Franco but were terrified of another civil war'. Consequently, either Britain accepted the indefinite prolongation of the present situation: this would preserve British economic and immediate political interests while leaving the government free to alter its policy later if required, although it would also discourage the moderate Spanish opposition and strengthen the extremists. Or Britain could take active steps to encourage the peaceful replacement of Franco by some alternative regime resulting from the discussions between Prieto and Gil-Robles: this would remove Franco and establish a regime orientated towards the west, with which Britain could resume normal relations and do business to the general advantage of Europe. However, if the new regime proved unacceptable, the sponsors of the scheme would have to beat a retreat, or, even if Franco were removed peacefully, the disruptive forces in the new regime might be greater than the forces of order, which would lead again to anarchy and the renewal of civil war. If the British government did decide to take action, then the first step, Curle suggested, would be to find out whether the Americans, and later the French, would enter joint discussions with the Vatican. However, if the Pope subsequently declined to play his part or Franco refused to go, Britain, Curle concluded, would have to resign itself to the fact that the peaceful removal of Franco was impossible and plan its policy on the basis that he would remain in power for the foreseeable future.[76]

Gil-Robles' option, however, was rejected by Curle's superiors. Crosthwaite minuted that it was premature to consider the idea of the three governments asking the Vatican to make a secret approach to Franco or to discuss it with the USA until Prieto and Gil-Robles had resolved their differences over the institutional question. He thought, instead, that all they needed to do at that stage was to inform Prieto and Gil-Robles that their memoranda had been carefully studied, that the British government was encouraged by the large measure of agreement already reached and that it would be interested in being kept informed of developments. In addition, Prieto should be told that the British government was firmly opposed to economic sanctions or further UN intervention and would have to say so publicly if the question were brought up in New York. Harvey and Sargent agreed with Crosthwaite, and on 22 November Howard was informed that Bevin had sent messages to Prieto and Gil-Robles along the lines suggested by Crosthwaite.[77]

Evidence of the Foreign Office's return to a non-committal policy on the Spanish opposition was soon provided when Don Juan came to London for the wedding of Princess Elizabeth and Lieutenant Philip Mountbatten on 20 November. On the day of the wedding Araquistain had written to Curle asking if Don Juan could be informed that Antonio Pérez, who had since been co-opted onto the PSOE Special Committee, and Trifón Gómez were arriving in London in four days' time and would like to meet Don Juan. Crosthwaite agreed that it would be a good idea to pass on the message, but Bevin minuted that he would not mention it when he met the Pretender.[78] Instead, after Don Juan's opening remark, at their five minute meeting on 24 November, that he wanted a constitutional monarchy to replace Franco, Bevin simply made the point that Britain was eager for good relations with the Spanish people and that the British government was most anxious not to see civil war in Spain again. He concluded, somewhat lamely, that if Franco were a patriotic man, he would see that his duty lay in making way for another regime, which would allow Spain to become part of Western Europe and join in its economic benefits. Bevin gave no indication whatsoever that the British would do anything practical towards a monarchist restoration.[79]

To a large extent Bevin's reluctance to go beyond these platitudinous reassurances or to broker a second republican-monarchist meeting in London can be explained by the decision reached on Spain in the UN only the week before. The UN General Assembly had referred the question of 'Relations of Members of the United Nations with Spain' to its First Committee on 23 September, although discussion had not begun until 11 November. By then the Committee had before it three resolutions on Spain. A Polish resolution reaffirmed the UN resolution of

December 1946 and called upon the Security Council to consider the Spanish question within one month and take adequate measures to remedy the situation. A second resolution, proposed by a group of Spanish American countries – Cuba, Guatemala, Mexico, Panama, Uruguay – also reaffirmed the 1946 resolution but went on merely to express confidence that the Security Council would assume its responsibilities under the Charter if it thought the situation in Spain so demanded. The third and weakest resolution, proposed by Belgium, Luxembourg and the Netherlands, omitted all direct reference to the 1946 resolution and, instead, regretted that the invitation to member states to withdraw their ambassadors and ministers plenipotentiary from Madrid had not been fully applied; it then expressed confidence that the Security Council would fulfill its obligations to maintain international peace and security as soon as the Spanish question required the adoption of measures (*sic*).[80]

The Polish resolution was backed only by the USSR, and the other Eastern bloc states then represented in the UN – Czechoslovakia, Byelorussia and Yugoslavia. Consequently, after a drafting sub-committee was set up on 12 November, the three-paragraph resolution it brought back to the First Committee combined only the Cuban and Belgian joint resolutions and rejected the Polish 'maximalist' position.[81] The First Committee forwarded this resolution to a plenary session of the General Assembly where each paragraph was voted on separately. The second paragraph, which reaffirmed the 1946 December resolution, failed to receive the necessary two-thirds vote and was lost. As a result, the UN resolution on Spain of November 1947 stated:

> Whereas the Secretary-General in his annual report has informed the General Assembly of the steps taken by the States Members of the organisation in pursuance of its recommendations of 12 December 1946, the General Assembly expresses its confidence that the Security Council will exercise its responsibilities under the Charter as soon as it considers that the situation in regard to Spain so requires.[82]

For the British government, the November resolution came as an undoubted relief. In a Cabinet paper of 17 December Bevin acknowledged that by avoiding 'fruitless discussion' on disarmament, the presence of British troops in foreign countries, the revision of the Italian Treaty and, lastly, Spain, 'in a negative sense at any rate, this year's Assembly was considerably more successful than last year's'. The Foreign Office believed, moreover, that from then on the Security Council would be called upon to consider further action only if Spain became a threat to world peace.[83] Yet, while it was recognised that the failure in November 1947 to reaffirm the resolution of December 1946 had rendered it, in a certain sense, invalid, the British government adhered to the strictly legalistic view that it remained in force until formally repealed by a two-thirds majority vote of the General Assembly. The advantages of this position, Curle noted, were that it preserved Britain's economic interests and the government's immediate political interests, while, by fulfilling Britain's obligations under the 1946 Resolution, it gave 'vent to ideological dislike of Franco' and left some freedom of manœuvre if future circumstances required. None the less, Spain's exclusion from international meetings and agreements did cause practical difficulties. Furthermore, Curle minuted, the Spanish Government, 'in their present exuberant confidence', seemed no longer willing to 'meet us in economic matters whilst receiving political kicks at the same time . . .'[84]

As for the Spanish opposition, the British government's attitude to it was inevitably affected by the UN November resolution. Howard went further than most in the Foreign Office but captured the new mood in a private letter to Crosthwaite of 25 November. In it he pitied the opposition, 'poor things', for having 'again missed the bus and taken a knock'. There was, he said, really no use banking on these 'hopeless opposition people getting together to bring anything effective'. However unpalatable it was, he felt, they had to stomach the fact that Franco was stronger than ever and that Spain was not in the mood for dangerous changes. His conclusion was blunt: if there was any chance of a change, he noted, 'by all means let us pin our hopes on the Opposition. But in the absence of any alternative it seems to me we stand to gain damn all and lose quite a deal by clutching on to our ideological distaste for the regime.'[85]

During 1947, in sharp contrast to the previous year, the British government faced little pressure from the French for action against Spain. This in turn reflected a gradual shift in Franco-Spanish relations from confrontation to mutual forbearance. To an extent the reorientation of French foreign policy away from the USSR and towards Britain and the USA in the spring of 1947 eased the path to improved relations. But it was more the self-inflicted damage to French economic interests caused by the closure of the Franco-Spanish border in February 1946 that provided the chief incentive for the French government to seek a new *modus vivendi* with Spain.[86]

Franco-Spanish negotiations on the border issue had, in fact, begun within days of the original closure. It was rapidly agreed, for example, to re-open the border between 25 March and 30 April 1946 to enable stranded French and Spanish nationals to return home. Other agreements soon dealt with the transit of third countries' nationals and goods through France and Spain. These temporary concessions, however, did not alleviate the economic and human hardships suffered by the estimated 20000 strong French colony in Spain as well as the difficulties faced by some 80000 French nationals in French Morocco waiting, since 1944, to return to France. This placed the Spanish government in a strong bargaining position, which it was eager to exploit to secure closer relations with France than the French wanted. Far from bringing Franco down, the closure of the border was therefore acknowledged by the Quai d'Orsay to have been '*un calcul politique erroné*' serving only to strengthen Spain's position *vis-à-vis* France.[87]

This unsatisfactory situation continued until the summer of 1947, when the French government, freed at last from communist pressure, decided to begin discreet negotiations for the eventual re-opening of the border. French proposals were put to Spain in August offering Spanish nationals transit rights through France in return for reciprocal rights for French nationals through Spain. It was not lost upon the Spanish Ministry of Foreign Affairs, however, that the main beneficiaries of the offer would be the stranded French in North Africa, and so it pressed for more concessions. These were accepted by the French a month later, but when the Spaniards went on to raise the question of the transit of Spanish goods through France, the French balked, saying that they would agree to it only when 'technically and politically possible'. This proved unacceptable to Spain and the negotiations were broken off. By the end of 1947, however, the Spanish government itself saw the value of re-establishing Franco-Spanish trading links as soon as possible and so early in December it offered the phased reopening of Spain's border with France in return for a French commitment to a new commercial agreement with Spain. Negotiations were resumed and culminated in the reopening of the Franco-Spanish border on 10 February 1948.[88]

The lowering of tension between the two countries was reflected in the relative lack of interest shown Spain by the French National Assembly in 1947 compared with the previous year. Indeed, not until 30 December was an anti-Franco resolution adopted, in protest at the execution of two political prisoners, Agustín Zoroa Sánchez and Lucas Nuño Bao. The following day the *Conseil de la République* (the Fourth Republic's Upper House) approved a similar resolution, and the executions were discussed in the Foreign Affairs Committee. Otherwise, Spain was mentioned only five times in the National Assembly during the whole of 1947.[89] France's contribution, too, to the UN debate on Spain in November 1947 was negligible, Alexandre Parodi, the French delegate, intervening only once, on the afternoon of 11 November, to argue against reaffirming the December 1946 resolution and to indicate French support for the joint resolutions of Cuba and Belgium.[90]

In 1947 British contacts with the anti-Franco opposition were a continuing irritant in Anglo-Spanish relations. As has been seen, the activities of the British Embassy in Madrid had drawn a protest from Martín Artajo at the end of 1946 and, as a result, Howard thought it wise to keep a low profile until 'the excitement over the wretched business of the Embassy's intrigues in Spain had died down'.[91] Even so, Embassy involvement in intelligence gathering was not curtailed. In April a Spanish police report on the arrest of a Basque nationalist, Santiago Goicoechea Egarte, drew attention to the fact that the British Consul in San Sebastián, William Goodman, was an agent of the British Intelligence Services and that in Bayonne there still existed an organisation, *Servicio X2*, of Basque 'ultra-nationalists' who had worked for the British Intelligence Services during the World War.[92] The following month the Spanish government protested that a lawyer, Francisco López Fernández, had admitted receiving monthly payments since 1942 for information handed over to British Embassy officials and that towards the end of 1943 he had also bribed a sergeant of the Civil Guard, Santiago Rojo García, to provide information. Yet again, at the end of June, the Marqués de Santa Cruz, the Spanish Chargé d'Affaires in London, was instructed to make a vigorous protest to the Foreign Office that the Director of the British Institute in Seville, Archie Colquhoun, was involved in subversion.[93]

By contrast, British contacts with the exiled Spanish opposition were more open. On 19 February, Bevin stated, in reply to a parliamentary question from Francis Noel-Baker, that the British Embassy in Paris had had mutual 'unofficial contacts' with the Llopis' government-in-exile. At the end of July, moreover, the Foreign Office told Howard that his Embassy staff were free to meet opposition leaders when outside Spain, although there were also 'suitable channels through which we can maintain such contact as seems suitable with Spanish exiles, without risk of unfortunate consequences to those concerned'. On 13 December, just before Harvey took up his new post as British Ambassador to France, Santa Cruz told Manuel Aguirre de Cárcer, the Spanish Chargé d'Affaires in Paris, that Harvey's past contacts with Spanish *émigrés* had indeed been proven by a letter from Harvey addressed to Pablo de Azcárate y Flórez, a republican Ambassador to London during the Civil War, which had been sent in error to the Spanish Embassy![94]

Certainly, no effort was made by the British government to conceal Prieto's interview with Bevin on 26 September, nor British involvement in the subsequent London meetings between Prieto and Gil-Robles in October. These were bitterly denounced by the Spanish government, in a *note verbale* of 22 October, as 'a violation of respect' due the independent sovereign government of Spain and 'an unfriendly act' towards a nation with which the British government had long maintained friendly relations. Bevin's reply of 12 November, however, was unapologetic. While not seeking to intervene in internal Spanish affairs, it said, the British government had made no secret of its dislike for the Franco regime nor of its hope for its replacement. In the curcumstances, it therefore reserved for itself the right to receive any visitors it liked.[95]

When Howard communicated Bevin's reply to Juan Sebastián de Erice, Director General of External Policy in the Foreign Ministry, three days later, he also pointed out, informally, that the British government had consistently resisted what seemed to them to be 'unjustifiable attempts' at the UN to intervene in the internal affairs of Spain. But a further Spanish note, received in the Foreign Office on 23 November, showed that the British reply had not satisfied the Spanish government. It expressed surprise and displeasure at the unjust and unfriendly action of the English (*sic*) representative at the last UN General Assembly over the Spanish question. It repudiated what it described as the unexpected reiteration of displeasure in the British note and expressed the hope that Britain would not forget the services offered and promises made in the 'solemn moments of England's life'.[96] Thus, 1947 ended as it had begun, with Anglo-Spanish relations temporarily ruffled over the Spanish opposition.

Conclusion

As a consequence of the international declarations on Spain in 1946 the interests of the Spanish anti-Franco opposition and of the British government briefly coincided for some eleven months in 1947. For the Spanish opposition its unification was a pre-condition of international recognition and support while for the British government it offered a means by which to pre-empt damaging international action against Spain.

In 1947 the impetus for unity within the democratic Spanish

opposition came originally from three directions: the republican government-in-exile, the interior ANFD-monarchist grouping, and the exiled Lisbon monarchists and *prietista* socialists. Despite Llopis' evident pragmatism, the association in monarchists' minds of his government-in-exile with atavistic republicanism precluded any republican-monarchist *rapprochement* on his terms. Conversely, apprehension over excessive monarchist concessions to republicanism dissuaded the Lisbon monarchists from endorsing the ANFD-interior monarchist agreement of December 1946. It compromised the *gil-roblista* option of retaining the Spanish Right as a reserve route to a monarchist restoration. However, when this option was forfeited through Don Juan's public opposition to the elective monarchy proposed in Franco's Law of Succession, the isolated Lisbon monarchists had little choice but to turn to the moderate Left represented by the exiled PSOE. This, by late July, had accepted the *prietista* thesis that a unified Spanish opposition could not be realised on the basis of pure republicanism but only through republican–monarchist compromise.

Before the *gil-roblista-prietista* convergence of mid-1947 the British government had had little incentive to abandon its passivity. What international pressure it faced came now not from the French but the USA. Acheson's initiative, an early response to the incipient Cold War, envisaged economic aid as an arm against communism in Spain, but, addressed, over the heads of the organised opposition, to Spanish moderates in general, the plan was dismissed in July by Britain as impractical.

It was, though, just at this time that Gil-Robles and Prieto appeared to offer the possibility of a durable republican-monarchist agreement. The Foreign Office saw in this an opportunity, albeit slight, for a resolution of British difficulties over Spain, for by leaving the initiative for an anti-Franco coalition to Spaniards, the impression of direct Anglo-American interference in Spain's internal affairs, which the McNeil-Acheson proposals entailed, was conveniently avoided and the risk of confrontation with Franco correspondingly reduced. At the same time it allowed the British government to argue that the formation of a Spanish anti-Franco front rendered an escalation of UN action superfluous. For their part, Prieto and Gil-Robles needed the backing of the British government not only for their own credibility but to neutralise each other's proposals for the post-Franco transition. Out of this coincidence of interests came the October talks in London.

Despite their fundamental differences, Prieto and Gil-Robles managed to establish a basis for future PSOE-CEFM negotiations. Yet, within a few days of the London talks' conclusion, the UN resolution of 17 November removed much of the incentive for the British government to remain actively involved. Whether, in the face of declining British interest and the international context of the Cold War, Prieto and Gil-Robles would continue to feel the need to work for an agreement between them will be considered in the next chapter.

6
1948–1950: The Frustration of the Anti-Franco Impulse

The immediate effect of the UN General Assembly's resolution on Spain of November 1947 was to bolster the Franco regime and correspondingly weaken the anti-Franco opposition. If, then, the latter was to retain any hope of recognition from the western democracies, it urgently needed to demonstrate its unity of principle and purpose. It was vital, therefore, that the negotiations begun in October 1947 between the PSOE and the CEFM resumed. But the Spanish opposition was also wholly dependent on unflagging international commitment to the restoration of democracy to Spain. From 1948 to 1950 this commitment was inevitably affected by the Cold War. The repercussions this had on British relations with the Spanish opposition, as it evolved in this period, are the subject of this chapter.

The anti-Franco opposition

In an exchange of letters in May 1948 Prieto and Gil-Robles explained their motives for wishing to continue the PSOE-CEFM negotiations. According to Prieto, it would prevent the western powers from 'washing their hands' of Spain on the pretext that Spaniards were a 'race of intolerant fanatics' who were incapable of finding a solution to the problem of Spain. For Gil-Robles, an agreement would help allay foreign governments' fears by guaranteeing that the removal of the Franco regime would not lead to renewed violence.[1] Gil-Robles had earlier confided to Vejarano that with Franco gaining ground the anti-Franco opposition had to reach agreement quickly, since once strategic considerations became predominant, or conservative administrations coincided, in Britain, France and the USA, Franco's position would be consolidated for the rest of his life.[2]

Both men, too, were aware of the USA's changing attitude towards Spain. Prieto, in particular, voiced his misgivings to Crosthwaite, Head of the Foreign Office Western Department, on 16 March 1948, when passing through London *en route* from the USA to France. He criticised the 'Pilate-like gesture' of George Marshall, the American Secretary of State, for leaving the final decision on Spain's inclusion in the European Recovery Programme (ERP) to the European governments even though the State Department itself was simultaneously encouraging negotiations between American and Spanish banking groups. By doing this, Prieto argued, the USA was repudiating the Tripartite Declaration pledge of March 1946 to give aid to a provisional Spanish government, was morally disavowing the 16 nations in the ERP and rushing to the rescue of Franco just when his regime was on the point of economic collapse. As for the anti-Franco opposition, Prieto feared that American aid to Spain would destroy the position of Spanish democrats like himself.[3]

Thus, the incentive for resuming socialist-monarchist negotiations was strong. They were conducted mainly through correspondence between Gil-Robles, in Portugal, and Prieto, first in Mexico and then, from spring 1948, in France. Their chief intermediary was Vejarano, whom Prieto saw for the first time in New York prior to embarking for Europe in March 1948 and then met occasionally in France, often in Saint Jean-de-Luz, South-West France. In general, negotiations proceeded according to the pattern established in London the previous October: the monarchists would propose draft agreements, which would then be commented upon by Prieto in consultation with his three colleagues of the PSOE Special Committee.[4]

The monarchist position at the beginning of 1948 was outlined in a memorandum drawn up for Don Juan's guidance before he met State Department officials on a visit to the USA in the spring. On the premise that a solution to the Spanish problem had to guarantee against a return to 1936 if it was to appeal to the opportunist Spanish Right, it was argued that Spain needed a strong, 'homogeneous', transitional regime. This would best be achieved through a regency-government made up of 'political elements from the Centre', excluding all 'totalitarian tendencies', and with the participation of 'observers' from the non-communist Left. The proposed regency-government would concentrate, initially, on liquidating the Franco regime and the gradual restoration of political freedom, before consulting the electorate on the new regime's institutions through either a referendum or a constituent assembly. Only then would it be possible to incorporate elements of the non-communist Left into public life. Spain, the memorandum emphasised, with the American audience clearly in its sights, could and should be an 'essential factor' in the fight against communism, and only a restored monarchy could facilitate her incorporation into the western bloc.[5]

Vejarano communicated this programme in a letter which Prieto received on 9 January 1948. It carefully omitted all reference to the participation of the Left as *observers* in a transitional government but in all other respects was identical to the memorandum prepared for Don Juan. In his reply, Prieto objected to the regency-government and to referendums, which, he said, had been discredited by Franco. But otherwise he was broadly in agreement with the monarchists' proposals.[6] After that, no significant exchanges took place until after Prieto's arrival in France on 19 March.

Once in France Prieto had his policy of socialist–monarchist *rapprochement* endorsed by the Third Congress of the PSOE-in-exile in Toulouse – postponed, at his request, from February to the last week of March. In debate Prieto reaffirmed his personal commitment to republicanism but reminded his audience that only his policy of compromise would win the support of the western powers. Following this, a large Congress majority approved the pro-*prietista* resolutions taken at the Assembly of PSOE Regional Delegates the previous July and expressed its confidence in the Special Committee subsequently set up. Party confidence in Prieto was further demonstrated when he was elected President of the incoming executive committee, with Trifón Gómez as Vice-President and Llopis General Secretary.[7]

A letter from Gil-Robles, which Prieto received in Saint Jean-de-Luz on 1 May, restarted negotiations. Partly because of Prieto's poor health, but mainly because of practical difficulties in communication, these then continued for another four months. Apart from the procedure for publicising any eventual agreement, on which Gil-Robles would not compromise (see below), the monarchists' approach throughout was to avoid specific commitments. Clearly, this worked to the socialists' disadvantage. Except for the idea of a regency-government with limited Left participation, which the monarchists dropped after Prieto threatened to return to Mexico, other contentious issues were skirted round. Thus, Prieto's wish to specify the modalities of a post-Franco electoral consultation evinced from Gil-Robles no more than the vague assurance that the 'will of the Nation' would be consulted 'either directly or through its representatives'. Reference to the Tripartite Declaration of March 1946, which was central to Prieto's oppositional strategy, was not taken up by Gil-Robles, who looked instead to a 'gradual crisis'

(*crisis evolutiva*) of the Franco regime to bring about the restoration of political freedom. Only on the desirability of a permanent Liaison Committee to coordinate future action in and outside Spain were monarchists and socialists readily agreed.[8]

Prieto's letters attest to his spirited defence of republican interests, but he was in a weak bargaining position. Indeed, it was Gil-Robles who pointed out to him that if their negotiations did collapse and the Franco regime had in the meantime disintegrated, the most probable outcome would be a move by the Dictator's former supporters to restore the monarchy; alternatively, if the situation in Spain became critical, the western powers would most likely offer Franco economic aid and so prop up his regime *sine die*. Consequently, short of abandoning his policy of *rapprochement*, Prieto had little choice but to settle for a joint socialist-monarchist declaration couched only in the broadest terms.[9] Subsequently known as the Pact of Saint-Jean-de-Luz, this was signed on 30 August by Francisco Moreno y Herrera, the Conde de los Andes, for the CEFM, and Prieto for the PSOE.

The Pact's first seven points covered a general amnesty for political offences and a legal statute regulating the 'use of the rights of man', as well as a system of judicial appeals against abuses of power, the strict maintenance of public order to prevent reprisals on religious, social or political grounds, a reform of the 'shattered' national economy in co-operation with 'all the elements interested in production', the exclusion of totalitarian groups and influence of whatever complexion from the country's political leadership, Spain's inclusion in the ERP and the five-power Brussels Pact, and freedom of religion and thought, together with due consideration for the Catholic religion. On the vexed question of electoral consultation the eighth point pledged, once civil liberties had been restored,

> [. . .] with the greatest speed permitted by circumstances, to consult the Nation to the effect of establishing a definitive political régime, either in a direct vote or through representatives, but in any case by secret vote, to which all Spaniards of either sex with full political capacity will be entitled. The government presiding this consultation, by its composition and the significance of its members, must be an efficient guarantee of impartiality.[10]

In addition, both sides agreed to the setting up of a Liaison Committee to monitor their reciprocal compliance with the Pact's eight points.

Yet, apart from the reference to Spain's incorporation into Europe's new economic and defence arrangements, the Pact amounted to little more than a restatement of the proposals first put forward by Gil-Robles in London the previous October. As such, it was a declaration of common principles rather than a detailed prescription for a post-Franco transitional regime. The eighth point, for example, did not specify the form the electoral consultation might take – whether by plebiscite *a priori*, elections *a posteriori* under a restored monarchy, or otherwise. As Prieto's colleague on the PSOE Special Committee, Jiménez de Asúa, later pointed out, both parties remained free to bring Franco down unilaterally and install the regime of their choice, since obligations under the Pact applied only *after* the establishment of the new regime.[11] Nevertheless, the unification of the Spanish opposition had moved a step forward, negotiations were ongoing, and by late autumn the Pact had been ratified by the monarchists and approved by the exiled and interior PSOE and UGT executive committees and the resurrected ANFD.[12]

Yet, its international impact fell far short of its authors' expectations. Disagreement over the publication of the Pact was partly to blame. Prieto saw the propaganda value of a joint *communiqué* to foreign governments. Gil-Robles, on the other hand, ever anxious not to provoke the Spanish Right, preferred the more discreet procedure of separate declarations from each side.[13] His view prevailed but even then it was not until October that copies of the Pact were finally delivered by the monarchists to embassies in Madrid, and by the PSOE to the French Foreign Ministry and embassies in Paris.[14] Unfortunately, the British Foreign Office erroneously identified Gil-Robles as the monarchist signatory to the agreement, obliging him to issue an immediate press denial. Inevitably, the month and a half delay in publicising the Pact and Gil-Robles' *démenti* served only to confuse foreign governments and discouraged expressions of support.[15]

Far more damaging were the repercussions of a meeting between the Spanish Pretender and Franco, which took place on 25 August, barely five days before the signing of the Pact of Saint Jean-de-Luz. By the beginning of 1948 Don Juan had become increasingly doubtful of Anglo-American support for his return to the Spanish throne. As has been noted, Bevin was singularly unforthcoming during their brief conversation in November 1947, and during his visit to the USA the following spring Don Juan had been repeatedly assured by government officials, politicians and Church leaders that, if the prospects of war with the USSR increased, Franco would receive all the American aid he wanted. Were Don Juan to reach an agreement with Franco, moreover, the USA would regard it with the utmost pleasure. In short, by the summer of 1948, Don Juan was close to accepting that only through Franco would the monarchy ever return to Spain.[16] This gave the *franquista* monarchists their chance. Prominent amongst these was Julio Danvila Rivera, formerly Vice-President of the monarchist party, *Renovación Española*, and by 1948 a director of the Bank of Spain, who had long pressed for a collaborationist *juanista* policy.[17] Early in 1948 he was authorised by Don Juan to approach Franco on his behalf, although it was not until 6 July that the Spanish leader consented to meet the Pretender. Danvila then spent another six weeks attempting to bring both sides together before finally arranging for Don Juan, who was sailing back to Portugal from the Cowes Olympic Regatta, to rendezvous with Franco's yacht, the *Azor*, off the coast of San Sebastián in the Bay of Biscay. There, because of the sea-swell, it was easier for Don Juan to transfer to the *Azor* rather than receive Franco on board his own yacht, the *Saltillo*.[18]

The *Azor* meeting lasted three hours but, according to Don Juan, who provided the only first-hand account, little was conceded by either side. Franco assured Don Juan that he would remain in power for another 20 years. Then, with tears in his eyes, he declared himself a 'fervent monarchist' but remained adamant that the monarchy could not provide Spain with the firm rule needed. For his part, the Pretender pointed out that he had been effectively by-passed by the Law of Succession and, no doubt with Kindelán's recent arrest and imprisonment in mind, complained of Franco's anti-monarchist measures.[19] If Don Juan is to be believed, nothing was agreed concerning the education of his son, Juan Carlos (see below); he went no further than saying that he had no objection to Juan Carlos' spending some time in Spain, provided he was with people of Don Juan's choosing. Yet, when Don Juan made it a condition that before Juan Carlos went to Spain, anti-monarchist propaganda should be toned down, which Franco accepted, the makings of a deal were struck.[20]

The *Azor* meeting was a propaganda *coup* for Franco.[21] The apparent reconciliation of the two men and rumours of a possible deal dismayed many *juanista* monarchists, including Gil-Robles, who was understandably upset at having been kept in the dark.[22] Certainly, Don Juan, who had sailed on to another international regatta off Cascais at the mouth of the Tagus, seemed in no hurry to contact him. And yet, on 1 September, when Don Juan finally gave him an account of the meeting, Gil-Robles was initially reassured that Don Juan had shown he was not the weak character Franco supposed him to be. Nevertheless, Gil-Robles thought it important to correct any impression of a reconciliation, and, as a preliminary precaution, it was decided that, unless specifically asked by Franco to meet him, Don Juan would arrange to be in Switzerland during a state visit by the Spanish Head of State to Portugal planned for that autumn.[23]

The visit, in fact, was postponed until the following year, and both Franco and the *juanistas* turned instead to the question of Juan Carlos' schooling. Having completed his primary education in Freiburg, Germany, and celebrated his tenth birthday on 5 January 1948, Don Juan's son was of an age to start his *bachillerato* (secondary education) in the autumn of that year. Where Juan Carlos studied thus became a matter of political concern. For Franco, a decision to send Juan Carlos to Spain would signal *juanista* capitulation and undermine the Spanish opposition's new found unity in the Pact of Saint Jean-de-Luz. At first, Don Juan seemed well aware of this danger and on 6 October Juan Carlos departed for Switzerland with his preceptor, Eugenio Vegas Latapié. Three weeks later, however, the Pretender changed his mind, probably in return for guarantees from Franco that sanctions against monarchists and the monarchist newspaper, *ABC*, would be lifted. Juan Carlos arrived in Madrid on 10 November, and Vegas Latapié promptly lost his job![24]

Don Juan's change of heart was widely believed to be part of a secret agreement with Franco for a monarchist restoration, but Prieto, albeit demoralised, still saw no alternative to a republican-monarchist *rapprochement*.[25] That autumn, however, his personal responsibility for implementing the policy was unexpectedly challenged by a newly reconstituted ANFD. On 6 September, at its first session since 1947, the ANFD's national committee decided to set up an 'Exterior Committee', comprising two delegates – from the interior and exiled oppositions respectively – from each of the ANFD's three component organisations. The intention was that the Exterior Committee, as the '*única y genuina representación*' of the Left, would have sole responsibility for all future negotiations with the CEFM. Although it fully endorsed *prietista* policy towards the monarchists and, indeed, designated Prieto as a delegate to its Exterior Committee, this decision by the ANFD necessarily implied the winding up of the PSOE Special Committee and the cancellation of the planned Liaison Committee.[26]

The ANFD's move can be seen, partly, as an attempt by the neglected libertarians to reassert their authority in the Spanish opposition. It seems, though, that the challenge to *prietista* dominance was mounted chiefly by the interior PSOE. Prieto had long paid lip-service to the primacy of the interior socialists but, in reality, had little confidence in their negotiating competence or their ability to resist excessive concessions to the monarchists. Consequently, at a meeting in Toulouse of the PSOE-in-exile's executive committee on 29 December the resurrection of the ANFD was described as a 'political error' and its Exterior Committee dismissed as unworkable. The decision was taken to inform the interior PSOE of the catastrophic consequences of disbanding the Special Committee, which, in any case, they would also be told, had already been instructed to set up the Liaison Committee. Without the support of the PSOE-in-exile the interior PSOE executive committee backed down on 1 February 1949 and the proposal for an Exterior Committee was abandoned.[27]

The way was now cleared for the formal constitution of the Liaison Committee on 2 March 1949. It had two members: Prieto, for the PSOE, with Trifón Gómez as his substitute, and Sainz Rodríguez, who was unable to leave Portugal, for the CEFM, with Vejarano as his substitute. Unfortunately, however, hopes of a united Spanish opposition front were immediately dashed by the creation in Spain the very next day of a *Comité Interior de Coordinación* (CIC). Chaired by Aranda, with the monarchist Lieutenant-Colonel José Pardo Andrade as Secretary, and with socialist, libertaran and *republican* adherence, the CIC could justly aim to be a more representative body than the small exiled Liaison Committee. The creation of this rival organisation, which subsequently replaced the ANFD, was made necessary, so its proponents claimed, by difficulties in communicating with the exiled opposition. It seemed, however, more a concerted attempt by the interior republican-monarchist opposition to regain the initiative lost in 1947.[28]

Not surprisingly, the PSOE-in-exile was thrown off guard by the formation of the CIC. The disadvantage of three opposition committees functioning simultaneously was recognised and Prieto foresaw confusion: monarchist demands would be accommodated in Spain while resisted in France; at monarchist invitation the libertarians had been admitted to the Pact of Saint Jean-de-Luz but without necessarily accepting all its points; and there were differences over adherence to the Atlantic Pact.[29] Nor were his apprehensions eased by news that, at the CIC's fourth meeting of 3 June, a monarchist memorandum had been endorsed by all parties, including the PSOE, according to which the Franco regime would be replaced only by the *juanista* monarchy. Such an assumption clearly negated all Prieto's previous endeavours to guard against an automatic restoration of the monarchy.[30]

On 23–24 July the Special Committee therefore sought to renew its mandate from a second PSOE Assembly of Regional Delegates. The *prietista* policy endorsed at the first Assembly of Regional Delegates of July 1947 and ratified by the Third PSOE Congress the following March was reaffirmed by a majority of the delegates. It was also agreed that there should be only one committee to negotiate with the monarchists and that any organisation that had not signed the Pact of Saint Jean-de-Luz – a clear allusion to the CNT/MLE – would not be consulted. The CIC's acceptance of a monarchist restoration was rejected. In the light of these decisions, the PSOE-in-exile's executive committee immediately wrote to the interior socialists instructing them to withdraw from the CIC. A few weeks later, however, a number of the CIC's members were arrested and, on 17 August, Aranda, at the age of 60, was placed on the reserve list.[31] Although it survived in rudimentary form until well into 1952, and the interior PSOE collaborated with it until March 1951, after the arrests the CIC ceased to play a significant role in the Spanish opposition.

This left the Liaison Committee free once more to continue its negotiations on arrangements for a post-Franco transitional regime. Yet, although Prieto informed Vejarano that he dissociated himself entirely from the CIC's acceptance of the monarchist memorandum, his position remained weak. Indeed, according to Vejarano, who saw Gil-Robles in Paris at the end of August 1949, by then the socialists were ready to accept a monarchist restoration without a plebiscite *a priori* as well as the postponement of electoral consultation for several years. With this information Gil-Robles instructed Vejarano a few days later to tell Prieto that the time had finally come for a restoration of the monarchy on the basis of Franco's Law of Succession, with an electoral consultation delayed until the 'normalisation of national life'. Not surprisingly, Gil-Robles' reversion to this hard-line position proved unacceptable to Prieto and the PSOE-CEFM negotiations reached stalemate.[32]

In the meantime, Franco's position, far from weakening, had been strengthened by international developments. The consolidation of Soviet rule in Eastern Europe, the signing of the North Atlantic Treaty in April 1949 during the last few weeks of the Soviet blockade of West Berlin, the explosion of the USSR's first atomic bomb on 22 August and Mao Zedong's proclamation of the Chinese People's Republic a month later heightened east-west confrontation. In the midst of this, the UN General Assembly failed on 16 May 1949 to reaffirm its resolution on Spain of December 1946, and in January 1950 the State Department signalled a more pro-Franco position.

Still, the Liaison Committee continued to meet during 1950. In May, for example, it decided that Prieto should present NATO foreign ministers with a memorandum reaffirming the Pact of Saint Jean-de-Luz as a basis for Spain's incorporation into the West. But, in reality, the Liaison Committee's impetus was lost. The outbreak of war in Korea in June was a further blow to any lingering hopes of western action against Franco and, at the Fourth Congress of the PSOE-in-exile of 22–25 August 1950, a letter from Prieto, who was too ill to attend, admitted that his policy had had little success. On 4 November the UN General Assembly voted to lift its ban on ambassadors returning to Madrid. Two days later, a bitterly disappointed Prieto resigned from the Liaison Committee and as President of the PSOE-in-exile and, on 9 November, sailed in secret for America. An Extraordinary PSOE Congress of 31 March–1 April 1951 voted to continue Prieto's policy. But in the light of the USA's decision in July that year to reach agreement with Franco on military bases in Spain and Don Juan's consequent surrender to Franco, the Fifth PSOE Congress in Toulouse was left with no choice but to disown the Pact of Saint Jean-de-Luz in August 1952.[33]

Although the possibility of a *juanista* restoration through Franco was exploited by Gil-Robles in his negotiations with the PSOE, Don Juan's capitulation over his son's education had not in fact ushered in the period of cordial relations with Franco that might have been expected. In his speech of 30 March 1949 on the eve of Victory Day, Franco reaffirmed his determination to hold on to power.[34] And even the *franquista* Danvila had to admit, after a three hour interview with Franco towards the end of June, that his policy of reconciliation had failed. Don Juan, therefore, informed Kindelán that he had no objection to the monarchists in Spain discreetly resuming their activities and, for a moment, even contemplated using a visit to his ailing father-in-law in Spain to proclaim himself king.[35]

After spending most of the summer of 1949 away from Portugal, Gil-Robles returned to the question of Juan Carlos' education in the autumn. Despite a warning from Nicolás Franco on 25 September that his brother would pass a law through the *Cortes* expressly excluding Don Juan from the throne, should Juan Carlos not return to Spain, Gil-Robles drew up a *note verbale* for Franco stating that Juan Carlos' presence in Spain was prolonging a 'policy of confusionism'. Franco's uncompromising reply emphasised that he had made no promises on the *Azor*, that Don Juan should be thankful for the Law of Succession, and that Juan Carlos' education in Spain was of benefit to him and his dynasty and gave rise to no misunderstandings. Franco blamed Don Juan's attitude on the bad advice he was receiving and added, pointedly, that monarchist restorations were 'nowadays very difficult'.[36]

An indication of the new coolness in relations was Don Juan's decision not to meet Franco, during his postponed state visit to Portugal of 22–29 October 1949, unless at the Pretender's own residence in Estoril or some other 'neutral' location. For his part Franco refused to meet anywhere except at the Palace of Queluz, where his party was staying, and so, despite a number of appeals, Don Juan stayed away. Had an interview taken place, Don Juan would have used the occasion only to press Franco on whether he was moving towards the restoration of the *juanista* monarchy or not.[37]

Relations worsened when Juan Carlos remained in Portugal rather than return to Spain for the new school year. Yet Don Juan continued to listen to the *franquista* monarchists and, in yet another apparent change of heart, warned Kindelán in December that he would not support 'hostile campaigns of a negative kind' against Franco.[38] Added strain came when the Spanish press reported later that month that Don Jaime, the Pretender's brother, had revived his claim to the Spanish throne. The Spanish government made no move to exploit the situation but the threat remained that Franco might designate Don Jaime's son, Don Alfonso de Borbón Dampierre – who was to marry Franco's grand-daughter, Carmen Martínez Bordíu in 1972 – as the future king of Spain.[39] It was therefore reluctantly accepted by Don Juan's advisers that Juan Carlos should resume his education in Spain in the autumn of 1950. On 10 July 1951 Don Juan's capitulation was complete: in a letter to Franco he stressed that he had always identified with the National Movement, that he was not bound by any pact, and, since the monarchy was the only possible alternative to his regime, he was asking Franco to reach an agreement with him. As Gil-Robles had already noted, the *juanista* monarchists were, for the foreseeable future, 'no more than a memory in Spanish politics'.[40]

British reaction to the anti-Franco opposition

For as long as the British government treated the Franco regime as an aberrant and transitory dictatorship, the Spanish anti-Franco opposition could still count as a factor in Britain's overall policy towards Spain. But the reverse equally applied: any reconciliation between the two governments would reduce the Spanish opposition to an irrelevancy in British calculations. Before 1948 there was little call, either international or domestic, for the British government to normalise its relations with

Franco Spain. However, as the Cold War intensified and communism eclipsed fascism as the perceived threat to the world order, international hostility to the Franco regime declined. Consequently, during the years 1948 to 1950, the attitude of the British government towards the Spanish anti-Franco opposition was affected not only by the evolution of the opposition itself but also by Britain's response to increasing pressure for the normalisation of Anglo-Spanish relations.

Outside the communist bloc, much of the post-war animus against Franco Spain had come from France. The re-opening of the Franco-Spanish border on 10 February 1948, however, confirmed the French government's retreat from confrontation and the abandonment of its pretension to leadership of an international combination against Spain.[41] To a considerable extent the damage done to French economic and cultural interests during the border closure accounted for this reorientation of policy. But French identification with a largely Soviet inspired anti-Franco campaign was no longer compatible with the new conjuncture of the Cold War. Even so, the Quai d'Orsay could not ignore the lasting antipathy of the French public towards the Franco regime and had, consequently, to settle for a policy of 'silent' *rapprochement*, distancing itself from any pro-Franco initiatives it thought likely to exacerbate internal dissent.[42] For this reason, as Robert Schuman, appointed Foreign Minister in July 1948, assured the French cabinet the following November, France remained firmly opposed to Spain's participation in the ERP and to her membership of the UN.[43] By the autumn of 1948 the French government was far from providing a stimulus for vigorous anti-Franco action. Instead, its position on Spain was virtually indistinguishable from Britain's own passive policy of *attentisme*.

Of greater concern to the British government was the attitude of the USA, where the rehabilitation of the Franco regime was increasingly seen as a necessary preliminary to a greater Spanish contribution to the defence of the West.[44] However, a normalisation of American-Spanish relations was bound to strengthen the Spanish dictatorship beyond the point of removal, leaving the British government little choice but to compose its differences with the regime or risk permanent diplomatic and economic exclusion from it. There was a danger, too, that Anglo-

American amity could be strained over Spain at a critical moment for Western European security. Consequently, the British response, for most of 1948 to 1950, was to apply discreet pressure on the American government in the hope of keeping its pro-Franco impulse in check.

The question of economic aid was a case in point. In the late 1940s, the main channel for American aid to Europe was the ERP, established at the Paris Conference of July 1947, and for George Marshall, the Secretary of State, there was no reason to exclude Spain from this initiative.[45] The British government took the opposite view. Bevin conveniently overlooked Britain's own Monetary Agreement with Spain of March 1947 – to be followed by a Commercial Agreement in June 1948, a Payments Agreement the following December and another Commercial and Payments Agreement in June 1949 – and was adamant that under no conditions could Britain work with Franco Spain in the ERP. It would, he protested, cause a 'complete revolt' in the Labour Party, as well as among many conservatives with bitter memories, and would make the whole Marshall proposal appear a 'line-up behind fascism and reaction'.[46] Behind this principled stand, there was also apprehension that any ERP allocation to Spain would reduce the overall sum available to the other 16 participants.[47]

In fact, British reservations concerning the ERP did not go unheeded. In April 1948, Robert Lovett, Acting Secretary of State, made it clear to Paul Culbertson, the American Chargé d'Affaires in Madrid, that, Franco's anti-communist record notwithstanding, it would be 'manifestly contrary' to the ERP's principles of 'individual liberty, free institutions and genuine independence in Europe' to admit Spain into the programme.[48] And, for a while at least, the State Department was careful to emphasise, both to its European partners and to the Spanish government, that, while Franco's departure was no longer a *sine qua non* of American aid, the latter was still conditional on the Spanish leader's commitment to the 'gradual and orderly liberalisation' of his regime.[49]

Yet, while prepared to exclude government aid to Spain, the State Department saw no reason to curtail private initiatives. A policy statement of 26 July 1948 stated that it was happy to encourage private trade with Spain, and private investment, 'on a purely business basis' – as well as informal contact between the Spanish and American military authorities.[50] In February 1949 the Chase Manhattan and National City Banks of New York accordingly announced loans to the Spanish government totalling $25 million.[51] Two months later, Acheson, Secretary of State since January 1949, informed the American Embassy in Madrid that government restrictions on applications to the Export-Import Bank, the American government's official lending agency, for credits to facilitate

American-Spanish trade had been lifted. Culbertson was also instructed to raise with the Spanish government the possibility of a 'modern and comprehensive Treaty of Friendship, Commerce and Navigation' with Spain, similar to the one the USA had signed with Italy in February 1948.[52]

In the meantime, the diplomatic rehabilitation of the Franco regime continued to be frustrated by the UN resolution of December 1946. And again, as on the question of economic aid to Spain, British and American views did not coincide. The State Department wanted the 1946 resolution amended so as to allow Spain's entry into the UN's technical agencies and the return of ambassadors to Madrid. In July, Marshall further indicated that the USA was no longer insisting on the reform of the Franco regime as a pre-condition for these concessions.[53] William Dunham, of the Division of Western European Affairs, had explained the reasons for this change in March 1949. The return of ambassadors, he maintained, should constitute the next step towards a normalisation of American-Spanish relations, which, he recalled, had been determined to be in the national interest. The ineffectiveness and violations of the 1946 resolution were adversely affecting the UN's prestige; periodic discussion of the Spanish question had distorted the problem out of all proportion, to the propaganda advantage of the USSR; and, finally, the resolution had completely failed in its purpose of bringing about change in Spain.[54]

The Foreign Office recognised, too, that the validity of the UN ban on ambassadorial representation in Madrid had been undermined by the inconclusive resolution of November 1947. Indeed, four days after Dunham's memorandum, Charles Shuckburgh, Head of the Western Department since January 1949, minuted that, taking British interests alone into account, a lot could be said for British support for an amendment to the 1946 resolution, particularly if the USA took the same line. It would ensure the amendment was carried, and the British ambassador would return to Madrid in a favourable atmosphere. This was, though, Shuckburgh admitted, 'hardly practical politics'. Voting to restore full diplomatic relations with Franco Spain would be a reversal of Britain's attitude towards Franco. It would draw criticism from the Labour government's supporters and be depicted in Soviet propaganda as a 'surrender to fascist Spain'. It would also prove an embarrassing distraction for European public opinion at a moment when it was being asked to accept the Atlantic Pact and the Council of Europe.[55]

British reluctance to back an amendment to UN policy on Spain was evident throughout 1948. Thus, in June Britain voted to defeat a Soviet proposal to return Spain to the Council's agenda.[56] Then, after the

Spanish question was placed on the agenda of the Third Session of the UN General Assembly, on 23 September, and referred the next day to its First Committee, Britain's UN delegation was reminded that its government opposed any attempt to 'whitewash' the Franco regime and would not accept either Spain's incorporation into the UN's technical agencies or the return of ambassadors to Madrid.[57] The following month, Bevin and Schuman took advantage of Marshall's presence in Paris for the General Assembly to secure his commitment to 'play down' any action on the Spanish question in the UN.[58]

In the event, a crowded agenda meant that the First Committee could not turn its attention to Spain until after the opening of the Second Part of the Third Session of the General Assembly in New York in April 1949. By this time, the Anglo-American positions on Spain had converged. Acheson, now Secretary of State, placed more importance than his predecessor on Western European goodwill and agreed with the American delegation to the UN that the USA should be seen to oppose all totalitarian regimes, whether communist or not. The delegation was accordingly instructed to abstain on the question of returning ambassadors to Madrid, although it could still vote for Spain's admittance into the technical agencies.[59] After talks in Washington, Bevin, too, recognised that since a change in American policy might lead to the end of Franco's isolation, it was in Britain's long-term interest to assist Spain's integration into the European bloc. So, although he did not, that spring, go as far as the USA in supporting Spain's entry into the UN's technical agencies, he did not oppose it, while on the question of the return of ambassadors to Spain the British delegation was instructed to follow the American lead and abstain.[60] Thus, by May 1949, Washington and London were agreed that while neither government would initiate action on Spain in the UN, they would not – albeit to varying degree – oppose some modification of the resolution of December 1946.[61]

When the First Committee finally turned to Spain on 4 May 1949, it had before it two draft resolutions, one Polish and one Brazilian. The Polish resolution insisted that internal repression in Spain had worsened since November 1947, and that several member states, notably Britain and the USA, had violated the principles of the UN Charter and the 1946 resolution and had prevented the establishment of democracy in Spain by strengthening their political and commercial ties with the Franco regime. The Polish resolution, therefore, called for an immediate halt to all armaments exports to Spain and to all negotiations for agreements with her. Only when a democratic government was in place would Spain be welcome to join the UN and its technical agencies. Until then, it was expected that the Security Council should keep the situation under continuous review and fulfil its responsibilities under the Charter.[62]

The second resolution, sponsored by Brazil, jointly with Bolivia, Colombia and Peru, called on the General Assembly to grant member states complete freedom of action in their diplomatic relations with Spain, arguing that as the 1946 resolution had not been reaffirmed the following year, a number of governments were now uncertain as to how to interpret the 1947 resolution. Furthermore, because the 1946 resolution had not banned all political and commercial relations with Spain, several members of the UN had concluded bilateral agreements with the Spanish government to the disadvantage of other, economically weaker, states. At American prompting, a clause recommending Spain's entry into the technical agencies was later inserted into the Brazilian resolution.[63]

At the end of the First Committee's four day debate, a predominantly Latin American group voted for the Brazilian resolution. A second group took its lead from the USSR and supported the Polish resolution, whilst the remainder, which included the USA, Britain and Western Europe, and a smaller number of Latin American countries, opposed the Polish resolution and abstained on the Brazilian one. On 16 May the two resolutions were debated at a plenary session of the General Assembly and the same pattern of voting emerged, with Britain, France, and the USA abstaining as before. Both resolutions failed to achieve the two-thirds majority required for the repeal of the 1946 resolution, but it was significant that the Brazilian resolution – with 26 for, 15 against and 16 abstentions – was only one vote short.[64] Thus, the 1946 resolution still stood, but bereft of authority.

Here, brief mention should be made of the domestic constraints upon Britain's Spanish policy. In May 1947 the Labour government had been criticised in a left-wing pamphlet, *Keep Left*, for failing to implement a truly socialist foreign policy. Amongst other things, Bevin was accused of supporting a fascist Spain. Bevin's outspoken remark before the Commons on 19 June that he 'hated' the Franco regime can thus be seen as a deliberate attempt to give the lie to the *Keep Left* charges.[65]

None the less, for the next three years, government statements to both Houses of Parliament repeatedly condemned Franco's fascist regime and reaffirmed Britain's commitment to the UN resolution of 1946 and to Spain's exclusion from the ERP, the Western Union and the North Atlantic Treaty Organisation (NATO). Combined with popular enthusiasm for Marshall Aid, growing apprehension over the USSR, and Bevin's promotion of an ethically based Western Union, the effect of these statements was to secure the quiescence of the broad political Left.[66] What pressure there was for a radical change in Spanish policy came instead from members of the British Right sympathetic to the Franco regime, a number of whom, including Winston Churchill, called frequently for the normalisation of Anglo-Spanish relations in the face of the Soviet threat. The Labour government, of course, had no intention of bowing to the demands of its conservative critics, since, even had it wanted to, any major initiative to improve relations with Franco Spain risked reactivating left-wing opposition. The inevitable consequence, however, was that Britain's foreign policy makers saw little alternative to a continuing policy of passivity towards Franco Spain. It was against this background of domestic stalemate, and weakening international resolve, that the British government's relations with the Spanish anti-Franco opposition were played out.

The re-opening of the Franco-Spanish border in February 1948 prompted a Foreign Office review of policy on Franco Spain. In April, Ashley Clarke, Minister at the Paris Embassy, supported by Howard, the Chargé d'Affaires in Madrid, called for Spain's military and economic incorporation into Western Europe. But Clarke and Howard's views were not shared by Harvey, the British Ambassador to France, who preferred to 'let sleeping dogs lie', nor by the Western Department, which had been told that Western European defence did not in fact depend on Spain, that an improvement in political relations would not affect Anglo-Spanish commercial negotiations then under way and that Spain's early association with the ERP would bring no immediate benefit to Europe. Yet, the conclusion drawn in the Foreign Office did not advance the Spanish opposition's cause. Franco's position was thought to be almost unassailable and his admission into the 'family circle' only a matter of time. Moreover, even if the Spanish republican and monarchist opposition did manage to reach agreement, there was still no great chance, according to Crosthwaite, that Franco would go. It was noticeable, too, that when Sir Ivone Kirkpatrick, recently appointed a Deputy

Under-Secretary in the Foreign Office, drew the debate on Anglo-Spanish relations to a close on 23 May, he did so without any reference to the Spanish opposition. He simply recommended, 'lest worse befall', continuing the 'admittedly unsatisfactory policy of waiting for something to turn up'. There was thus no departure from Bevin's policy of inaction.[67]

Given this inertia, it was only to be expected that the Foreign Office should have had reservations about the negotiations in 1948 between Prieto and Gil-Robles. Admittedly, news from Prieto in January that they were being resumed was received sympathetically, and, in May, when their break-down seemed possible, Crosthwaite suggested that Bevin should express his disappointment.[68] To an extent, however, this reflected little more than the Spanish opposition's continuing usefulness in providing the Foreign Office with an alibi for resisting the pro-Franco inclinations of the State Department. For, despite the view that a republican-monarchist agreement would be a 'good augury' for the future of Spain, it was recognised that there was no realistic prospect of Franco's replacement by a PSOE–CEFM coalition.[69] Open declarations of British support for the negotiations were therefore unforthcoming. Against the view expressed by Prieto during his meeting with Crosthwaite on 16 March, that their endorsement by the western powers would leave the Spanish problem 'as good as solved', Crosthwaite merely observed that as yet the Spanish opposition had not reached agreement.[70]

After receiving a copy of Prieto's letter of 2 May rejecting Gil-Robles' proposed regency-government, Crosthwaite minuted that it was 'utterly unrealistic' to suppose that the co-victors of the Civil War would ever hand over power to the losers, since they feared that any shift of power to the feckless republicans would end in communist ascendancy and a recrudescence of civil war. Furthermore, even if Gil-Robles and Prieto did establish a perfect agreement, the essential part of the Spanish problem remained unsolved, for who, Horsfall Carter pointedly asked, was going to bell the cat? When, on 27 May, Prieto forwarded his next exchange of letters with Gil-Robles, Roderick Parkes, a newcomer to the Western Department, commented that it would not be their agreement that eventually destroyed the Franco regime but Spain's economic paralysis. Again, at the end of June, after receiving a copy of Prieto's reply to Gil-Robles' proposals of 31 May, the normally sympathetic Horsfall Carter minuted that what chiefly emerged from the discussions was their 'futility', and the next day Parkes noted that they were likely to result only in 'exasperation and eventual breakdown'.[71]

On 28 August Crosthwaite provided the Foreign Office's first reaction to the *Azor* meeting. The possibility of Don Juan's son, Juan Carlos, start-ing his secondary education in Spain would, he admitted, be a great victory for Franco. But he very much doubted whether the Pretender, whose intention it had always been to enter Spain as king of *all* Spaniards, was trying to come to terms with Franco. Crosthwaite thought it more likely that Don Juan wanted to impress upon the Spanish leader in person the need for reconciliation with the Left before his return to Spain, especially as he was then in a position to disclose that a republican-monarchist agreement was imminent. With reports coming in that Prieto's negotiations were still proceeding in a friendly atmosphere, Crosthwaite therefore considered it best to suspend judge-ment until Don Juan was back in Portugal.[72]

Over the next few weeks the Western Department received reassur-ances from both Prieto and Gil-Robles that a deal between Don Juan and Franco had not been struck. In a letter to the State Department of 21 September, forwarded to the Foreign Office Research Department, Prieto insisted that the Pact of Saint Jean-de-Luz had Don Juan's 'express assent', and that Don Juan, who had agreed to meet Franco only because he believed it could be kept secret, was now repenting of having gone behind his advisors' backs. On 6 October Gil-Robles similarly wrote to Bevin that Don Juan viewed with approval the PSOE-CEFM negotiations and that neither directly nor indirectly had there been any talk at the *Azor* meeting of Don Juan's abdication or renunciation of his rights. Admittedly, the question of Juan Carlos' education had been raised, but the boy would definitely not be returning to Spain until there was con-crete evidence of a substantial change in Franco's policy towards the *juanista* monarchy. Since the *Azor* meeting there had been no further contacts between Don Juan and Franco.[73]

But other reports on the *Azor* meeting were less encouraging. Accord-ing to Howard, the view in Spain in early September was that Franco had delivered a 'master-stroke'. He had swept away the monarchist opposition in Spain and thwarted the Pact of Saint Jean-de-Luz, and Don Juan, like Franco, was now repudiated by the entire Left. In October, Sir Charles Johnston, transferred the previous month to the Madrid Embassy as First Secretary, wrote that 'all shades of opinion' known to him were agreed that the Pact of Saint Jean-de-Luz had little practical value and could emerge from the shadows only after Franco departed. Even then, once the Army was in power, he could not see the generals 'voluntarily availing themselves of the services' of the parties to the Pact. Juan Carlos' arrival in Madrid on 10 November further com-promised his father's independent position in the eyes of the Foreign

Office, so that by the end of the year scant faith was placed in the Pact of Saint Jean-de-Luz as an effective motor for change in Spain.[74]

With the appointment in February 1949 of William Ivo Mallet, until then Consul-General in Tangier, as an Assistant Under-Secretary of State in the Foreign Office, came one last proposal to use the Spanish opposition against Franco. Mallet's initiative began with a request to the Madrid Embassy for their assessment of Britain's current policy towards Spain. Howard's reply of 10 May was a persuasive indictment. Britain's policy, he wrote, had done more than almost anything else to strengthen Franco's position. It was considered by the broad mass of Spaniards to be 'hypocritical, short-sighted, illogical and intensely stupid', and Britain was identified by the Spanish government as 'Public Enemy No. 1' and as the biggest obstacle to Spain's economic rehabilitation and acceptance in the western world. Even the French, who periodically came in for a 'bit of venom', Howard pointed out, were for the first time in living memory less criticised than the British. In addition, Anglo-Spanish commercial relations were strained because Britain's inability to take more Spanish goods was depriving Spain of sterling. There was a dearth, too, of military intelligence at a time of 'immense' opportunities for armaments exports, without which, Howard warned, Spain would be a heavy liability rather than a valuable ally 'when the balloon goes up'. Only the USSR was benefiting from the bad relations between Spain and the Western Powers. In short, British interests were 'prejudiced by our present policy'.[75]

On 28 May Mallet saw the Duque de San Lúcar la Mayor, who twelve months earlier had replaced the Marqués de Santa Cruz as Spain's Chargé d'Affaires in London. Britain's policy, San Lúcar was told, was unaffected by the recent UN resolution on Spain, and until Franco's replacement by a democratic government international recognition and support would continue to be withheld. This firmness, however, was deceptive. In a minute on his interview, Mallet acknowledged that if 'most of us' did not send ambassadors back to Madrid and Spain received no loans, the Army, or even Franco, might resolve on a change of regime. This possibility, though, was 'very slight', so that sooner or later, he feared, they would have to modify a policy which until then had succeeded only in strengthening Franco's political hold and in harming British interests and the Spanish people. Mallet therefore proposed an approach to the American and French governments. If they thought a change of regime in Spain still possible, they could then, with Britain, agree on economic pressure against Franco and on opposition to the return of ambassadors; if, though, change was considered unlikely, Mallet suggested that joint consultations should follow on how to end a policy, 'the failure and disadvantages of which we shall then be obliged to recognise'.[76]

To an extent the Foreign Office's own estimation of the likelihood of change in Spain depended on its assessment of the interior CIC, formed on 3 March 1949. Immediate reaction from John Russell, Assistant Head of the Western Department, was hardly encouraging: 'Department of glorious political prose', he noted with some irritation, 'Spanish division, half-in half-out, full of sound and fury . . . *Arriba* you and me and all our friends! Down with Franco, hard work and reality! Up the café-rebels.'[77] Early reports that the CIC republicans were willing to accept a constitutional monarchy – welcomed as 'remarkable' by Howard – were also treated with caution by Russell. In a minute of 7 May he queried the true extent of left-wing representation on the CIC and thought its programme most likely to result in a semi-military 'cabal or *junta*' after Franco's removal. Shuckburgh thought the CIC 'realistic', but then criticised it for its excessive reliance on foreign intervention against Franco. The following month, doubts were also expressed by Hoyer Millar, former Head of the Western Department but by then Minister in the Washington Embassy. The CIC's scheme, he commented, sounded 'painfully familiar' and not unlike the optimistic information received two or three years before. Thomas Achilles, Director of the Office of Western European Affairs in the State Department, whom Hoyer Millar saw on 7 June, had not, he said, even heard of the CIC.[78]

Perhaps in view of his monarchist leanings, Mallet was less dismissive of the CIC. In a memorandum drawn up on 8 August, following a discussion with Sir William Strang, the Foreign Office Permanent Under-Secretary, and Sir Roger Makins, a Deputy Under-Secretary, he contended that since British policy had clearly failed to bring about Franco's removal, it might be worth examining whether there were any means by which the British and American governments could support the recent CIC agreement to restore the monarchy. Views should also be exchanged with the French government. Until his proposal was adopted, it was still essential, Mallet insisted, that neither Britain nor the Americans, nor, if possible, anyone else, should encourage Franco by offering loans or advocating the return of ambassadors to Madrid. Britain should therefore abstain on the question of ambassadors at the next UN General Assembly, despite the fact that the 'illogicality of such a line' was likely to expose the British government to even more criticism than before and the difficulties of maintaining the policy could become still more apparent.[79] A few days before Mallet's memorandum, however, news had reached the Foreign Office that much of the CIC's membership had been arrested, gone into hiding or, in Aranda's case, been placed on the reserve list. For Russell, this immediately confirmed Aranda's final disappearance from the political scene and represented a serious blow to Spanish moderates. Nothing, he concluded, could now be done except to 'sit quietly back and await further developments'. Two months later, Shuckburgh similarly observed that the effect of Franco's move against the CIC had been to put a timely and effective check upon those elements inside Spain 'on whom we were relying as the focus of a possible move against him'. Yet, even without the arrests, reaction to Mallet's proposed reliance on the Spanish opposition was unenthusiastic. Howard, for one, doubted the CIC's importance and drew attention to the lack of support for Aranda from Franco's Captains-General. Only Strang favoured sounding out the French and American governments along the lines suggested by Mallet.[80]

Yet the rejection of the Spanish opposition option did not automatically imply a readiness to normalise Anglo-Spanish relations. For Bevin the second part of Mallet's advice was more pertinent; change, he noted, was best avoided, at least for another year. Britain's ambassadors in Paris and Washington were accordingly instructed to resist any American moves to return ambassadors to Madrid, and, at a meeting on 14 September, Bevin told Acheson that he wanted to 'let sleeping dogs lie'.[81]

The designation in September 1949 of Robin Hankey, former Head of the Northern Department, as the new Chargé d'Affaires in Madrid provided Bevin with an opportunity for a comprehensive restatement of his policy on Spain. When he saw Hankey on 31 October Bevin dismissed the Spanish opposition as not 'very serious': he thought Don Juan's arrangements with Franco showed that he was playing with both sides, Prieto he no longer considered 'much of a force', and even Trifón Gómez, according to Bevin, believed that the Spanish opposition could do no more. Nevertheless, as Hankey's subsequent instructions of 14 November made clear, Britain still adhered to the Tripartite Declaration on Spain of March 1946. Originally, of course, Bevin had opposed the decision to withdraw ambassadors from Madrid, but now, Hankey was reminded, the British government considered itself bound by the UN resolution of December 1946 until it was revoked. It was not, furthermore, prepared to vote for the resolution's revocation, since that would be interpreted as a change of heart towards the Franco regime, 'and this

His Majesty's Government cannot at present accept'. This position, Hankey was told, was admittedly unsatisfactory, but it was such that the government could 'neither advance nor withdraw'. As the prospects of a change of regime appeared increasingly remote, the best that could be reasonably looked for was some gradual improvement in the character of the existing regime.[82]

Hankey was also instructed to pay attention to any signs of a change of policy towards Spain on the part of the USA, or of conflict between the American State and Armed Services Departments. He was asked, in particular, to report any evidence that the American, or French, governments were breaking their undertaking not to discuss strategic questions with Franco or to supply him with military equipment. Before Hankey could act, however, a shift in American policy had already occurred. On 18 January 1950, the *New York Times* published a letter, approved by President Truman, from Acheson to Thomas Connally, Chairman of the Senate Foreign Relations Committee, announcing that the USA was now prepared to vote for a UN resolution which left member states free to send ambassadors to Spain. This vote, the Secretary of State insisted, would in no sense signify approval of the Franco regime; it merely indicated a desire, 'in the interests of orderly international intercourse', to return to normal practice in exchanging diplomatic representation.[83] The strategic concerns of the Pentagon, publicly endorsed by a vociferous and influential pro-Franco lobby, had evidently won out against the State Department's greater political caution.[84] More important for the British government, however, was the fact that the Anglo-American consensus on abstaining over Spain in the UN had been broken.

After Acheson's announcement the Western Department briefly reconsidered the prospects of the CIC. Its value, Hankey had earlier observed in his annual report for 1949, was still its potential usefulness in any confused situation arising at the end of the Franco regime, when, with most moderate socialist and left-wing leaders under arrest, there would be no moderate leadership to resist communist demagogy. By February, however, Hankey was less certain. The CIC had, he admitted, done well to survive Franco's attempt to break it up the previous summer, but now the effect of the change in the American government's attitude to Franco, combined with the 'inefficiency and doubtful judgement' of Don Juan's advisors in Portugal and the disillusionment of the moderate Left, would probably be to provoke a crisis in it in the near future. Such a crisis, he warned, could lead to the disappearance of the moderate anti-Franco opposition inside and outside Spain and to both the stabilisation of the Franco regime in the short run and the strengthening of the 'forces of violent subversion' in the long run. Peter Laurence, who had since taken over responsibility from Curle for Spain and Portugal in the Western Department, felt therefore that nothing should be done to discourage the CIC, the 'only representative body of moderate Spanish opinion which is at all articulate', and Russell, who freely admitted never having been impressed by the CIC, also agreed that it should be kept alive, if only because of the role reserved for it in the future. However, they had not, he noted, been able to assess the value of the new PSOE and CNT members of the CIC since the arrests of August 1949, and with the monarchist organisation 'heavily penetrated and as rotten as a pear', he wondered whether the CIC, too, had been penetrated by Franco's agents. It remained to be seen, Russell concluded, whether the CIC would be totally liquidated in the autumn, or given recognition and even legitimation.[85]

Of greater concern to the Foreign Office was whether Britain should follow the American lead when, as was predicted, the Spanish question came before the UN General Assembly in the autumn of 1950. Officially, there was no change in policy, and, at the end of March, Britain's delegation to the UN was informed that the intention was still to abstain over the return of ambassadors and Spain's admittance to the technical agencies. But, in private, Bevin wondered whether, since 'we were agreed' (*sic*) on the desirability of sending back heads of missions to Madrid, it was desirable to come out into the open and vote in favour of such a resolution. For the moment, though, he felt there was no point in discussing the question until nearer the time of the General Assembly.[86]

By then, the outbreak of the Korean War in June had convinced Mallet of the necessity for Britain to vote with the USA over Spain. In a memorandum to Bevin of 2 August, he argued that with the West obviously threatened with a fight for existence against Russia, it was 'illogical' to exclude Spain from the 'western front', despite its deplorable, and even fascist, regime. It had to be accepted that henceforth any change in policy would be 'in spite of Franco', and not for the purpose of removing him, and that it should not be conditional upon a prior commitment in Spain to any particular form of government. The CIC, whom Mallet now saw as taking 'a hand in affairs' only *after* the regime's liberalisation, might, he admitted, be discouraged by this *rapprochement*, but it could be explained to them that, barring revolution, it was only by working through Franco that his regime might be modified in the direction wished for by the British government and the Spanish opposition. Mallet's views were supported by Strang and Makins, whereas for Kenneth Younger, the new Minister of State, political objections still outweighed the case for a change in policy. Still, with the next session of the UN General Assembly fast approaching, Bevin decided that the time had come for Britain's policy on Spain to be considered by the Cabinet.[87]

The question immediately at issue, Bevin's preparatory Cabinet paper of 23 August made clear, was whether Britain should abstain or vote for an amendment of the 1946 resolution in favour of Spain. A vote for the return of heads of mission to Madrid would, it was recognised, encourage Franco and discourage his opponents. On the other hand, a vote in favour did not in any way imply approval of the Franco regime; besides, since a two-thirds majority in the General Assembly was expected to vote for the return of ambassadors, would it not be better – if Britain's ambassador was subsequently to have any influence or even to be accepted in Madrid – that Britain should vote for the amendment in the autumn rather than abstain? There was even less reason for voting against Spain's admission to the UN technical agencies, since, it was argued, it was difficult to justify a country's exclusion from international organisations and agreements whose sole purpose was to ensure safety at sea, a wider knowledge of agricultural science and the prevention of disease.

As regards Britain's overall policy on Spain, it was candidly admitted that it had not succeeded because they had not been prepared to take measures to upset Franco which would have hurt British interests. As the object of Britain's policy was to secure the liberalisation of the Spanish government so that Spain could resume her proper place among the western countries, it was necessary to create the possibility of an alternative form of government. But as neither monarchists nor republicans were in a position to do this, the only alternatives to Franco were another military government or chaos. Since, rather than face another civil war, which a more liberal regime might introduce, the vast majority of Spaniards preferred Franco, his regime would not be replaced by a better government until the foundations for a more liberal regime had been laid. However, experience had shown that Franco would not liberalise his regime while under attack from abroad, so that British policy should be to liberalise the regime 'in spite of Franco' rather than try to get rid of him.

It was not envisaged that Spain would immediately join NATO or the Council of Europe, or, 'from one day to another', adopt representative government on the models of Westminster or Washington. Rather, the return of ambassadors and Spain's admittance into the UN technical agencies would merely be regarded as a first step towards Spain's return to civilised society. In this way Franco would be convinced that the democracies were not out to smash his regime, thus making it possible for him to introduce a programme of reforms, which in turn would enable the western governments to 'raise the iron curtain', and, as Spain became more integrated into Western Europe, use their influence to secure the modifications to his regime they wanted.

Against this, the paper argued, there were considerable political objections to a change in Britain's policy over Spain. The origins and nature of the Franco regime and the fact that it was the last survivor of the nazi-fascist group of governments which had instigated World War II had real importance for the morale of Western Europe. Nor could it be said that Britain's economic interests were particularly affected by the current state of Anglo-Spanish relations nor that the question of supplying military equipment to Spain was urgent. A change of policy would weaken the ideological basis of the western front against the USSR, and the feelings of the Labour Party, Trade Unions, and Co-operative Movement could not be ignored. Even if Britain's policy had not succeeded, the paper concluded, it had done no harm.[88]

When the Cabinet discussed Bevin's paper on 6 September, it was these objections which carried the day. Since Anglo-Spanish commercial relations were not hindered by Britain's political attitude to the Franco regime and – although Spain was of undoubted strategic importance to the defence of Western Europe – a change in Britain's policy would have no immediate effect on the availability of Spanish forces in an emergency, the Cabinet agreed that it was inadvisable to make any change in general policy towards Spain. Britain would abstain from supporting any proposal in the UN to amend the resolution of 1946.[89]

The Fifth Session of the UN General Assembly opened on 19 September 1950. One week later, the question of 'Relations of Member States and specialised agencies with Spain' was placed on its agenda and then referred to the Special *Ad Hoc* Political Committee (as the First Committee was now known). When debate began on 27 October the Committee had before it a draft Latin American resolution, which called for the repeal of the 1946 resolution on the grounds that it constituted intervention into the internal affairs of a state in violation of the UN Charter. The Latin American resolution was opposed by the communist bloc countries, but, as anticipated, supported by the USA. In accordance with the Cabinet decision the previous month the British representative maintained that since nothing had taken place to justify any change in the British attitude towards the Franco regime, he would abstain from voting on the resolution, which was approved by 37 votes to 10, with 12 abstentions.[90]

The General Assembly then debated the resolution in plenary session on 4 November. The, by now, well worn arguments were rehearsed, following which 38 members, including the USA, voted for the resolution's first recommendation, 10 voted against, and 12, including Britain and France, abstained; 39 voted for the second recommendation, 10 against and 11 abstained. Thus, it was finally resolved:

> 1. To revoke the recommendations for the withdrawal of Ambassadors and Ministers from Madrid, contained in the General Assembly resolution 39 (1) of 12 December 1946;
> 2. To revoke the recommendation intended to debar Spain from membership in international agencies established by or brought into relationship with the United Nations, which recommendation is part of the same resolution adopted by the General Assembly in 1946 concerning relations of Members of the United Nations with Spain.[91]

The fact that the original paragraphs of the 1946 resolution relative to the history of the Franco regime and its condemnation by the UN still stood had scant political significance.

Almost immediately, on 9 November, the British Cabinet approved a proposal from the Foreign Secretary to appoint an ambassador to Spain and, two days later, it authorised Bevin to inform the Commons that there would be no delay in giving effect to the UN resolution.[92] Sir John Balfour, the Ambassador to Argentina, was appointed Ambassador to Spain and presented his credentials to Franco on 15 March 1951. The Marqués de Estella, Miguel Primo de Rivera, brother of the founder of the *Falange*, was Franco's defiant, albeit second, choice of ambassador for London.[93] The Franco regime, although technically only back in the position it had been in 1945, was immeasurably strengthened. But, under the new dispensation, the Spanish opposition ceased to play a role in Britain's Spanish policy.

Brief mention must be made of the effect on Anglo-Spanish diplomatic relations in this period of Britain's attitude towards the Spanish anti-Franco opposition. As already noted, relations were certainly at a low ebb in 1948–1950. This was, however, hardly due to any overt British encouragement of the Spanish opposition but was rather a consequence of the Spanish perception that Britain was the 'main obstruction' to Spain's joining the concert of Western Europe.[94] There was, in fact, only one occasion after October 1947 when an assumption of British support for the Spanish opposition came anywhere near making relations between London and Madrid worse than they already were. Following the BBC announcement in October 1948 of the Pact of Saint Jean-de-Luz, Foreign Office complicity was immediately taken for granted in the Spanish Foreign Ministry. Franco was particularly incensed by the suspicion that behind the Pact lay the intention of Spanish 'leftist exiles', working on the left wing of the British Labour Party, to counteract the course of American policy towards Spain. San Lúcar, the Chargé d'Affaires in London, duly protested to Kirkpatrick, and, in reprisal, a few British citizens were expelled from Spain. These included an Information Officer, recently arrived in Barcelona, accused of helping escaped prisoners during the Civil War, and a second British subject, who was allegedly in contact with the anti-Franco opposition in León.[95] Apart from this one incident Britain's attitude to the Spanish opposition contributed only minimally to the poor state of Anglo-Spanish relations in 1948–50.[96]

Conclusion

The Pact of Saint Jean-de-Luz of August 1948 represented the culmination of the efforts of the exiled Spanish opposition to establish a united moderate front which would finally win recognition and support from the western democracies. That it failed in this was due in part to the confusion caused in foreign governments' minds by the parallel *Azor* meeting, subsequent monarchist reticence over the Pact's publication, the unexpected revival of the ANFD and the emergence of its successor, the CIC. More than this, however, it was due primarily to the impact of the Cold War.

For the British government the implications of the Cold War for its policy on Spain were contradictory. On the one hand, a *rapprochement* with the anti-communist Franco regime was strategically inviting. On the other, the need to retain the moral high ground in the fight against communism made cooperation with a reactionary regime undesirable. Furthermore, while the long-term advantages of Spain's economic integration into Western Europe were undeniable, the immediate dilution of Marshall Aid at the expense of the existing ERP beneficiaries was unacceptable. In the circumstances, the only response left the British government was to maintain its policy of inaction. This, of course, ran counter to American decisions for an *entente* with Franco Spain, and although British pressure ensured Spain's permanent exclusion from the ERP and, for a while, American abstention over the repeal of the UN 1946 resolution, once the resolution of May 1949 had signalled the collapse of international opposition to the Franco regime, Britain was no longer in a position to prevent the normalisation of American-Spanish relations.

Of course, full British acquiescence in the definitive legitimation of the Franco regime remained politically unrealisable in 1950. Yet, an anti-Franco policy pursued in isolation would not only have harmed Britain's commercial and financial interests in Spain, it also risked compromising American-European solidarity at a critical moment in the Cold War. Thus, the decision was immediately taken to re-appoint a British Ambassador to Madrid after the UN vote of November 1950. Paradoxically, at a time when Anglo-Spanish diplomatic relations were worse than at any time since World War II, the Spanish opposition was finally dismissed as a factor in Britain's policy towards Spain. By winning his diplomatic battle with the western democracies, Franco had ensured the survival of his regime and the defeat of the Spanish opposition. No wonder that a disillusioned Prieto resigned from the Presidency of the exiled PSOE and returned to Mexico in November 1950.

7
Conclusion

Somos espectadores de la historia,
hemos dejado de ser actores.
Somos una fuerza negativa,
de repulsión, de exclusión.[1]

There is no denying that the disunity of the Spanish anti-Franco opposition in the 1940s contributed to the longevity of the dictatorship of General Francisco Franco.[2] It would, of course, be a crude misrepresentation to attribute this disunity to fecklessness or, as was sometimes thought at the time, to an inherent flaw in the Spanish character.[3] Nor – albeit more plausibly – can it be fully accounted for by reference to the ideological legacy of the Second Republic and the Civil War. A more satisfactory explanation for the absence of a united Spanish anti-Franco front, this study has suggested, is to see it as one consequence of *British* policy towards the Spanish opposition.

In the 1940s Spanish and British opposition to Franco was far from uniform in its motivation. For Spanish republicans, the defeated party in the Civil War, the Franco dictatorship was, in essence and in practice, the antithesis of democracy, and, as such, could lay no claim to legitimacy. The opposition of Spanish monarchists, on the other hand, did not spring from any attachment to the Second Republic, in whose destruction Alfonso XIII and his son, Don Juan, had been willing accomplices, but from frustration at Franco's refusal to put his newly established dictatorship at the service of the Bourbon cause. Britain's anti-Franco opposition similarly reflected different political allegiances – from left-wing identification with republican intransigence to right-wing endorsement of monarchist opportunism – but in general it derived from a common resentment over Franco's wartime cooperation with the Axis powers and from a sense of his regime's anomalous position in post-fascist Europe. Not surprisingly, these perceptions translated into different and, at times, incompatible oppositional strategies.

To reverse the verdict of the Civil War and single-handedly remove the Franco regime by military force, whether conventional or guerrilla, was never a practical proposition for the republican democrats. Yet, while they acknowledged their consequent reliance on foreign intervention, there was disagreement amongst them on how to secure it. One option was to maintain the fiction of an undefeated Second Republic providing a credible and functioning alternative to the Franco dictatorship. This 'pure' republican approach, however, was never acceptable to the British government. A revived *Frente Popular*, it feared, especially with communist participation, would mark the first step towards civil war in Spain and put Britain's commercial and strategic interests in the Iberian Peninsula at risk. Hence the hostility of the British government towards Juan Negrín during World War II and its indifference to the governments-in-exile of José Giral and his successors from 1945 on.

This coolness towards the republicans notwithstanding, many Spaniards expected a move by Britain and her allies against the Franco dictatorship at the end of World War II. Indeed, it was partly this perception which, though subsequently proved wrong, led to the emergence of the Spanish monarchist opposition. Collaboration with Franco – the *franquista* option – risked permanent *juanista* exclusion from any post-Franco settlement, from which a small number of monarchists concluded that an alternative strategy was necessary. Simply breaking with Franco was clearly not enough, since, it was acknowledged, any attempt to re-impose the monarchy on Spain without popular consent was as likely in British eyes to destabilise the Iberian Peninsula as was the unmediated restoration of the Second Republic. If, then, the monarchy were to receive British backing, without which a restoration 'against Franco' was unlikely, it was expedient to reach some form of agreement with the moderate republicans. The formation of a broad anti-Franco front, it was believed, would allay British fears of a violent post-Franco transition and thus assure the monarchy a future in Spain.

Similar conclusions, though for opposite reasons, were reached by some sections of the republican opposition. If a restored republic were to remain an option after Franco's departure, then Britain's antipathy towards 'pure' republicanism would, again, be circumvented only by the 'moderate' alternative of a republican-monarchist *entente*. Concessions to the monarchists could be made, the *prietistas* in particular argued, safe in the knowledge that not only would a subsequent plebiscite of the Spanish people automatically return a republican majority, but, more importantly, their electoral verdict would be guaranteed by Britain and her allies. So, in 1944, the republican ANFD made contact with a small group of dissident monarchists in Spain, grouped around General

Aranda. By the end of the year a basis for future negotiations had been reached and, one year later, an agreement on the post-Franco transition needed only Don Juan's ratification.

It was at this point, however, that the perceptions of the interior and exiled monarchist oppositions diverged. For the Lisbon group, led by Gil-Robles, the *juanistas*, isolated in their opposition to Franco and yet uncertain of foreign support, could ill afford to alienate their natural constituency in Spain: the Spanish Right. It was therefore essential, if the Pretender were to counter nationalist accusations of deficient patriotism and leftist sympathies, to keep concessions to the republicans to a minimum. This, the Lisbon group believed, the ANFD-monarchist agreement of December 1945 had signally failed to do, and so the following October they proposed instead their Estoril Agreement. When this, in its turn, was rejected by the republicans, the ANFD-monarchist talks stalled. With the ANFD then incapacitated by police action, the initiative passed to the exiled opposition and the anti-Franco front strategy entered its second stage: one bringing direct British involvement.

The assumption by the Spanish opposition that a mutual detestation of fascism was of itself sufficient to guarantee British commitment to their cause was naive. The truth was that British support for the opposition was entirely conditional upon its capacity at any one time to advance or retard Britain's national interests. Thus, during the German occupation of France, the opposition was dismissed by the Foreign Office as irrelevant. Certainly, contingency plans were drawn up to use republican *guerrilleros* and a monarchist 'government of national resistance' in the event of a German invasion of the Iberian Peninsula, and several monarchist generals were bribed to keep Franco's pro-Axis inclinations in check. Otherwise, any suggestion of cooperation with Franco's opponents was rejected as likely to lose Britain the advantage of Spain's war-time neutrality.

Nor was this policy changed by the Liberation of France. As it confirmed by its 'warning' to Franco of January 1945, the Churchill government, and its Labour successor, remained firmly opposed to direct confrontation with the Spanish Dictator. Churchill, somewhat nebulously, assigned responsibility for his removal to the Spanish 'moderates', but, apart from this, the Spanish opposition was not a factor in British calculations. Accordingly, of the three major opposition developments in 1945, the first – Don Juan's Lausanne Manifesto in March – was regarded by the Foreign Office as a 'damp squib', the second – Giral's first republican government-in-exile in August – a reversion to the divisions of the Civil War, and the third – the ANFD-monarchist agreement in December – insufficiently advanced to warrant sustained attention.

Nevertheless, the British government could not avoid engagement with the Spanish opposition indefinitely. In December 1945 the Foreign Office had rejected a French call for action against Spain on the grounds that it might have prejudiced the ANFD-monarchist negotiations then under way. A meeting between Don Juan and Franco, predicted for the following February, was similarly used to parry an American proposal to assist the French government by means of a joint anti-Franco declaration. When, as had been anticipated, these two Spanish initiatives came to nothing and French demands for anti-Franco action grew more insistent, the British government was forced to agree to the Tripartite Declaration of March 1946. Intended originally, by Britain at least, as no more than a sop to ease the domestic predicament of the French government, its appeal to 'leading patriotic and liberal-minded Spaniards' to overthrow Franco, together with the promise of recognition of a transitional regime, marked a significant advance in Britain's moral commitment to the Spanish anti-Franco opposition.

For the British government the implications of this commitment were brought home by the UN General Assembly's resolution on Spain of December 1946. Though mild in its immediate recommendations, the resolution nevertheless left open the possibility of more stringent UN sanctions in the future. If these were then to be ignored by the British government, the Tripartite Declaration's pledge to democracy in Spain would be exposed as a sham, and the UN's authority dangerously undermined. Equally, compliance with anti-Franco sanctions, so obviously at odds with the policy of non-intervention, would threaten British interests in Spain. The response of the American State Department, which coincided with a proposal from Hector McNeil, the British Minister of State for Foreign Affairs, was to offer the 'moderates' in Spain recognition and economic assistance if they removed Franco. For the Foreign Office, however, this still smacked too much of direct intervention in Spain's internal affairs. If, instead, the British government could point to a moderate anti-Franco front, formed on Spanish inititiative alone, then the impression of intervention in Spain's affairs might be avoided, and with it probable confrontation with General Franco. Even more importantly, tougher UN measures against Franco Spain would be shown to be superfluous. Thus, the Spanish opposition could be exploited, paradoxically, to *prevent* rather than initiate action against the Spanish dictatorship. Nevertheless, for this strategy to succeed, a moderate anti-Franco front had actually to exist. So, in 1947, the Foreign Office took upon itself the task of bringing together the two Spanish opposition leaders then thought most able to deliver a republican-monarchist agreement: Indalecio Prieto and José María Gil-Robles.

From the outset, the difficulties facing Prieto and Gil-Robles were considerable. Both men, former ministers of the Second Republic, which they had, respectively, defended and attacked, were faced with the daunting task of concluding what amounted, in effect, to a peace settlement of the Spanish Civil War. With each suspecting the other's ulterior motives, it was not surprising, therefore, that the culmination of ten months of intermittent negotiations – from the London talks of October 1947 to the Pact of Saint Jean-de-Luz of August 1948 – should amount to little more than a declaration of principles rather than a detailed prescription for the post-Franco transition. Yet, partial responsibility for this inconclusive outcome must be borne by the British government, for whom it was above all the *demonstration* of the Spanish opposition's unity of purpose rather than the actual content of any agreement that really mattered. In fact, once the UN General Assembly's vote of November 1947 removed the threat of international sanctions against Spain, the incentive for continuing British involvement in a republican-monarchist reconciliation had gone.[4]

Although negotiations between Prieto and Gil-Robles carried on well into 1949, partly under their own momentum and partly for want of an alternative, the united front strategy was nevertheless dealt a serious blow by Don Juan's reversion to *franquista* collaborationism. His meeting with Franco on board the *Azor*, only a few days before the Pact of Saint Jean-de-Luz, followed by his decision, in the autumn of 1948, to send Juan Carlos to Spain for his secondary education presaged the suspension of *juanista* opposition in July 1951.[5] Yet, to blame the collapse of the united front strategy on Don Juan alone would be unfair. In the final years of the decade the Pretender saw only too well that the intensifying Cold War, with its promise of American-Spanish *rapprochement*, was making Franco's hold on power increasingly secure. If, the Pretender concluded, the monarchist opening to the left, even when brokered by the Foreign Office, had not brought British commitment, then what choice did he have but to turn to the right – and Franco – or risk his dynasty's permanent exclusion from the Spanish throne?

From time to time, as this study has shown, a case was made out in the Foreign Office, at junior and senior level, for greater support of the Spanish opposition; usually at some new stage in its evolution. Thus, in December 1945, Robert Sloan, responsible for Spain in the Western Department, recommended British recognition of the proposed ANFD-monarchist *Frente Nacional Democrático*, and, in the same month, in response to the French plea for action, Philip Noel-Baker, Minister of State for Foreign Affairs, pressed Attlee to recall Sir Victor Mallet, the British Ambassador, from Madrid. In January 1946, rumours of a forth-coming meeting between Don Juan and Franco prompted Mallet himself to argue that support for a constitutional monarchy in Spain 'might just turn the scale' against Franco; he was backed by Sir Oliver Harvey, Assistant Under-Secretary, and Sir Orme Sargent, the Permanent Under-Secretary. In November 1946, as pressure in the UN mounted for action against Spain, even Bevin briefly considered appealing in the General Assembly for a united Spanish opposition. In the spring of 1947, the proposal from McNeil, Noel-Baker's successor as Minister of State, for a joint approach, with France and the USA, to the Spanish 'moderates' coincided with a similar call from Dean Acheson, Acting Secretary of State, for a more 'positive policy' on Spain; and this stim-ulated a four month debate in the Foreign Office on policy towards the anti-Franco opposition. This continued, in the autumn, after John Curle, Sloan's replacement in the Western Department, warned of the 'final frustration' of the Spanish opposition, if the Prieto–Gil-Robles talks were not supported. Finally, in the summer of 1949, William Ivo Mallet, newly appointed Assistant Under-Secretary, had the backing of Sir Roger Makins, Deputy Under-Secretary, and Sir William Strang, the new Permanent Under-Secretary, when he recommended the interior *Comité Interior de Coordinación* as a potential nexus of government in the post-Franco transition.

Except during the initial Prieto–Gil-Robles *rapprochement*, however, Bevin consistently refused to adopt a proactive policy towards the Spanish opposition.[6] To an extent, this position reflected a basic premise of Foreign Office thinking, which tended to reassert itself after every call for a firmer pro-oppositional stance: that the Franco dictatorship could be brought down by diplomatic admonition alone. According to this untested assumption, warnings, such as the one delivered in February 1945, would of themselves convince Franco of the error of his ways, or else inspire Spain's disaffected 'moderates' to press for his departure. By the same token, any encouragement of the organised anti-Franco opposition was to be avoided since it invariably provoked a nationalist reaction in Spain and drove the moderates into Franco's arms. It was, moreover, British policy not to recognise 'shadow' gov-ernments until they were assured of firm indigenous support. What, short of guaranteed British recognition, would have rallied Spain's principal power broker – the Army – to an alternative government or inspired a moderate *Fronde* of the sort imagined by the Foreign Office was never clarified.

More than anything, however, Bevin's policy towards the Spanish opposition accorded with his overall policy towards Spain itself. As has been repeatedly said, Britain's post-war commercial and strategic interests in the Iberian Peninsula were not threatened by the existence of the Franco dictatorship. Moreover, its removal by military force alone was improbable, and, at the time, international cooperation over economic sanctions thought doubtful. This passivity has since been challenged by Qasim Ahmad, who argues that contemporary analysts exaggerated the predicted effect of sanctions on the British economy.[7] Even so, as Ahmad himself admits, Britain's economy would not have escaped unscathed, and it is debatable how far Attlee's Labour government could have imposed further hardships, however minor, on the population of war-torn Britain.

Yet, over and above economic considerations, Ahmad insists that what was really at stake was a moral issue: whether the post-war British government was committed or not to the extirpation of fascism in Europe. This view might have been disregarded on the grounds that the defence of national interests without moral reference has been legitimated by long precedent. On this count, therefore, no blame should necessarily be attached to Bevin's policy towards Spain and the Spanish opposition. However, by his laying claim to the *moral* leadership of western civilisation, Bevin in fact committed the Labour government to an ethical foreign policy and thereby exposed his Spanish *Realpolitik* to a moral evaluation it would not otherwise have incurred.[8]

From the perspective of half a century later, Britain's restrained relationship with the Spanish opposition in the 1940s might appear to have had little moral consequence. British disengagement from the anti-Franco struggle forced Don Juan to an accommodation of sorts with the Franco dictatorship, and in 1969 his son, Juan Carlos, was designated Franco's successor. Indeed, contrary to Prieto's forebodings thirty years before, after Franco's death in November 1975 it was the monarchy *in situ* rather than a provisional republic that ensured Spain's peaceful transition to democracy in the face of determined opposition from a reactionary Francoist minority. The problem of the plebiscite, moreover, whose timing had so vexed Prieto and Gil-Robles, resolved itself. After elections in 1977 for a constituent assembly, in which all political parties including the communists participated, a referendum of the

Spanish people in January 1978 – in other words, a plebiscite *a posteriori* – approved Spain's transformation into a parliamentary democracy under a constitutional monarchy. The transitional process was completed in October 1982 when the formation of a socialist government under Felipe González signalled the final reconciliation of the erstwhile republican PSOE with the Bourbon monarchy.[9]

To exculpate a policy on the basis of developments fifty years later is, of course, anachronistic. After 1944, Britain's reluctance to inspire either an international anti-Franco combination or to guarantee recognition of a united Spanish opposition front, while pragmatically defensible, was also partly responsible for the perpetuation of a vicious dictatorship. While the strength of anti-Franco feeling in Churchill's War Cabinet was always questionable, the Spanish Civil War had struck deep roots into the collective consciousness of the British and international Left so that there was no doubting the bitter animosity of the Attlee Cabinet towards the Franco regime. For all that, though, its attitude was essentially sentimental, substituting anti-Franco rhetoric for action and seeing no contradiction in simultaneously pursuing normal commercial and financial Anglo-Spanish relations. Thus, a policy of diplomatic 'pinpricks' was adopted, officially on the grounds that it brought home to Franco his regime's pariah status, but, in reality, because it helped defuse left-wing criticism of Britain's inaction. A similar function was performed by the Spanish opposition. In its dealings with it, the British government must be credited for making no secret of its commitment to non-intervention, but its anti-Franco rhetoric raised expectations which it was never prepared to meet. Nor was the temptation resisted to use the Spanish opposition to quieten Labour discontent at home and to meet the threat of UN action. In terms of *Realpolitik*, Britain's policy towards the Spanish opposition cannot be censured. As an example of ethical foreign policy, however, it does not redound to Britain's credit.

Notes

Introduction

1. W. Ewer, 'The Labour Government's Record in Foreign Policy', *The Political Quarterly*, XX, 2 (1949), p. 118. Ewer was the diplomatic correspondent of the *Daily Herald* and generally a supporter of the British Foreign Secretary, Ernest Bevin.

2. For the British government's attitude towards Franco during the Civil War, see, for example, J. Edwards, *The British Government and the Spanish Civil War* (London: Macmillan, 1979); E. Moradiellos García, *Neutralidad Benévola* (Oviedo: Pentalfa, 1990); *La Perfidia de Albión; el Gobierno Británico y la Guerra Civil Española* (Madrid: Siglo XXI de España, 1996); 'Appeasement and Non-Intervention: British policy during the Spanish Civil War', in P. Catterall and C. Morris (eds), *Britain and the Threat to Stability in Europe, 1918–1945* (London: Leicester University Press, 1993), pp. 94–104; D. Smyth, *Diplomacy and Strategy of Survival: British Policy and Franco's Spain, 1940–41* (Cambridge University Press, 1986) especially, pp. 10–71.

3. On 12 June 1940 Franco moved from *neutrality* to *non-belligerence*; on 23 October 1943 he returned to *neutrality*. For Franco's relations with the Axis Powers during World War II, see L. Suárez Fernández, *España, Franco y la Segunda Guerra Mundial desde 1939 hasta 1945* (Madrid: Actas, 1997); J. Tusell, *Franco, España y la II Guerra Mundial. Entre el Eje y la Neutralidad* (Madrid: Temas de Hoy, 1995). See also A. Egido León, 'Franco y las Potencias del Eje. La Tentación Intervencionista de España en la Segunda Guerra Mundial', *Espacio, Forma y Tiempo*, 2 (1989) 191–208; J. Fusi, *Franco: Autoritarismo y Poder Personal* (Madrid: Ediciones El País, 1985), pp. 76–100; A. Marquina Barrio, 'La Neutralidad o la Pérdida de la Neutralidad en la Segunda Guerra Mundial. Cuestiones Pendientes de un Debate Todavía Inconcluso', *Cuadernos de Historia Contemporánea*, 17 (1995) 313–22; V. Morales Lezcano, 'L'Espagne des Années de Guerre et son Isolement d'Après-Guerre (1939–1953)', in Table Ronde de l'Equipe Défense et Diplomatie des Moyennes Puissances, *La Moyenne Puissance au XX° Siècle: Recherche d'une Définition* (Paris: Institut d'Histoire des Conflits Contemporains, 1989), pp. 157–8; P. Preston, *The Politics of Revenge: Fascism and the Military in Twentieth Century Spain* (London: Unwin Hyman, 1990), pp. 51–84; *Franco* (London: Harper Collins, 1993), pp. 333–87; D. Smyth, *Diplomacy and Strategy*, pp. 245–6. For an apologia for Franco's pro-Axis policy, see J. Doussinague, *España Tenía Razón (1939–1945)*, 2nd edn (Madrid: Espasa-Calpe, 1950), pp. 41–50.

4. Churchill enunciated his 'tests of freedom' during a visit to Italy in August 1944: W. Churchill, *The Second World War. Triumph and Tragedy*, VI (London: Cassel, 1954), pp. 111–12.

5. Britain's post-war commitment to the liberal order was made clear in O. Sargent's memorandum, 'Stocktaking after VE-Day', 11 July 1945: R. Bullen

and M. Pelly (eds), *Documents on British Policy Overseas, Series 1*, I (London: HMSO, 1984) no. 102, p. 187 (henceforth cited as *DBPO*).

6. For a conceptual framework within which to treat the Spanish opposition and its periodisation, see M. Tuñón de Lara, 'Sobre la Historia de la Oposición al Franquismo: Balance y Perspectivas', in J. Tusell, A. Alted, A. Mateos *et al.*, *La Oposición al Régimen de Franco: Estado de la Cuestión y Metodología de la Investigación*, II (Madrid: UNED, 1990), pp. 421–6. Whether the monarchists in the 1940s constituted an opposition to Franco in the full sense of the term is debated in P. Malerbe, *La Oposición al Franquismo 1939/1975* (Madrid: Ediciones Naranco, 1977), p. 10; J. Toquero, *Franco y Don Juan: la Oposición Monárquica al Franquismo* (Barcelona: Plaza & Janés, 1989), pp. 12, 379; J. Tusell, *La España del Siglo XX: desde Alfonso XIII a la Muerte de Carrero Blanco* (Madrid: Dopesa, 1975), pp. 387–90. The title of J. Tusell's *La Oposición Democrática al Franquismo (1939–1962)* (Barcelona: Planeta, 1977) is also indicative of Tusell's position. Linz's classification of the monarchists as a 'semi-opposition' is an acceptable compromise: J. Linz, 'Opposition in and under an Authoritarian Regime: the Case of Spain' in R. Dahl, *Regimes and Oppositions* (Newhaven & London: Yale University Press, 1973), pp. 191–9.

7. The term 'family' is taken from A. de Miguel, *Sociología del Franquismo* (Barcelona: Euros, 1975).

8. Tusell's *Foreword* in F. Portero, *Franco Aislado: La Cuestión Española (1945–1950)* (Madrid: Aguilar, 1989), p. 16.

9. In February 1936 the anarcho-syndicalist *Confederación Nacional de Trabajo, Federación Anarquista Ibérica* and *Federación Ibérica de Juventudes Libertarias* came together to form the *Movimiento Libertario Español* (MLE).

10. This study does not deal, either, with workers' strikes as a form of opposition, on which see, for example, J. Jímenez de Aberasturi, *La Huelga General del 1° de Mayo de 1947* (San Sebastián: Eusko Ikaskuntza, 1991).

11. P. Preston, 'The Anti-Francoist Opposition: the Long March to Unity' in P. Preston (ed.), *Spain in Crisis: the Evolution and Decline of the Franco Regime* (Hassocks: Harvester Press, 1976), pp. 133–6.

12. In March 1947 the British Ambassador to Spain, Sir Victor Mallet, observed that the autonomists' attempt to lobby foreign support was 'just as reprehensible as if the Scottish Nationalists were to start lobbying in Moscow or New York': Hoyer-Millar's minute, 1 April 1947: Public Record Office (henceforth cited as PRO) FO 371/67872, Z3208/16/41. During the Civil War the Spanish President, Manuel Azaña, dismissed Basque-Catalan nationalism as the 'Barcelona-Bilbao Axis': R. de la Cierva, *Don Juan de Borbón: Por Fin Toda la Verdad. Las Aportaciones Definitivas* (Madrid: Fénix, 1997), pp. 489–90.

13. Undoubtedly, many leading *republicans* were freemasons, as for example, the first President of the exiled republic, Diego Martínez Barrio, who was Grand Master of the Spanish Grand Orient Lodge.

14. Although the monarchy was restored by military *pronunciamiento* in December 1874, a monarchist constitution was not ready until 1876. Alfonso XII died in 1885 and, as his son, Alfonso XIII, was born posthumously in 1886, there followed a regency under Alfonso XII's wife, María Cristina of Austria, until Alfonso XIII ascended the throne in 1902.

15. For an excellent survey of Carlism from its inception until the Second Repub-

lic, see M. Blinkhorn, *Carlism and Crisis in Spain 1931–1939* (Cambridge University Press, 1975), pp. 1–40; see also M. Blinkhorn, 'Elites in Search of Masses: the Traditionalist Communion and the Carlist Party, 1937–1975', in F. Lannon and P. Preston (eds), *Elites and Power in Twentieth Century Spain: Essays in Honour of Sir Raymond Carr* (Oxford: Clarendon Press, 1990), pp. 179–201; J. Clemente, *El Carlismo en la España de Franco (Bases Documentales 1936–1977)* (Madrid: Editorial Fundamentos, 1994).

16. Linz's 'Opposition in and under an Authoritarian Regime: the Case of Spain' and Preston's 'The Anti-Francoist Opposition: the Long March to Unity' and *Politics of Revenge* are cited above. P. Fagen, *Exiles and Citizens: Spanish Republicans in Mexico* (Austin & London: University of Texas Press, 1973); R. Gillespie, *The Spanish Socialist Party: a History of Factionalism* (Oxford: Clarendon, 1989); P. Preston, *Franco* (London: Harper Collins, 1993); D. Pike, *In the Service of Stalin: the Spanish Communists in Exile, 1939–1945* (Oxford: Clarendon Press, 1993); L. Stein, *Beyond Death and Exile: the Spanish Republicans in France, 1939–1955* (Cambridge, Massachusetts & London: Harvard University Press, 1979).

17. D. Smyth, 'The Politics of Asylum, Juan Negrín and the British Government in 1940' in R. Langhorne (ed.), *Diplomacy and Intelligence during the Second World War. Essays in Honour of F.H. Hinsley* (Cambridge University Press, 1985), pp. 126–46; *Diplomacy and Strategy of Survival: British Policy and Franco's Spain, 1940–41* (Cambridge University Press, 1986); G. Stone, 'Britain, France and Franco's Spain in the Aftermath of the Spanish Civil War', *Diplomacy and Statecraft*, 6, 2 (1995) 373–407; 'The Degree of British Commitment to the Restoration of Democracy in Spain, 1939–1946' in C. Leitz and D. Dunthorn (eds), *Spain in an International Context, 1936–1959* (New York & Oxford: Berghahn, 1999), pp. 191–217; Q. Ahmad, *Britain, Franco Spain and the Cold War, 1945–1950*, revised edn (Kuala Lumpur: A.S. Noordee, 1995). See also, in French, D. Smyth, ' "Les Chevaliers de Saint-George": la Grande-Bretagne et la Corruption des Généraux Espagnols (1940–1942)', *Guerres Mondiales et Conflits Contemporains*, 162 (1991) 29–54. For a useful survey, in Spanish, of recent British historiography on Spain, see A. Guerrero and A. Mateos, 'Algunas Notas sobre el Hispanismo Británico del *Laberinto Español* de Brenan al *Franco* de Preston', *Spagna Contemporanea*, 8 (1995) 133–47.

18. An exception is the author's 'The Prieto–Gil-Robles meeting of October 1947: Britain and the Failure of the Spanish anti-Franco Coalition, 1945–50', *European History Quarterly*, 30, 1 (2000) 49–76, much of which has been incorporated into the present study.

19. H. Heine, *La Oposición Política al Franquismo de 1939 a 1952* (Barcelona: Editorial Crítica, 1983); J. Tusell, *La Oposición Democrática al Franquismo (1939–1962)* (Barcelona: Planeta, 1977); *Franco y los Católicos. La Política Interior Española entre 1945–57* (Madrid: Alianza, 1984); R. de la Cierva, *Don Juan de Borbón: Por Fin Toda la Verdad. Las Aportaciones Definitivas* (Madrid: Fénix, 1997). De la Cierva's description of Preston as 'la manipulación histórica más rabiosamente antifranquista según las directrices de la masonería y la Internacional Socialista' gives a flavour of his rancor: *ibid.*, p. 967.

20. José Carlos Gibaja has also made extensive use of the *Fundación Pablo Iglesias'* archives for his own, very useful, political biography of Prieto:

J. Gibaja Velázquez, *Indalecio Prieto y el Socialismo Español* (Madrid: Editorial Pablo Iglesias, 1995).

21. Archival material from the *Fundación Nacional Francisco Franco* forms the basis of Suárez's eight-volume *Francisco Franco y Su Tiempo* (Madrid: Fundación Francisco Franco, 1984) and his *España, Franco y la Segunda Guerra Mundial desde 1939 hasta 1945*. A published collection of the *Fundación's* primary material had only reached December 1943 by mid-1999: Fundación Nacional Francisco Franco, *Documentos Inéditos para la Historia del Generalísimo Franco*, II-1, II-2, III, IV (Madrid: Azor, 1992, 1992, 1993, 1994).

22. One such protest is found in J. Tusell, S. Sueiro, J.M.ª Marín, M. Casanova, *El Régimen de Franco: Política y Relaciones Exteriores*, I (Madrid: UNED, 1993), p. 11.

23. Bevin's autonomy in foreign affairs in general has been remarked upon by his principal private secretary, Sir Roderick Barclay: R. Barclay, *Ernest Bevin and the Foreign Office 1932–69* (London: published by author, 1975), pp. 78, 84. See also P. Hennessy and A. Arends, 'Mr. Attlee's Engine Room. Cabinet Committee Structure and the Labour Government 1945–1951', *Strathclyde Papers on Government and Politics*, 26 (1983) 11–12; K. Morgan, *Labour in Power 1945–1951* (Oxford: Clarendon, 1984), p. 236; H. Pelling, *The Labour Governments, 1945–51* (London: Macmillan, 1984), pp. 139–41.

1   Spanish Opposition before 1945

1. Republican distrust of Franco was evident even before the July 1936 insurrection: hence the government's decision in February 1936 to terminate Franco's position as Chief of the General Staff in Madrid and appoint him Commander-General in the Canaries: Preston, *Franco*, pp. 120–1; S. Ellwood, *Franco* (London: Longman, 1995), pp. 63–4.

2. Republican refugees scattered eventually to some 23 countries: V. Llorens, 'La Emigración Republicana de 1939' in J.L. Abellán (ed.), *El Exilio Español de 1939*, 1, *La Emigración Republicana* (Madrid: Taurus, 1976), pp. 97–200.

3. Accounts of the exiled Spanish republicans' experiences are found in M. Alexander, 'France, the Collapse of Republican Spain and the Approach of General War: National Security, War Economics and the Spanish Refugees, 1938–1940', in Leitz and Dunthorn, *Spain in an International Context*, pp. 105–28; J. Alfaya, 'Españoles en los Campos de Concentración' in J.L. Abellán (ed.), *El Exilio Español de 1939*, 2, *Guerra y Política* (Madrid: Taurus, 1976); J. Borras Llop, *Política de los Exiliados Españoles 1944–1950* (Paris: Ruedo Ibérico, 1976); F. Caudet, *Hipótesis sobre el Exilio Republicano de 1939* (Madrid: Fundación Universitaria Española, 1997); I. de Palencia, *Smouldering Freedom: the Story of the Spanish Republicans in Exile* (London: Gollancz, 1946); Pike, *In the Service of Stalin*; E. Pons Prades, *Los Derrotados y el Exilio* (Barcelona: Bruguera, 1977); M. Sanz, *Los Guerrilleros Españoles en Francia, 1940–1945* (Havana: Editorial de Ciencias Sociales del Instituto Cubano del Libro, 1971); Stein, *Beyond Death and Exile*. For the eventual integration of Spanish refugees into France, see A. Angoustures, 'Les Réfugiés Espagnols en France de 1945 à 1981', *Revue d'Histoire Moderne et Contemporaine*, 44, 3 (1997) 457–83.

4. Borras Llop, *Política de los Exiliados Españoles*, pp. 145–63; J. Estruch Tobella, *El PCE en la Clandestinidad, 1939–1956* (Madrid: Siglo Veintiuno de España Editores, 1982), pp. 48–65; Fernández, 'Las Formaciones Políticas del Exilio' in Abellán, *Exilio Español*, 2, pp. 167–72; Heine, *Oposición*, pp. 95–102; G. Morán, *Miseria y Grandeza del Partido Comunista de España* (Barcelona: Planeta, 1976), pp. 21–9.

5. Heine, *Oposición*, pp. 56–8, 123–4. Although the most serious, the *negrinista* division was far from being the only one affecting the exiled PSOE; see Gibaja, *Prieto*, pp. 207–13.

6. Azaña was followed a few hours later by the heads of the Catalan and Basque governments, Lluís Companys y Jover and José Antonio Aguirre y Lecube respectively: F. Giral and P. Santidrian, *La República en el Exilio* (Madrid: Historia Secreta del Franquismo Ediciones, 1977), pp. 13–16. Negrín returned to Spain a second time on 10 February, where he remained until the Casado *coup* in Madrid of 4 March finally obliged him to leave for France the next day; M. Tuñón de Lara, R. Miralles, B. Díaz Chico, *Juan Negrín López, el Hombre Necesario* (Las Palmas: Gobierno de Canarias, 1996), pp. 127–44.

7. For the text of Azaña's letter of resignation, see Borras Llop, *Política de los Exiliados Españoles*, p. 12. According to Articles 68 and 74 of Spain's 1931 Constitution the President of the *Cortes* assumed the functions of the President of the Republic for a maximum period of 38 days, at the end of which the approval of both the *Cortes* and an equal number of delegates elected by popular vote was required; it was obviously impossible to meet either condition. The 21 seats on the *Diputación Permanente* were allocated to political parties in proportion to their representation in the *Cortes*. D. Martínez Barrio, *Memorias* (Barcelona: Planeta, 1983), pp. 410–15; Giral and Santidrian, *República en el Exilio*, pp. 18–20; J. Mª del Valle, *Las Instituciones de la República Española en el Exilio* (Paris: Ruedo Ibérico, 1976), pp. 9–32.

8. On the Casado *coup*, see H. Graham, *Socialism and War: the Spanish Socialist Party in Power and Crisis, 1936–1939* (Cambridge University Press, 1991), pp. 232–44. Allegations of involvement by British intelligence in the Casado *coup* are denied in Horsfall-Carter's minute, 24 October 1945: PRO FO 371/49594, Z9928/234/41.

9. For the text of the *Diputación Permanente*'s declaration of 26 July 1939, see C. and J. Martínez Cobo, *La Primera Renovación. Intrahistoria del PSOE, 1 (1939–1945)* (Barcelona: Plaza & Janés, 1989), pp. 363–4.

10. S. de Madariaga, *Spain: a Modern History* (London: Jonathan Cape, 1972; first published USA, 1942), p. 590.

11. Before the Civil War Prieto's pragmatism had often set him at odds with other factions within the PSOE: see Gibaja, *Prieto*, pp. 89–130; Gillespie, *Spanish Socialist Party*, pp. 89–169.

12. Gibaja, *Prieto*, pp. 170–92.

13. Ostensibly for use by the *Servicio de Emigración de Republicanos Españoles*, an organisation set up by Negrín to assist refugees, the funds were also intended to strengthen Negrín's political influence; but, at its meeting of 26 July 1939, the *Diputación Permanente* claimed exclusive authority over the Republic's assets and a few days later established the *Junta de Auxilio a los Republicanos Españoles* to administer them: Fagen, *Exiles and Citizens*, pp. 34–6; Gibaja,

Prieto, pp. 213–14; Giral and Santidrian, *República en el Exilio*, pp. 39–44; Heine, *Oposición*, pp. 31–2.

14. Martínez Cobo, *Primera Renovación*, pp. 180–98.
15. J. Marichal, 'Juan Negrín y la Continuidad de la Segunda República' in Tusell *et al.*, *Oposición al Régimen de Franco*, pp. 67–72.
16. S. Cabeza Sánchez-Albornoz, *Historia Política de la Segunda República en el Exilio* (Madrid: Fundación Universitaria Española, 1997), pp. 29–30. The ARE established a delegation in Britain: Garran, 'Spanish Republican Refugees: the Present Situation', 8 February 1945: PRO FO 371/49554, Z2035/18/41. In another attempt to unite the republican camp an *Alianza Democrática Española* (ADE) was formed in Bordeaux in December 1939 and, the following summer, reconstituted itself in London as the *junta delegada* of the ADE; it was, though, little more than a façade for British intelligence services and their Spanish agents in Spain: Heine, *Oposición*, pp. 34–40.
17. The UDE established a delegation in Britain known as the *Coalición Republicana Española*.
18. Heine, *Oposición*, pp. 102–13.
19. Valle, *Instituciones*, pp. 72–8.
20. The JEL manifesto is in PRO FO 371/39703, C3524/107/41.
21. Prieto, 'Puntualizaciones. Respuesta a una Carta Abierta', 1959: *Fundación Pablo Iglesias* (henceforth cited as FPI) ALJA 419–33.
22. Gibaja, *Prieto*, pp. 270–3.
23. Nor did the JEL in Mexico gain by the creation in October 1944 in Toulouse, of the JEL (*Comité de Francia*). This met regularly until May 1945, though not formally dissolved until September 1947: Martínez Cobo, *Primera Renovación*, pp. 312–15.
24. Borras Llop, *Política de los Exiliados Españoles*, pp. 85–106. Anti-communist resolutions passed at the PSOE Congress and at the UGT Congress in November also isolated the *negrinistas*, who then formed the *Unión Socialista Española*. Despite its pro-communist reputation, it was rejected by the PCE. It lasted until the XIII PSOE Congress of 1965: Fernández, 'Las Formaciones Políticas del Exilio', pp. 160–7.
25. Heine, *Oposición*, pp. 164–6.
26. It has been claimed that over 30 per cent of male republican exiles participated in the French Resistance: A. Fernández, *La España de los Maquis* (Mexico: Ediciones Era, 1971), pp. 24–8, 36–106. See also Pike, *In the Service of Stalin*, pp. 84–107, 194–235.
27. Numerous reports of republican *guerrilleros* on the Franco-Spanish border are found in PRO FO 371/39817-8.
28. Heine, *Oposición*, pp. 421–71. Studies of anti-Franco guerrilla activity in Spain include: F. Aguado Sánchez, *El Maquis en España. Su Historia* (Madrid: San Martín, 1975); V. Fernández Vargas, *La Resistencia Interior en la España de Franco* (Madrid: Ediciones Istmo, 1981); R. Garriga, *Los Validos de Franco* (Barcelona: Planeta, 1981); F. Jáuregui and P. Vega, *Crónica del Anti-Franquismo: los Hombres que Lucharon por Devolver la Democracia a España*, 1 (Madrid: Argos Vergara, 1983); E. Pons Prades, *Guerrillas Españolas 1936–1960* (Barcelona: Planeta, 1977); F. Romeu Alfaro, 'Panorámica Socio-Política de los Primeros Movimientos Guerrilleros en la España del 39 al 46' in J. García Delgado (ed.), *El Primer Franquismo. España durante la Segunda Guerra Mundial*

(Madrid: Siglo Veintiuno Editores, 1989); J. Solé Tura, 'Unidad y Diversidad en la Oposición Comunista al Franquismo' in J. Fontana (ed.), *España bajo el Franquismo* (Barcelona: Editorial Crítica – Grupo Editorial Grijalbo, 1986); A. Sorel, *Búsqueda, Reconstrucción e Historia de la Guerrilla Española del Siglo XX, a través de sus Documentos, Relatos y Protagonistas* (Paris: Librairie du Globe, 1970). An MLE report to the ANFD in June 1946 cast considerable doubt on the guerrilla threat to the Franco regime: E.M. Nadal, *Todos contra Franco – La Alianza Nacional de Fuerzas Democráticas 1944/1947* (Madrid: Queimada Ediciones, 1982) p. 95. For Stalin's attitude towards the guerrilla struggle in Spain, see G. Swain, 'Stalin and Spain, 1944–1948' in Leitz and Dunthorn, *Spain in an International Context*, pp. 245–64.

29. Heine, *Oposición*, pp. 202–5. Hoare thought the JSUNE's importance 'vastly exaggerated': Hoare to Foreign Office, 6 April 1944: PRO FO 371/39741, C4939/264/41.
30. Preston maintains that the ANFD's creation was the most significant move towards the unification of the anti-Franco opposition before 1974: Preston (ed.), *Spain in Crisis*, p. 132. For an account of the ANFD from its inception until the end of 1948, see Foreign Office Research Department, 'The Alianza Nacional de Fuerzas Democráticas', 2 December 1948: PRO FO 371/73360A, Z10440/1027/41.
31. Tusell, *Oposición Democrática*, p. 90; see also Valle, *Instituciones*, pp. 78–9.
32. Heine, *Oposición*, pp. 246–51, 283–95; see also Suárez, *España, Franco y la Segunda Guerra Mundial*, pp. 609–10. For reports on the widespread arrests, see Bowker to Eden, 9 January, 24 March 1945: PRO FO 425/423, Z381, 4228/233/41.
33. Alfonso XIII went first to Marseilles and then to Paris to rejoin his family; his wife, Queen Victoria Eugenia, left him shortly afterwards because of his adulterous behaviour and moved to England, while Alfonso eventually took up residence in Italy: R. Borràs Betriu, *El Rey de los Rojos: Don Juan de Borbón: una Figura Tergiversada*, 3rd edn (Barcelona: Plaza & Janés, 1996), pp. 67–8.
34. The term, 'Alfonsist insurrectionaries', is taken from P. Preston, 'Alfonsist Monarchism and the Coming of the Spanish Civil War' in M. Blinkhorn (ed.), *Spain in Conflict 1931–1939: Democracy and Its Enemies* (London: Sage, 1986), pp. 160–82.
35. A. Kindelán, *La Verdad de Mis Relaciones con Franco* (Barcelona: Planeta, 1981), pp. 37–41.
36. According to Kindelán's son, also called Alfredo, almost all the rebel generals were monarchists: A. Kindelán, *Mis Cuadernos de Guerra* (Barcelona: Planeta, 1982), pp. 59–60.
37. *Acción Española*, founded in 1931, resumed its meetings in October 1939 as *Cultura Española* until closed down in the summer of 1942: E. Vegas Latapié, *La Frustración en la Victoria: Memorias Políticas 1938–1942* (Madrid: Actas, 1995), pp. 141–4.
38. Ibid., pp. 314–30; Tusell, *Oposición Democrática*, pp. 36–43.
39. P. Sainz Rodríguez, *Testimonio y Recuerdos* (Barcelona: Planeta, 1978), pp. 275–89, 335; see also Hoare to Foreign Office, 18 September 1941: PRO FO 371/26898, C10462/33/41.
40. Heine, *Oposición*, pp. 253–7; Preston, *Politics of Revenge*, pp. 86–96. See also

Hoare to Foreign Office, 22, 28 November, Yencken to Strang, Yencken to Cadogan, 28 November 1941: PRO FO 371/26899, C12972, 13211, 13262, 13886/33/41.

41. Kindelán, *Relaciones*, pp. 55–6.
42. J. Mª Gil-Robles, *La Monarquía por la que Luché. Páginas de un Diario (1941–1954)* (Madrid: Taurus, 1976), p. 61; P. Preston, 'Franco et ses Généraux (1939–1945)', *Guerres Mondiales et Conflits Contemporains*, 162 (1991) 7–28; P. Sainz Rodríguez, *Un Reinado en la Sombra* (Barcelona: Planeta, 1981), p. 161. See also Admiralty Intelligence report, 16 August 1943: PRO FO 371/34821, C9692/217/41.
43. For an English translation of the generals' letter, see Yencken to Foreign Office, 30 September 1943: PRO FO 371/34821, C11895/217/41. See also Suárez, *Francisco Franco*, III, pp. 431–3.
44. Don Juan moved to Italy from France in 1936 after the French *Front Populaire* electoral victory. In an interview with Sainz Rodríguez in March 1978, he claimed he wanted to move to Switzerland once Italy entered the war but because of his father's death could not leave until April or May 1941: Sainz, *Reinado*, p. 258. H. Grant claimed in 1947 that Don Juan had remained in Italy until late 1942: H. Grant, 'The Situation in Spain', *International Affairs*, XII (1946) 404; but this is contradicted in J. Tusell, *Juan Carlos I. La Restauración de la Monarquía* (Madrid: Temas de Hoy, 1995), p. 60.
45. Much of the correspondence between Don Juan and Franco is reproduced in Sainz, *Reinado*, and in L. López Rodó, *La Larga Marcha hacia la Monarquía* (Barcelona: Plaza & Janés, 1979).
46. Sainz, *Reinado*, p. 324.
47. Ibid., pp. 330–2.
48. Toquero's emphasis on Don Juan's liberalism between 1942 and 1945 is therefore open to challenge: J. Toquero, *Don Juan de Borbón, el Rey Padre* (Barcelona: Plaza & Janés, 1992), pp. 111–14.
49. Sainz, *Reinado*, pp. 350–1; Suárez, *Francisco Franco*, III, pp. 312–13.
50. For the importance of the 'Catholic monarchs' to Franco, see J. Gilmour, 'Reliving an Imperialist Past – the Extreme Right, Franco and the Catholic Monarchs', *Tesserae*, 1, 2 (1995) 201–21; M. Blinkhorn, 'Spain: the "Spanish Problem" and the Imperial Myth', *Journal of Contemporary History*, 15 (1980) 21–2.
51. Sainz, *Reinado*, p. 329.
52. Ibid., p. 362.
53. Ibid., pp. 330–1, 363.
54. Gil-Robles' involvement in the 1936 military rebellion has been debated; he was certainly aware of the conspiracy: J. Mª Gil-Robles, *No Fue Posible la Paz* (Barcelona: Ediciones Ariel, 1968), pp. 797–8, 800; de la Cierva claims that Gil-Robles was briefly a propagandist for Franco: R. de la Cierva, *Don Juan de Borbón*, pp. 219–23; see also P. Preston, *The Coming of the Spanish Civil War: Reform, Reaction and Revolution in the Second Republic*, 2nd edn (London: Routledge, 1994), pp. 241–4.
55. Gil-Robles, *Monarquía*, pp. 339–40. See also Foreign Office Research Department, 'José-María Gil Robles', 24 January 1945: PRO FO 371/60374, Z7448/41/41.
56. Gil-Robles' political ideas are dealt with briefly in J. Tusell, *Historia de la*

Democracia Cristiana en España. I. Los antecedentes: la Ceda y la II República (Madrid: Editorial Cuadernos para el Diálogo, Edicusa, 1974), pp. 362–6. For a sympathetic treatment of his ideas, see J. Mª García Escudero, *Vista a la Derecha* (Madrid: Ediciones Rialp, 1988), pp. 179–226.
57. Tusell, *Oposición Democrática*, p. 89.

2   Britain and the Spanish Opposition until 1944

1. For the strategic importance of Spain's neutrality, see Nicholl to Strang, 7 August 1940: PRO FO 371/24516, C8045/113/4; 'Spain', report by the Chiefs of Staff, 23 November 1940: PRO CAB 66/13, WP (40) 460. See also J. Edwards, *The British Government and the Spanish Civil War* (London: Macmillan, 1979), pp. 228–32; J. Lewis, *Changing Direction: British Military Planning for Post-War Strategic Defence, 1942–1947* (London: Sherwood Press, 1988), pp. 75–9; J. Saville, *The Politics of Continuity: British Foreign Policy and the Labour Government, 1945–46* (London: Verso, 1993), pp. 34–9; G. Stone, 'The European Great Powers and the Spanish Civil War, 1936–1939' in R. Boyce and E. Robertson (eds), *Paths to War: New Essays on the Origins of the Second World War* (London: Macmillan, 1989), pp. 215–16; ——'Britain, France and Franco's Spain', p. 375.
2. For Britain's attitude to 'early' Franco Spain, see Moradiellos, *Neutralidad Benévola*, pp. 77–106; Smyth, *Diplomacy and Strategy of Survival*, pp. 10–25; 'Franco Cunctator', *The International History Review*, XVIII, 3 (1996) 629–40.
3. Eden's memorandum, 'Our Policy in Spain', 20 July 1941: PRO CAB 66/17, WP (41) 174.
4. For the background to the 'wolfram question' see Hoare to Eden, 10 May 1944, PRO FO 371/39654, C6240/2/41; C. Leitz, *Economic Relations between Nazi Germany and Franco's Spain 1936–1945* (Oxford University Press, 1996), pp. 170–99; see also the Spanish Foreign Ministry's summary of an interview between Franco, Jordana and Hoare on 28 January 1944: *Archivo de la Presidencia del Gobierno: Fondos de la Jefatura del Estado* (henceforth cited as APG JE) *leg.* 3, *exp.* 1, *no.* 4. The full text of the wolfram agreement with Spain is found in Hoare's letter to Jordana, 1 May 1944: PRO FO 371/39654, C6241/2/4. For an account of the evolution of Anglo-American relations with Spain during the Second World War, see C. Collado Seidel, '¿De Hendaya a San Francisco? Londres y Washington contra Franco y la Falange (1942–1945)' in *España y la Segunda Guerra Mundial* (Madrid, *Espacio, Tiempo y Forma*, Series V, 7, 1994), pp. 51–84.
5. Alba to *Ministerio de Asuntos Exteriores*, 29 April, 31 May 1944: APG JE *caja* 6718 (H.2); *Hansard Parliamentary Debates* (Commons), (henceforth cited as *Hansard*) 5th Ser. Vol. 400, cs. 768–72. Churchill later explained the strategic considerations behind his speech in a letter to Roosevelt: 'I do not care about Franco but I do not wish to have the Iberian Peninsula hostile to the British after the war. I do not know how I can depend on a de Gaullist France. Germany would have to be held down by main force, and we have a 20-years alliance with Russia . . .': Churchill to Roosevelt, 4 June 1944: PRO FO 954, SP/44/68; also in FO 371/39669, C7647/23/41.
6. Hoare to Foreign Office, 12 June 1944: PRO FO 371/39669, C8346/23/41.

7. Hoare's memorandum, 'The Allied Attitude Towards the Franco Government', 16 October 1944: PRO CAB 66/58, WP (44) 665. For the advantages of leaving relations with Spain unchanged, see also Garran's minute, 24 October 1944: PRO FO 371/39761, C14492/23/41.

8. Cadogan's minute, 27 October 1944: PRO FO 371/39761, C14492/23/41.

9. In February 1939 Attlee had denounced Britain's recognition of Franco's government as 'a gross betrayal of a friendly Government, a gross betrayal of democracy': J. Dugdale (ed.), *War Comes to Britain: Speeches of the Rt. Hon. C. R. Attlee, M.P.* (London: Gollancz, 1940), p. 218. Attlee had also demonstrated his support for the Second Republic in December 1937 when, as a member of a fraternal delegation from the Labour Party National Executive Committee, he visited Negrín in Barcelona and inspected the British contingent of the International Brigade in Madrid: C. Attlee, *As It Happened* (London: Heinemann, 1954), pp. 94–5; K. Harris, *Attlee* (London: Weidenfeld & Nicolson, 1982), pp. 138–9.

10. Attlee's note, 'Policy towards Spain. Note by the Lord President of the Council and Deputy Prime Minister', 4 November, Eden to Halifax, 9 November 1944: PRO PREM 8/106.

11. Churchill's minute, 10 November 1944: PRO PREM 8/106; Selborne's memorandum, 'Policy Towards Spain', 15 November 1944: PRO CAB 66/58, WP (44) 651. Selborne had earlier expressed his sympathy for Spain and his desire for increased Anglo-Spanish trade at a dinner with Alba at the Spanish Embassy in July 1944: Alba to *Ministerio de Asuntos Exteriores*, 31 July 1944: Archivo General de la Administración, Asuntos Exteriores (henceforth cited as AGA AE) *caja* 6718 (H.2).

12. Alba, 'Informe Político', 1 October, 30 November 1944: AGA AE *caja* 6718 (H.2).

13. Alba to *Ministerio de Asuntos Exteriores*, 22 November 1944: APG JE *leg.* 4, *exp.* 6, no. 1. Franco's letter accompanied Eden's memorandum, 'Spain', 25 November 1944: PRO CAB 66/58, WP (44) 691.

14. Eden's memorandum, 'Policy Towards Spain', 18 November 1944: PRO CAB 66/58, WP (44) 665; PRO CAB 65/43, WM 157 (44) 3, 27 November 1944 (the record of the Cabinet discussion is in the Confidential Annex, CAB 65/48); PRO CAB 65/44, WM 171 (44) 4, 18 December 1944.

15. Portero, *Franco Aislado*, p. 52.

16. Churchill to Franco, 15 January, Franco to Churchill, 20 February 1945: PRO PREM 8/106. Preston aptly speaks of a 'British rhetoric of hostility behind which lay an innocuous policy of non-intervention . . .': Preston, *Franco*, p. 523. On 17 March 1945, the Marqués de Santa Cruz, Spain's Chargé d'Affaires in London, even questioned, in a personal letter to Lequerica, the necessity for Anglo-Spanish 'cordiality': after all, he pondered, when, down through the centuries, were relations between the two countries really cordial? Santa Cruz to Lequerica, 17 March 1945: APG JE *leg.* 5, *exp.* 3, *no.* 2.

17. See, for example, the Foreign Secretary's reference to a 'victory of Fascist or Communist' in a Foreign Office minute of 30 August 1936: W. Medlicott and D. Dakin (eds), *Documents on British Foreign Policy 1919–1939, Second Series*, XVII (London: HMSO, 1979) no. 157, n. 1, p. 209; E Moradiellos, 'El General Apacible. La Imagen Oficial Británico de Franco durante la Guerra Civil', in J. Tusell, S. Sueiro, J. Mª Marín, M. Casanova, *El Régimen de Franco: Política y*

Relaciones Exteriores, 2 (Madrid: UNED, 1993) pp. 131–43; Smyth, *Diplomacy and Strategy of Survival*, pp. 21–2; Stone, 'The European Great Powers', pp. 213–14. Foreign Office prejudice against the *Frente Popular* was strengthened by memoranda, such as one from the Madrid Embassy Press Department in April 1944, in which the *Frente Popular* was blamed for ruining the Second Republic by its 'violent sectarianism and its anti-constitutional acts which culminated in a shocking *crime d'État*, in anarchy and in civil war followed by the Franco administration – the most tyrannical regime that has ever ruled the country': Hoare to Churchill, 15 April 1944: PRO FO 425/422, C5151/26/41.

18. Hoare to Eden, 28 December 1940: PRO FO 371/26904, C49/46/41.
19. Roberts to Leggett, 17 March 1944: PRO FO 371/39703, C3076/107/41.
20. Jordana communication, 1 December 1943: Fundación Nacional Francisco Franco, *Documentos Inéditos para la Historia del Generalísimo Franco*, IV (Madrid: Azor, 1994) pp. 636–9. In December 1944 Lequerica also instructed all Spain's Embassies abroad to stress that the total number of Spanish expatriate 'reds' in Latin America amounted to some ten thousand at the most, compared with the 27 million Spaniards in Spain who wanted peace; 'The only way to avoid a fratricidal struggle in Spain was to cease making declarations supporting those whose only interest was to incite it': Lequerica to Ambassadors in London, Washington, Rio de Janeiro, Lima, and all Legations in Latin America, 13 December 1944: APG JE *leg.* 4, *exp.* 7, *no.* 1.
21. PRO CAB 65/8, WM 191 (40) 7, 2 July 1940; WM 215 (40) 4, 30 July 1940. On 20 November 1940, R. Butler, Parliamentary Under-Secretary for Foreign Affairs, denied that the government had taken any steps to oblige Negrín to leave: *Hansard* (Commons), 5th Ser. Vol. 408, cs. 1954–5.
22. Alba had been authorised by Madrid to hire a retired London policeman at £6 a week to spy on the *émigré* republicans in London: Alba to Domingo de las Bárcenas, Under-Secretary at the Ministry of Foreign Affairs, 14 July and 31 August 1939: AGA AE *caja* 6914 (E-14. A 252). For Spanish complaints about Negrín's presence in London, see PRO FO 371/24527, C7501/7501/41; see also R. Rodríguez-Moñino Soriano, *La Misión Diplomática del XVII Duque de Alba: en la Embajada de España en Londres (1937–1945)* (Valencia: Castalia, 1971), pp. 16, 47–54.
23. Hoare to Foreign Office, 22 October 1940: PRO FO 371/24508, C11460/40/41; PRO CAB 65/10, WM 281 (40) 6, 1 November, WM 285 (40) 8, 8 November, WM 298 (40) 3, 28 November 1940; D. Smyth, 'The Politics of Asylum, Juan Negrín and the British Government in 1940' in R. Langhorne (ed.), *Diplomacy and Intelligence during the Second World War: Essays in Honour of F. H. Hinsley* (Cambridge University Press, 1985), pp. 127–32, 139–46.
24. Eden's words were quoted in Morrison's memorandum, 'Exit Permit Applications by Dr. Negrín', 12 December 1944: PRO CAB 66/59, WP (44) 725; see also Eden's memorandum, 'Application by Dr. Negrín for Exit Permit to France', 18 December 1944: PRO CAB 66/59, WP (44) 744; PRO CAB 65/44, WM 171 (44) 4, 18 December 1944; Foreign Office to Halifax, 1 January 1945: PRO FO 371/49553, Z8/18/41.
25. Garran's minute, 24 November, Roberts to Holman, 30 November 1944: PRO FO 371/39837, C16234/16234/41.

26. R. Martínez Nadal, *Antonio Torres y la Política Española del Foreign Office (1940–1944)* (Madrid: Casariego, 1989), pp. 73–8, 97–190.

27. *Ministerio de Asuntos Exteriores* to Alba, 17 April 1944: APG JE *leg. 3, exp. 4, no. 1*; Alba to Eden, 26 July 1944: AGA AE *caja* 6719 (H.9.1); Alba to *Ministerio de Asuntos Exteriores*, 22, 30 November 1944: APG JE *leg. 4, exp. 1, nos. 1, 2.*

28. Bowker to Roberts, 29 December 1944: PRO FO 371/49592, Z399/234/41.

29. Foreign Office Research Department, 'Spanish Republican Refugees: the Present Situation', 17 January 1945, PRO FO 371/49553, Z1065/18/4.

30. D. Stafford, *Britain and European Resistance, 1940–1945: a Survey of the Special Operations Executive, with Documents* (London: Macmillan, 1980), pp. 2, 42–4, 55–6, 212–24; Makins' minute, 9 June 1941: PRO FO 371/26890, C6339/3/41.

31. The SOE, known as SO2 until August 1941, was formed in July 1940 under Hugh Dalton's chairmanship; the SIS, also known as MI6, was answerable to Kim Philby, head of the Iberian subsection of SIS Section V (Counter-Intelligence). The coordination of intelligence gathering was undertaken at the Madrid Embassy by, amongst others, Brigadier Torr, the Military Attaché, Alan Hillgarth, the Naval Attaché, Tom Burns, the Press Attaché, the Economic Counsellor and the Blacklist Section: K. Benton, 'The ISOS Years: Madrid 1941–3', *Journal of Contemporary History*, 30, 3 (1995) 359–410.

32. D. MacLachlan, *Room 39: Naval Intelligence in Action* (London: Weidenfeld & Nicolson, 1968), pp. 194–6.

33. 'Supplemental Agreement No. 1', 16 November 1942: PRO HS 3/56.

34. In October Supreme Headquarters Allied Expeditionary Force (SHAEF) was asked to provide details on the 'disorder' in south-west France; SHAEF estimated that there were approximately 20 000 Spanish guerrilla fighters in the region: H. Footitt and J. Simmonds, *France 1943–1945* (Leicester University Press, 1988), pp. 171, 178.

35. Foreign Office brief, 'Situation on the Franco-Spanish Frontier', 9 November 1944: PRO FO 371/39818, C15535/10324/41; FO 371/39817 contains numerous reports on the border situation.

36. Colville to Lawford, 1 February 1940, Williams' minute, 25 December 1941: PRO FO 371/26964, C1111, 14354/1111/41; Roberts' minute, 22 August 1940: PRO FO 371/24516, C88971/113/41.

37. Foreign Office Research Department, 'Draft Proclamation by Miguel Maura on Spain's need for a Republic', 20 March, minutes by Hoyer Millar and Garran, 29 March 1945: PRO FO 371/49554, Z3996/18/41.

38. In addition, a number of generals were bribed to support the Allies' cause: D. Smyth, ' "Les Chevaliers de Saint-George": la Grande-Bretagne et la Corruption des Généraux Espagnols (1940–1942)', *Guerres Mondiales et Conflits Contemporains*, 162 (1991) 29–32, 39–41; D. Stafford, *Churchill and Secret Service* (London: John Murray, 1997), pp. 202–3, 229.

39. Strang's minute, 30 October, Foreign Office to Yencken, 4 November 1941: PRO FO 371/26898, C11958/33/41.

40. Hoare to Foreign Office, minutes by Williams, Roberts, Strang, 5, 6, 7 August 1941: PRO FO 371/26895, C8727/24/41; Williams' minute, 28 August 1941: PRO FO 371/26895, C1037/24/41.

41. Hoare to Eden, 13 May 1942: PRO FO 945, SP/42/23; Eden to Hoare, 3 June 1942: PRO FO 954, SP/42/26.

42. L Suárez Fernández, *España, Franco y la Segunda Guerra Mundial desde 1939 hasta 1945* (Madrid: Actas, 1997) p. 587. Hoare's blatant monarchism had already been commented on in a report by the *Dirección General de Seguridad* of 20 December 1943: Fundación Nacional Francisco Franco, *Documentos Inéditos*, IV, pp. 683–724.

43. J. Toquero, *Franco y Don Juan: la Oposición Monárquica al Franquismo* (Barcelona: Plaza & Janés, 1989), pp. 78, 83, 92.

44. Cadogan's minute, 27 March 1944: PRO FO 371/39736, C3668/225/41.

45. Roberts' minutes, 26 October, 12 November 1944, Cadogan to Churchill, 27 October 1944: PRO FO 371/39736, C15053/225/41; Roberts to Lisbon, 23 November 1944: PRO FO 371/39736, C15806/225/41; Alba, 'Informe Político', 30 November 1944: AGA AE *caja* 6718 (H.2).

46. Hoare to Foreign Office, 27 July 1944: PRO FO 371/39742, C10173/264/41.

47. Hoare's memorandum, 15 January 1942: PRO FO 371/31234, C514/220/41; Heine, *Oposición*, pp. 244–5.

48. Extensive reports by the *Dirección General de Seguridad* for the years 1940–1943 are found in *Documentos Inéditos para la Historia del Generalísimo Franco*, II-1, II-2, III, IV (Madrid: Azor, 1992, 1992, 1993, 1994).

49. J Doussinague, *España Tenía Razón (1939–1945)* (Madrid: Espasa-Calpe, 1950), pp. 315–27.

50. Hoare to Foreign Office, 31 January 1941: PRO FO 371/26904, C986/46/41; Jordana's memorandum, 21 March 1944: APG JE *leg.* 3, *exp.* 3, *no.* 3; Jordana to Hoare, 31 March 1944: Ministerio de Asuntos Exteriores (henceforth cited as MAE) *leg.* R1371, *exp.* 1. On 28 December 1944 Bowker reported that during a conversation between the Spanish Under-Secretary for Popular Education and the Embassy Press Attaché, the former had said that 'Lord Templewood knew as well as he did that the British Intelligence Service had been active in Spain throughout the war. All the proofs had fallen into the hands of the Spanish Government's hands and the Ambassador was committed up to the neck. Twenty-six wireless transmitters of British origin had been hauled in by the police, and were still in their safe keeping . . .': Bowker to Foreign Office, 2 January 1945: PRO FO 371/49587, Z355/233/41.

51. Franco to Alba, 18 October 1944, enclosure in Eden's memorandum, 'Spain'. 25 November 1944: PRO CAB 66/58, WP (44) 691.

52. Roberts' 'Brief for conversation with M. Massigli on Monday August 28th': PRO FO 371/39817, C11471/10324/41.

3   1945: Adjusting to Peace

1. Cabeza Sánchez-Albornoz, *Segunda República*, pp. 36–87; Garran, 'Spanish Republican Refugees: the Present Situation', 8 February 1945: PRO FO 371/49554, Z2035/18/41.

2. Gibaja, *Prieto*, pp. 273, 369.

3. Valle, *Instituciones*, pp. 84–7; Prieto defended his actions in Prieto, 'Puntualizaciones. Respuesta a una Carta Abierta', 1959: FPI ALJA 419–33. If the deputies of all the *Cortes* political parties of the Second Republic were included, the number surviving in late 1944 stood at 344; of the *Frente Popular* parties only 309 deputies survived, of whom 205 lived in exile and

104 in Spain: Suárez, *España, Franco y la Segunda Guerra Mundial*, p. 619. The 'complete failure' of the *Cortes* session did not escape the attention of the Spanish Ambassador in the USA, Juan Francisco de Cárdenas, who attributed it to differences between the exiles and their realisation that they did not enjoy the support of Spanish public opinion: Cárdenas to *Ministerio de Asuntos Exteriores*, 24 January 1945: APG JE *leg.* 5, *exp.* 1, *no.* 1.

4. A Fernández, 'Las Formaciones Políticas del Exilio' in Abellán, *El Exilio Español de 1939, 2, Guerra y Política*, pp. 149–50.

5. At a press conference on 8 May, the JEL delegation launched *An Appeal from the Spanish Committee of Liberation to the San Francisco Conference* detailing the close links between Francoism and fascism during World War II: Valle, *Instituciones*, pp. 91–102. According to Cárdenas, the appeal was so long that most delegates dropped it into the waste-paper basket and a shorter version had to be produced! As for the Spanish monarchists, they made no contribution to the San Francisco Conference, Julio López Oliván attending only because of his position in the Court of International Justice: Sanz Briz to *Ministerio de Asuntos Exteriores*, 7 May 1945: APG JE *leg.* 6, *exp.* 1, *no.* 4.

6. Cárdenas to *Ministerio de Asuntos Exteriores*, 8 May 1945: APG JE *leg.* 6, *exp.* 1, *no.* 1; Valle, *Instituciones*, pp. 106–8.

7. Alpert, 'Don Juan Negrín en Londres, 1940–1956' in Tusell *et al.*, *Oposición al Régimen de Franco*, I-1, p. 86. For Negrín's attitude to the Spanish problem at the beginning of 1945, see Irujo to Ziauritz, 9 January 1945: PRO FO 371/49582, Z396/119/41; Azcárate's *aide-mémoire* to Cadogan, 26 January 1945: PRO FO 371/49554, Z1525/18/41; Bateman to Foreign Office, 18 May 1945: PRO FO 371/49555, Z6569/18/4; Heine, *Oposición*, pp. 157–63.

8. The PCE's new position – its third – was made clear in a letter to Giral from Dolores Ibárruri, who had returned to France in March 1945: Ibárruri to Giral, 19 December 1945: Fundación Universitaria Española (henceforth cited as FUE) P 655.2. For evidence of Negrín's change of tactic, see Lizaso to Aguirre, 21 November 1944: PRO FO 371/39744, C17567/309/41; Negrín to Velao Nápoles, 29 December 1944: PRO FO 371/49553, Z69/18/41; intercept letter, 17 April 1945, on a meeting between Negrín and the libertarian National Committee in Toulouse: PRO FO 371/49555, Z5896/18/41.

9. Cabeza Sánchez-Albornoz, *Segunda República*, pp. 41–4; Valle, *Instituciones*, pp. 115–16. Álvarez del Vayo claims that he and Negrín were 'chiefly responsible' for Martínez Barrio's nomination as provisional president: J. Álvarez del Vayo, *The Last Optimist* (London: Putman, 1950), pp. 327–30.

10. Gibaja, *Prieto*, pp. 372–3; Heine, *Oposición*, pp. 168–70; Valle, *Instituciones*, pp. 113–23. Prieto explained to a friend in March 1946 that he did not join Giral's government because it was a 'serious obstacle' to a solution of the Spanish problem: I. Prieto, *Epistolario, 1941–1946* (Eibarko: Udala, 1991) pp. 78–81. In December 1945 Negrín returned to Britain where, apart from occasional visits to France, he remained for the rest of his life.

11. Bateman to Foreign Office, 1 December 1945: PRO FO 371/49558, Z13180/18/41. For the Spanish text of Giral's speech, see *La Habana*, 11 November 1945: FUE P 720.1.

12. Gibaja, *Prieto*, pp. 374–5; see also Tusell, *Oposición Democrática*, pp. 138–43; I. Prieto, 'Puntualizaciones. Respuesta a una Carta Abierta', 1959: FPI ALJA

419–33; Spanish Chargé d'Affaires, USA, to *Ministerio de Asuntos Exteriores*, 17 November 1945: APG JE *leg. 7, exp. 2, no. 1.*

13. S. Cabeza Sánchez-Albornoz, 'Posición de la República Española en el Exilio ante el Ingreso de España en la ONU', *Cuadernos de Historia Contemporánea*, 17 (1995) 150; Cabeza Sánchez-Albornoz, *Segunda República*, pp. 52–4.
14. L. M. Anson, *Don Juan* (Barcelona: Plaza & Janés, 1994), pp. 223–6; Kindelán, *Relaciones*, pp. 61, 73–5.
15. Norton to Eden, Berne 27 March 1945: PRO FO 371/49629, Z4041/1484/41; the Spanish text is in Sainz, *Reinado*, pp. 324–5.
16. De la Cierva, *Don Juan de Borbón*, p. 389.
17. Heine, *Oposición*, pp. 294–5; Kindelán, *Relaciones*, pp. 229–38. Alba's farewell speech to the Embassy staff is in Santa Cruz to *Ministerio de Asuntos Exteriores*, 25 October 1945: AGA AE *caja* 6720 (H.2). Following Don Alfonso's resignation Kindelán effectively assumed the representation of Don Juan's cause in Spain.
18. Lequerica to Don Juan, 2 April 1945: L. de Llera and J. Andrés-Gallego, *La España de Posguerra: un Testimonio* (Madrid: Consejo Superior de Investigaciones Científicas, 1992), pp. 114–15; Lequerica to Ambassadors, Chargés d'Affaires, Consul Generals, etc., 7 April 1945: APG JE *leg. 5, exp. 4, no. 1*; Lequerica's circular, 13 April 1945: AGA AE *caja* 6845 (A-461). For the reply of 22 April 1945 which the Vizconde de Rocamora, Head of Don Juan's Household, wrote to Goicoechea on Don Juan's behalf, see Sainz, *Reinado*, pp. 333–6.
19. Portero, *Franco Aislado*, pp. 62–3; Tusell, *Franco y los Católicos*, pp. 144–6.
20. De la Cierva, *Don Juan de Borbón*, pp. 459–61; Sainz, *Reinado*, pp. 364–8; Suárez, *Francisco Franco*, IV, pp. 62–3.
21. Sainz, *Reinado*, pp. 336–7.
22. Preston, *Franco*, pp. 527–9; Bowker to Foreign Office, 27 March 1945: PRO FO 371/49587, Z4137/233/41; Mallet to Harvey, 4 August 1945: PRO FO 371/49589, Z9612/233/41.
23. Kindelán, *Relaciones*, pp. 261–5.
24. C. Fernández, *Tensiones Militares Durante el Franquismo* (Barcelona: Plaza & Janés, 1985), p. 124.
25. Gil-Robles, *Monarquía*, pp. 136–7; Heine, *Oposición*, 328–9; Sainz, *Reinado*, pp. 159–61; Suárez, *Francisco Franco*, IV, p. 66.
26. The election of a Labour government in Britain had at first raised ANFD hopes of greater British support for their cause; see, for example, the ANFD declaration of September 1945: FPI AE 637–5.
27. Heine, *Oposición*, p. 329.
28. Ibid., pp. 327–8; Sainz, *Reinado*, pp. 170–3; Tusell, *Oposición Democrática*, pp. 152–61.
29. This paragraph is taken from Dunthorn, 'The Prieto–Gil-Robles meeting of October 1947', 53–4.
30. Mallet to Bevin, 22 November 1945: PRO FO 371/49629, Z13177/14841; Heine, *Oposición*, p. 330; Toquero, *Franco y Don Juan*, pp. 198–200.
31. The PSOE-in-France believed that the communists could be better controlled within the ANFD and were, in any case, a force that could not be ignored: O'Malley's memorandum, undated: PRO FO 371/67874, Z1945/20/41.

32. C. and J. Martínez Cobo, *¿República? ¿Monarquía? En busca del Consenso. Intrahistoria del PSOE. Volumen II (1946–1954)* (Barcelona: Plaza & Janés, 1992) pp. 60–1; Heine, *Oposición*, pp. 228–31, 354–8.

33. Garran, 'Draft Directive for B.B.C. Broadcasts to Spain', 13 February 1945: PRO FO 371/49592, Z2147/234/41.

34. Minutes by Garran, Hoyer Millar and Cadogan, Eden's comment: 28, 29, 20 March 1945: PRO FO 954, SP/45/9; Eden to Nicolson, 4 April 1945: PRO FO 954, SP/45/11.

35. Sloan's minutes, 20, 25 August 1945: PRO FO 371/49613, Z9628/537/41, 371/49555, Z9740/18/41; Attlee's note, 28 August, Hoyer Millar's minute, Cadogan's memorandum, Bevin's minute, 1, 8, 10 September 1945: PRO FO 371/49556, Z10747/18/41. In May 1945 Santa Cruz, the Spanish Chargé d'Affaires in London, reported that Negrín was living a life of luxury beyond the reach of even the Presidents of the Council of Ministers of the regime which he attacked so much: Santa Cruz, 'Informe Político', 26 May 1945: AGA AE *caja* 6720 (H.2).

36. Minutes by Hoyer Millar, Garran, Harvey, 30, 31 August 1945: PRO FO 371/49555, Z10011/18/41.

37. Bateman to Foreign Office, 1 December, minutes by Sloan and Garran, 4, 6 December 1945: PRO FO 371/49558, Z13180/18/41.

38. Mallet to Foreign Office, 6 August 1945: PRO FO 371/49589, Z9328/233/41; Mallet to Harvey, 17 September, Mallet to Foreign Office, 6 October 1945: PRO FO 371/49590, Z11330, 11432/233/41.

39. Garran, 'Draft Directive for B.B.C. Broadcasts to Spain', 13 February 1945: PRO FO 371/49592, Z2147/234/41.

40. Bowker to Foreign Office, 16 June 1945: PRO FO 371/49593, Z7208/234/41; Mallet to Foreign Office, 10 September 1945: PRO FO 371/49594, Z0572/234/41; Grisewood to Harvey, 16 October, Garran's minute, 27 October, Woolf to Noel Baker, 22 November 1945: PRO FO 371/49595, Z11818, 12051, 13312/234/41.

41. Irujo's letters, 13, 19 September, minutes by Sloan, Hoyer Millar, Harvey, Cadogan, 26, 27, 28 September, minutes by Sloan, Hoyer Millar, Harvey, 28 September, 2 October 1945: PRO FO 371/49556, Z10807, 10910, 11085/18/41; Irujo's letter, 9 October, Garran's minute, 13 October, Pierson Dixon to Lizaso, 27 October 1945: PRO FO 371/49557, Z11555, 12974/18/41. British refusal to have any dealings with the exiled republicans did not prevent routine Spanish complaints about the presence of republicans in London: see Bárcenas to *Ministerio de Asuntos Exteriores*, 12 December 1945: APG JE *leg.* 7, *exp.* 3, no. 1; Bárcenas to Sargent, 19 December 1945: AGA AE *caja* 7281 (Q.18.j); Santa Cruz, 'Informe Político', 25 April 1945: AGA AE *caja* 6720 (H.2); Alba to *Ministerio de Asuntos Exteriores*, 19 September 1945: APG JE *leg.* 6, *exp.* 5, *no.* 1. Martín Artajo instructed Alba to remind influential people in London of what various prominent republicans stood for and of the need to counter Negrín's influence over leading members of the Labour Party: Martín Artajo to Alba, 22 August 1945: APG JE *leg.* 6, *exp.* 4, *no.* 2.

42. The phrase in English replaced the original Spanish – 'a desencadenar una acción violenta para el logro de sus derechos y aspiraciones' – which was crossed out.

43. Giral to 'Excelencies', 17 December 1945: FUE P 655.2.
44. Garran's draft letter, 10 December 1945: PRO FO 371/60333, Z9/9/41.
45. PRO CAB 65/49, WM 6 (45) 4, 5 January 1945. As Eden expected, once rumours reached the Spanish government of Prieto's intended visit to Britain, clarification was sought from the Foreign Office: Alba's *aide mémoire*, 16 January 1945: AGA AE *caja* 7281 (Q.18.i).
46. Sloan's minute, 4 December 1945: PRO FO 371/49558, Z13180/18/41.
47. Hoyer Millar's minute, 24 August 1945: PRO FO 371/49589, Z9816/233/41.
48. Anson, *Don Juan*, pp. 218–23; de la Cierva, *Don Juan de Borbón*, p. 964; Suárez, *España, Franco y la Segunda Guerra Mundial*, pp. 624–5. While there is no doubting Don Juan's contacts with A. Dulles (see Sainz, *Reinado*, p. 269), there is no reference to the Yalta plan in Don Juan's published correspondence; Anson's claim is dismissed in Tusell, *Juan Carlos*, pp. 88, 104–5, and in S Carrillo, *Juez y Parte. 15 Retratos Españoles* (Barcelona: Plaza & Janés, 1996), pp. 177–8.
49. Bowker to Foreign Office, 24, 27 March 1945: PRO FO 371/49629, Z3919/1484/41, 371/49611, Z4225/537/41; minutes by Garran, Hoyer Millar, Sargent, 22, 29 March, 2, 3, 6 April 1945: PRO FO 371/49629, Z3742, 4141, 4138/1484/41.
50. Mallet to Foreign Office, 22 September, minutes by Sloan, Garran, Hoyer Millar, 24, 26, 27 September 1945: PRO FO 371/49590, Z10932/233/41.
51. Mallet to Foreign Office, 22, 23 August 1945: PRO FO 371/49589, Z9816/233/41, 371/49590, Z9877/233/41; Mallet to Bevin, 3 December 1945: PRO FO 425/423, Z13504/18/41.
52. Torr, 'Conversations with Generals', 19, 20 January 1945: PRO FO 371/49587, Z1906/233/41.
53. Garran's minute, 1 November 1945: PRO FO 371/49629, Z12200/1484/41.
54. Bowker to Foreign Office, 3 May, Garran's minute, 23 May 1945: PRO FO 371/49611, Z5974/537/41.
55. Mallet to Foreign Office, 4 November, minutes by Sloan, Garran, Hoyer Millar, Harvey, 4, 6, 15, 16 November, Harvey to Mallet, 27 November 1945: PRO FO 371/49591, Z12196/233/41.
56. Foreign Office Research Department, 'José María Gil Robles', 24 January 1945: PRO FO 371/60374, Z7448/41/41.
57. Harvey's minute, 27 September 1945: PRO FO 371/49629, Z10593/1484/41; minutes by Garran, Hoyer Millar, Harvey, Bevin's comment, 21, 22, 23, 28 November 1945: PRO FO 371/49629, Z 2488/1484/41.
58. British Embassy, Madrid, to Spanish Ministry of Foreign Affairs, 27 December 1946: PRO FO 371/67867, Z77/3/41.
59. Mallet to Bevin, 3 December 1945: PRO FO 425/423, Z13504/18/G.
60. The reliability of Mallet's report is open to doubt, however, as he seems to confuse the ANFD with the executive committee of the PSOE: Mallet to Bevin, 6 October 1945: PRO FO 371/49590, Z11644/233/41.
61. Bowker, 'Report on Leading Personalities in Spain', 17 July 1945: PRO FO 371/49658A, Z8666/8666/41; Burns' report, 18 October 1945: PRO FO 425/423, Z12195/18/41.
62. Mallet to Foreign Office, 11 October 1945: PRO FO 371/49590, Z11640/233/41; Mallet to Bevin, 'Basis for Discussion proposed by the Monarchist Delegation', 22 November 1945: PRO FO 425/423, Z13277/1484/41.

63. Sloan's minute, 4 December, minutes by Garran and Hoyer Millar, 5 December, Cadogan's minute, 7 December 1945: PRO FO 371/49629, Z13177/1484/41.
64. Mallet to Harvey, 5 December 1945: PRO FO 371/49614, Z13581/537/41; minutes by Sloan, Garran, Hoyer Millar, 14, 15, 16 December 1945: PRO FO 371/49614, Z13581/537/41; Hoyer Millar's minute, 13 December 1945: PRO FO 371/49614, Z13730/537/41.
65. Harvey's minute, 11 December 1945: PRO FO 371/49591, Z13782/233/41.
66. Harvey's minute, 31 December 1945: PRO FO 371/60349, Z139/36/41.
67. At the same interview Mallet spoke to Martín Artajo about five 'respectable Spaniards' arrested in December 1944 for working for a republican-monarchist coalition: Mallet to Foreign Office, 22, 25, 28 September, 3 October 1945: PRO FO 371/49576, Z10933, 11097, 11193, 11351/89/41.
68. Sloan's minute, 24 September 1945: PRO FO 371/49576, Z10933/89/41.
69. Mallet to Hoyer Millar, 4 October 1945: PRO FO 371/49577, Z11968/89/41.
70. Garran's minute, 15 November 1945: PRO FO 371/49577, Z12888/89/41.
71. Mallet to Foreign Office, 27 July 1945: PRO FO 371/49617, Z8861/829/41; Mallet to Foreign Office, 14 August 1945: PRO FO 371/49590, Z9890/233/41.
72. *Hansard*, 5th Ser. Vol. 416, cs. 2314–15. Martín Artajo duly protested that Bevin's attitude 'contrasted strongly with the spirit of reciprocal tolerance and understanding which characterised Anglo-Spanish relations, notwithstanding the internal political vicissitudes of each country': a copy of the Note, undated, is in MAE *leg.* R2222, *exp.* 49.
73. *DBPO, Series 1*, I, no. 194, p. 426, no. 195, pp. 434–5, no. 603, p. 1274.
74. *Hansard* (Commons), 5th Ser. Vol. 413, c. 296.
75. Ellis-Rees, 'Anglo-Spanish Economic Relations, 1944', 3 October 1944: PRO FO 425/422, C13896/3/41; Mallet to Foreign Office, 6 October 1945: PRO FO 371/49590, Z11432/233/41. See also Foreign Office memorandum, 'The Effect of our External Financial Position on our Foreign Policy', 30 March 1945: PRO FO 185/1756, UE 813/813/53.
76. Hoyer Millar's minute, 15 October 1945: PRO FO 371/49660, Z11591/11591/41.
77. Bevin's memorandum 'The Supply of Equipment to Spain', 11 October 1945: PRO CAB 129/3, CP (45) 220; PRO CAB 128/1, CM 45 (45) 3, 23 October 1945; Sloan's minute, 15 November 1945: PRO FO 371/49617, Z12584/829/41.
78. PRO CAB 121/129: COS (45) 142, 1 June 1945; 'Security in the Western Mediterranean and the Eastern Atlantic: Report by the Post-Hostilities Planning Staff', 19 May 1945: PRO CAB 121/129: PHP (45) 6 (0) (Final).
79. PRO CAB 121/129: P.H.P. (44) 24 (0) (Final), 4 November 1944; C.O.S. (44) 966 (0), 'Situation in Tangier', 13 November 1944; Bevin's memorandum, 'Tangier', 3 August 1945: PRO CAB 66/67, CP (45) 93.
80. The Franco-Spanish treaty of 1912 had provided for the establishment of a French protectorate over the whole of Morocco and the 'leasing' of Northern Morocco to Spain; the international status of the Tangier Zone was defined by the Anglo-French-Spanish Tangier Statute of 18 December 1923 (modified in 1928). For the background to the establishment of the Tangier international zone, see Eden's memorandum, 'The Future of Tangier', 11 April 1945, CAB 66/64, WP (45) 236.

81. Eden's memorandum, 'The Future of Tangier', 11 April 1945, CAB 66/64, WP (45) 236; Foreign Office minute, 'Spain', 13 July 1945: PRO FO 371/49613, Z9237/537/41; see also P. Brundu, *Ostracismo e Realpolitik: gli Alleati e la Spagna Franchista negli Anni del Dopoguerra* (Università di Cagliari: Pubblicazioni della Facoltà di Scienze Politiche – Instituto Storico Politico, C.E.L.T. Editrice, 1984), pp. 49–50.

82. The Final Act of the Conference, 31 August 1945, incorporated two declarations – one Soviet and the other Anglo-French-American – making clear their disagreement over Spain's participation in the interim administration of the Tangier International Zone: 'Acte Final de la Conférence tenue à Paris au mois d'août 1945', 'Accord Franco-Britannique', PRO FO 371/49355, Z11183/16/28. Accounts of the meetings are in PRO FO 371/49352–3.

83. According to Hoyer Millar, Franco had 'a skin like a rhinoceros': Hoyer Millar's minute, 3 September 1945: PRO FO 371/49613, Z10105/537/41.

84. Santa Cruz to Lequerica, 17 March 1945: APG JE *leg. 5, exp. 3, no.* 2; Santa Cruz to Lequerica, 24 April 1945: APG JE *leg. 5, exp. 4, no.* 2; Bowker to Eden, 12 June 1945, PRO FO 425/423, Z7338/233/41.

85. J. Tusell, *Carrero: la Eminencia Gris del Régimen de Franco* (Madrid: Ediciones Temas de Hoy, 1993), pp. 112–18, 130.

86. Bárcenas to *Ministerio de Asuntos Exteriores*, 12 December 1945: APG JE *leg. 7, exp. 3, no.* 1.

87. Mallet to Foreign Office, 6 October 1945: PRO FO 371/49590, Z11432/233/41.

4   1946: International Confrontation

1. Even so, present in the large party welcoming Giral on his arrival in Paris on 8 February 1946 was a delegation from the French Constituent Assembly: Duff Cooper to Foreign Office, 9 February 1946: PRO FO 371/60333, Z1258/9/41.

2. Republican disappointment at Britain's refusal to recognise Giral did not escape the Spanish Foreign Ministry's notice: Sousa to *Ministerio de Asuntos Exteriores*, 29 August 1946: APG JE *leg. 9, exp. 2, no.* 1.

3. The Giral government was recognised by Poland, Romania, Yugoslavia, Hungary, Czechoslovakia, Bulgaria and Albania. For Giral's continuing attempts to gain the recognition of the major powers, see FUE P 675.5.

4. 'Mémorandum présenté à la sous-Commission du Conseil de Sécurité de la ONU par le Gouvernement Républicain Espagnol', 9 May 1946: FUE 712–3. On 24 May Giral presented a second memorandum.

5. 'Una nota del Gobierno Giral a los Cuatro Grandes y a la O.N.U.', n.d.: FUE P 675.5; see also Harvey to Hoyer Millar, Paris, 9 October 1946: PRO FO 371/60337, Z8720/9/41; Cabeza Sánchez-Albornoz, *Segunda República*, pp. 98–105, 109–13.

6. Ibid., pp. 116–19; Heine, *Oposición*, pp. 370–1.

7. Gibaja, *Prieto*, pp. 320–3; Martínez Cobo, *¿República? ¿Monarquía?*, pp. 82–6, 96–101, 347–8; Tusell, *Oposición Democrática*, pp. 146–8. Francis Noel-Baker, Labour MP, quoted Llopis as saying: 'We can only put forward the idea of a Republic, but we should not put obstacles in the way of another solution

brought about by legal means': Duff Cooper to Bevin, 3 June 1946: PRO FO 371/60335, Z5223/9/41.

8. For the text of the ANFD manifesto, see Nadal, *Todos contra Franco*, pp. 107–9; see also Martínez Cobo, *¿República? ¿Monarquía?*, pp. 75–7, 102–5; S. Vilar, *Historia del Anti-Franquismo 1939–1975* (Barcelona: Plaza & Janés, 1984), pp. 106–11.

9. J. Aróstegui, 'Nuevas Aportaciones al Estudio de la Oposición en el Exterior: Largo Caballero y la Política de "Transición y Plebiscito"', in García Delgado, *Primer Franquismo*, pp. 328–48.

10. Gibaja, *Prieto*, pp. 320, 322–3.

11. Mallet to Bevin, 31 December 1945, 7 January 1946: PRO FO 371/60372, Z41, 243/41/41; Portero, *Franco Aislado*, pp. 184–5.

12. Kindelán, *Relaciones*, pp. 79–82.

13. O'Malley to Foreign Office, 4 January, Mallet to Foreign Office, 7, 14, 18 January 1946: PRO FO 371/60372, Z145, 243, 475, 593/41/41.

14. De la Cierva, *Don Juan de Borbón*, pp. 470–1; Gil-Robles, *Monarquía*, pp. 152, 185–6; Sainz, *Reinado*, pp. 366–8.

15. During a brief stop-over in London Don Juan saw George VI and, among other important figures, the exiled diplomat and historian, Madariaga: O'Malley to Foreign Office, 10 February 1946: PRO FO 371/60375, Z1515/45/41.

16. Gil-Robles, *Monarquía*, pp. 158, 163; Kindelán, *Relaciones*, pp. 283–4; Sainz, *Reinado*, pp. 291–6.

17. Gil-Robles, *Monarquía*, pp. 166–9; Tusell, *Oposición Democrática*, pp. 116–20.

18. The text of the *Bases* is in Gil-Robles, *Monarquía*, pp. 383–5.

19. Even Kindelán thought they needed a 'democratic touch': Kindelán, *Relaciones*, p. 304.

20. Mallet to Foreign Office, 4 February 1946: PRO FO 371/60375, Z1078/45/41; Martínez Cobo, *¿República? ¿Monarquía?*, pp. 62–4.

21. Nadal, *Todos contra Franco*, pp. 103–6, 114–16.

22. Ibid., pp. 119–31; Suárez, *Franco*, IV, pp. 128–31.

23. According to Gil-Robles and Sainz Rodríguez, Santamaría's first name was Francisco, but according to Heine and Suárez Fernández, and a Foreign Office minute of 1948, it was Vicente: Foreign Office Research Department, 'The Alianza Nacional de Fuerzas Democráticas', 2 December 1948: PRO FO 371/73360A, Z10440/1027/41.

24. O'Malley's memorandum, undated: PRO FO 371/67874, Z1945/20/41; Gil-Robles, *Monarquía*, p. 191. See also Dunthorn, 'The Prieto–Gil-Robles meeting of October 1947', 55–6.

25. Gil-Robles, *Monarquía*, p. 386.

26. Ibid., pp. 192–5.

27. V. Alba, *Historia de la Resistencia Antifranquista 1939–1955* (Barcelona: Planeta, 1978), pp. 238–45; C. Mera, *Guerra, Exilio y Cárcel de un Anarcosindicalista* (Paris: Ruedo Ibérico, 1976), pp. 278–81.

28. Kindelán, *Relaciones*, pp. 292–4.

29. Mallet to Foreign Office, 13 December 1946: PRO FO 371/60379, Z10512/45/41. See also Malley's 'Conversation with General Aranda', 2 December 1946: PRO FO 371/60374, Z10279/41/41; Mallet to Foreign Office, 16, 23 December 1946: PRO FO 371/60379, Z10511, 10727/45/41; Howard to Foreign

Office, 4 January 1947: PRO FO 371/67874, Z191/20/41; Nadal, *Todos contra Franco*, pp. 189–216.

30. Howard to Foreign Office, 14 January 1947: PRO FO 371/67874, Z560/20/41.

31. P. Brundu, 'L'Espagne Franquiste et la Politique Étrangère de la France au Lendemain de la Deuxième Guerre Mondiale', *Relations Internationales*, 50 (1987) 167; P. Martínez Lillo, *Una Introducción al Estudio de las Relaciones Hispano-Francesas (1945–1951)* (Madrid: Fundación Juan March, 1985), pp. 13–14.

32. See, for example, de Gaulle's press conference of 12 October 1945: C. de Gaulle, *Discours et Messages: dans l'Attente Février 1946–Avril 1958* (Paris: Plon, 1970), pp. 639–41.

33. Brundu, 'L'Espagne Franquiste', 168–9; A. Dulphy, 'La Politique de la France à l'égard de l'Espagne Franquiste 1945–1949', *Revue d'Histoire Moderne et Contemporaine*, XXXV (1988) 124–5; Martínez Lillo, *Introducción*, pp. 13–20; P. Martínez Lillo, 'Una Aproximación al Estudio de las Relaciones Bilaterales Hispano–Francesas durante la Posguerra. El "Affaire" Fronterizo en la Perspectiva del Quai d'Orsay (1946–1948)', *Revista de Estudios Internacionales*, 6, 3 (1985) 588–9; R. Rodríguez Cruz, 'Relaciones Franco–Españolas al Término de la Segunda Guerra Mundial: de la Tirantez al Cierre de la Frontera', in *Españoles y Franceses en la Primera Mitad del Siglo XX* (Madrid: Consejo Superior de Investigaciones Científicas, 1986), pp. 236–41.

34. The text of the French note of 12 December 1945 is in PRO FO 371/49614, Z13588/537/41.

35. Noel-Baker to Attlee, Attlee's comment, 21, 22 December 1946: PRO PREM 8/353.

36. Foreign Office to Paris, 21 December 1945: PRO FO 371/49614, Z13532/537/41; see also Hoyer-Millar's minute, 13 December 1945: PRO FO 371/49614, Z13730/537/41.

37. Assemblée Nationale Constituante: *Journal Officiel de la République Française, Débats de l'Assemblée Constituante*, 1, pp. 3–4; 2, pp. 57–64; 3, pp. 81–103, 107; P. Martínez Lillo, 'La Perspectiva de la Ruptura Diplomática con la España Franquista en la Política Francesa (Noviembre–Diciembre de 1945–Enero de 1946)' in Tusell *et al.*, *Régimen de Franco*, II, pp. 371–80.

38. Foreign Office minute, 'Extract from the Secretary of State's Record of his conversation with Monsieur Bidault on 1st. February'; Foreign Office to Paris, 2 February 1946, 'Record of a Talk between the Secretary of State, M. Bidault and M. Massigli on Friday, February 1st, 1946'; Foreign Office to Madrid, 3 February 1946: PRO FO 371/60350, Z1296, 1062, 1218/36/41.

39. Garran's minute, 15 January, Mallet to Foreign Office, 18 January 1946: PRO FO 371/60372, Z446, 625/41/41.

40. Foreign Office to Mallet, 26 January 1946: PRO FO 371/60373, Z886/41/41.

41. Mallet to Foreign Office, 4 February, minutes by Sloan and Garran, 6 February 1946: PRO FO 371/60375, Z1078/45/41.

42. Mallet to Foreign Office, 7 January, minutes by Garran, Harvey, Cadogan, Bevin's comment, 8, 9 January, Foreign Office to Madrid, 10 January 1946: PRO FO 371/60372, Z244, 373/41/41; Foreign Office to Lisbon, 3 February 1946: PRO FO 371/60373, Z1055/41/41; PRO CAB 128/5, CM 11(46)4, 4 February 1946.

43. Harvey's minute, 7 February 1946: PRO FO 371/60350, Z1297/36/41.

44. Mallet to Bevin, 15 February 1946: PRO FO 371/60375, Z1717/45/41; Hoyer Millar's minute, 15 February 1946: PRO FO 371/60352, Z2124/36/41; Harvey's minute, 18 February 1946: PRO FO 371/60350, Z1708/36/41.
45. *Débats de l'Assemblée Constituante*, 3, p. 452.
46. In fact, the Spanish government anticipated the French move and closed the border on 27 February. The French *communiqué* on the closure of the border is in Duff Cooper to Foreign Office, 28 February 1946: PRO FO 371/60421, Z1932/619/41.
47. Attlee to Bevin, 26 February 1946: PRO FO 800/504, Sp/46/5; PRO CAB 128/5, CM 18(46)2, 25 February 1946; *Confidential Annexes and No Circulation Records* to CM 18(46)2 in PRO CAB 128/7.
48. The French note of 27 February 1946 is in PRO FO 371/60351, Z1868/36/41.
49. Hoyer Millar, 'Minutes of a Meeting held at the Foreign Office on the 28th February to consider the possible consequences of a rupture of relations with Spain', 2 March 1946: PRO FO 371/60351, Z1974/36/41.
50. Foreign Office to Paris, 2 March 1946: PRO PREM 8/353; British objections to the French proposal were summarised in Hoyer Millar's memorandum, 'Spain', 3 March 1946: PRO FO 371/60352, Z2103/36/41.
51. Foreign Office to Paris, 2 March 1946: PRO PREM 8/353.
52. On US–Spanish relations, see J. Cortada, *Two Nations over Time: Spain and the United States, 1776–1977* (London: Greenwood Press, 1978); J. Edwards, *Anglo-American Relations and the Franco Question 1945–1955* (Oxford: Clarendon Press, 1999); B. Liedtke, *Embracing a Dictatorship. US Relations with Spain* (London: Macmillan, 1998); see also Brundu, *Ostracismo*, pp. 19–25.
53. Dunn's memorandum, 19 December, Acheson to Caffery, 22 December 1945: United States Department of State: *Foreign Relations of the United States, 1945*, V (Washington DC: Government Printing House, 1967), pp. 701–4, 706–7 (cited henceforth as FRUS); Cárdenas to *Ministerio de Asuntos Exteriores*, 20 December 1945: APG JE *leg.* 7, *exp.* 3, *no.* 1.
54. Bevin's comment, 31 December 1945: PRO FO 371/60349, Z184/36/41.
55. Halifax to Foreign Office, 19 January 1946: PRO FO 371/60349, Z601/36/41.
56. Foreign Office to Washington, 26 January 1946: PRO FO 371/60349, Z601/36/41.
57. Halifax to Foreign Office, 28 January 1946: PRO FO 371/60349, Z882/36/41.
58. Hoyer-Millar's minute, 24 November 1945: PRO FO 371/49558, Z13279/18/41.
59. Washington to Foreign Office, 25 February, Bevin to Attlee, 27 February 1946: PRO PREM 8/354; Foreign Office to Washington, 27 February 1946: PRO FO 371/60351, Z1801/36/41; PRO CAB 128/5, CM 20 (46) 1, 4 March 1946.
60. Foreign Office to Moscow, Lisbon, Tangier, Madrid, 4 March 1946: PRO FO 371/60352, Z2128/36/41.
61. Bidault to Duff Cooper, 12 March 1946: PRO FO 371/60353, Z2518/36/41.
62. Hoyer Millar's minute, 13 March, Bevin to Duff Cooper, 19 March 1946: PRO FO 371/60353, Z2420, 2736/36/41.
63. Duff Cooper to Foreign Office, 25 March, Foreign Office to Paris, 6 April 1946: PRO FO 371/60354, Z2886, 2887, 2968, 3140/36/41; Duff Cooper to Foreign Office, 11 April 1946: PRO FO 371/60355, Z3566/36/41.
64. *United Nations Official Records of the General Assembly: First Session, Part 1, 1946*, annex 9, pp. 584–5 (cited henceforth as UNGA); *United Nations Security Council. Official Records. First Year. First Series, Supplement No. 2*, annexes

3a, 3b, pp. 54–5 (cited henceforth as UNSC). UN attention to the 'Spanish question' in 1946 is comprehensively covered in A. Lleonart y Anselem and F. Castiella y Maiz, *España y ONU (1945–1946)*. *Documentación básica, sistematizada y anotada* (Madrid: Consejo Superior de Investigaciones Científicas, 1978).

65. *UNSC, First Year. First Series*, pp. 155–67.
66. Ibid., pp. 180–5. The British and American governments wanted the Spanish question referred to the General Assembly without any Security Council recommendations because, as voting in the General Assembly was by two-thirds majority, both governments were confident that any resolution calling for action against Spain would be defeated; for the same reason, the USSR objected to the General Assembly having any say in the matter. Cadogan's speech in the Security Council was appreciated in the Spanish Foreign Ministry: *Ministerio de Asuntos Exteriores* to Bárcenas, 19 April 1946: APG JE *leg*. 8, *exp*. 3, *no*. 1.
67. Kennan to Byrnes, 3 February 1946: *FRUS, 1946, V* (Washington DC: Government Printing House, 1969), pp. 1033–6; *DBPO, Series I*, VI (London: HMSO, 1991), *no*. 78, pp. 297–301; Foreign Office to Paris, 2 March 1946: PRO PREM 8/353.
68. *UNSC, First Year. First Series*, 2, pp. 311–25; Lleonart and Castiella, *España y ONU (1945–1946)*, pp. 84–98; 'The Report of the Sub-Committee on the Spanish Question Appointed by the Security Council on 29 April 1946' is in PRO FO 371/60360, Z5299/36/41. Reports of the Security Council Sub-Committee's meetings are also in PRO FO 371/60358, Z4934/36/41.
69. *UNSC, First Year. First Series*, 2, pp. 325–446; Lleonart and Castiella, *España y ONU (1945–1946)*, pp. 97–100, 105–9, 130–97; *Documents on Australian Foreign Policy 1937–1949, IX, 1946* (Canberra: Department of Foreign Affairs and Trade – Australian Government Publishing Service, 1989), pp. 531–5, 546–8, 556–9.
70. Garran, 'Policy towards Spain', 7 June 1946: PRO FO 371/60360, Z5375/36/41; see also Garran, 'Report on a visit to Spain', 4 June 1946: PRO FO 371/60378, Z5378/45/41.
71. Mallet, 'Spain', 11 June 1946: PRO FO 371/60377, Z5305/45/41.
72. Sargent's minute, 29 June 1946: PRO FO 371/60377, Z5305/45/41.
73. Hoyer Millar's minute, 26 July 1946: PRO FO 371/60378, Z6771/45/41.
74. Sloan's minute, 28 August 1946: PRO FO 371/60363, Z7535/36/41.
75. A. Cordier and W. Foote, *Public Papers of the Secretaries-General of the United Nations. Volume 1: Trygve Lie 1946–1953* (London & New York: Columbia University Press, 1969), p. 64. On 6 November 1946 the Security Council formally removed Spain from its agenda, thus allowing the General Assembly to consider it: Lleonart and Castiella, *España y ONU (1945–1946)*, pp. 215–39.
76. Foreign Office to Madrid, 11 November 1946: PRO FO 371/60365, Z9415/36/41; Cadogan to Foreign Office, 19 November 1946: PRO FO 371/60367, Z9803/36/41.
77. *UNGA: First Session, Part II, 1946*, pp. 1161–222, annex 70, 1536–8; Lleonart and Castiella, *España y ONU (1945–1946)*, pp. 228–35, 259–60, 294–6, 342–9.
78. The text of the Resolution is found in Ahmad, *Britain, Franco Spain, and the Cold War*, pp. 236–8.
79. Protest letters against Franco Spain, 1945–46, are found in PRO FO

371/60349, Z185/36/41, FO 371/60355, Z3379/36/41 and in AGA AE *caja* 6850 (*signaturas* 962 (a) (b)).

80. Alba to *Ministerio de Asuntos Exteriores*, 28 September 1945: AGA AE, *caja* 6720 (H.2). Protest letters over the arrests of Zapirain and Alvarez are found in PRO FO 371/60324, Z1039, 1134, 1256, 1318, 1319, 1320/7/41 and in AGA AE, *caja* 7281 (Q.18.j).

81. *Hansard* (Commons), 5th Ser. Vol. 413, c. 296.

82. H. Berrington, *Backbench Opinion in the House of Commons 1945–55* (Oxford: Pergamon, 1973), pp. 56–9; A. Bullock, *Ernest Bevin: Foreign Secretary, 1945–1951* (London: Heinemann, 1983), pp. 70–1.

83. *Hansard* (Commons), 5th Ser. Vol. 416, cs. 2314–15, Vol. 418, c. 142. The Spanish government's protest at Bevin's statement of 5 December 1945 is in MAE *leg.* R2222, *exp.* 49.

84. *DBPO, Series I*, VII, no. 26i.

85. *Hansard* (Commons), 5th Ser. Vol. 420, cs. 17–19.

86. Ibid., Vol. 423, c. 2035.

87. Ahmad, *Britain, Franco Spain, and the Cold War*, pp. 195–6, 201–9.

88. *Hansard* (Commons), 5th Ser. Vol. 427, cs. 747–58, 1604–9.

89. The text is in Foreign Office to Madrid, 6 November 1946: PRO FO 371/60365, Z9337/36/41. For correspondence between the TUC and the Prime Minister in 1946, see: 'Draft paper covering the correspondence between the TUC and the Prime Minister', 11 September 1946: PRO FO 371/60364, Z8056/36/41.

90. Berrington, *Backbench Opinion*, pp. 54–8; Bullock, *Ernest Bevin*, pp. 70–1; H. Pelling, *The Labour Governments, 1945–51* (London: Macmillan, 1984), pp. 139–41.

91. Bárcenas to *Ministerio de Asuntos Exteriores*, 28 July 1946: APG JE *leg.* 9, *exp.* 1, no. 1.

92. 'Asunto C.N.T.', 20 October 1945: MAE *leg.* R2224, *exp.* 14; see also Nadal, *Todos contra Franco*, pp. 60–7.

93. *Jefatura Superior de Policía de Madrid*, 27 May 1946: MAE *leg.* R2224, *exp.* 14.

94. Martín Artajo to Mallet, 7 June, Mallet to Martín Artajo, 15 June 1946: PRO FO 371/60467, Z5808/5808/41; see also MAE *leg.* R2224, *exp.* 14. Barranco subsequently escaped to France.

95. *Hansard* (Commons), 5th Ser. Vol. 424, cs. 1760–1.

96. Hoyer Millar's draft letter to Ashley Clarke, 3 August 1946: PRO FO 371/60363, Z6819/36/41.

97. Inverchapel to Foreign Office, 19 December 1946: PRO FO 371/60371, Z10586/36/41; *Ministerio de Asuntos Exteriores* to British Embassy, Madrid, *note verbale*, 21 December 1946: MAE *leg.* R2224, *exp.* 14 (also in MAE *leg.* R3510, *exp.* 1); a summary of the *note* is in Mallet to Foreign Office, 22 December 1946: PRO FO 371/60371, Z10644/36/41. Spanish outrage at Britain's connections with the opposition was made clear by Carrero Blanco, writing under his *nom de plume*: Juan de la Cosa, *Spain and the World (Exposure of an Isolation)* (Madrid: Publicaciones Españolas, 1954), pp. 167–71.

98. Minutes by Hogg, Hoyer Millar, McNeil, Foreign Office to Madrid, 20, 23, 24 December 1946: PRO FO 371/60371, Z10586/36/41.

99. British Embassy, 27 December 1946: PRO FO 371/67867, Z77/3/41.

5   1947: British Intervention

1. In March 1947 Paul-Henri Spaak, Prime Minister of Belgium and President of the UN General Assembly in 1946, told Llopis that in his opinion the 'reasonable time' stipulated by the UN resolution extended at most for six months: Davies to McNeil, 1 April 1947: PRO FO 371/67872, Z3466/16/41.
2. Much of this chapter is based on Dunthorn, 'The Prieto–Gil-Robles meeting of October 1947', 60–4.
3. Duff Cooper to Foreign Office, 2, 20 February 1947: PRO FO 371/67872, Z1255, 1950/16/41.
4. Heine, *Oposición*, pp. 374–5.
5. Cabeza Sánchez-Albornoz, *Segunda República*, pp. 151–5; Duff Cooper to Foreign Office, 9 August 1947: PRO FO 371/67873, Z7277/16/41.
6. See, for example, Albornoz's government declaration of 2 September 1947: Tusell, *Oposición Democrática*, p. 184.
7. Cabeza Sánchez-Albornoz, 'Posición de la República Española', pp. 160–1; Martínez Cobo, *¿República? ¿Monarquía?*, pp. 146–9; Suárez, *Franco*, IV, pp. 187–8, 202. See also Prieto to Araquistain, 17 November 1947: FPI ALA 98–39.
8. Heine, *Oposición*, p. 385. The only organisation in which the republican government-in-exile continued to have a voice was the Interparliamentary Union, to which it was admitted in 1947: Álvarez del Vayo, *Last Optimist*, p. 382.
9. Howard to Foreign Office, 30 January, 28 February 1947: PRO FO 371/67874, Z1213, Z2282/20/41; Gil-Robles, *Monarquía*, pp. 387–8.
10. The CEFM replaced Gil-Robles' *Coalición Monárquica Nacional* formed the year before, which may account for the different dates given for the CEFM's founding by Heine and Tusell: Heine, *Oposición*, p. 376; Tusell, *Oposición Democrática*, p. 116.
11. B. Malley, 'Interview with General Aranda', 28 March 1947: PRO FO 371/67875, Z3594/20/41.
12. Heine, *Oposición*, pp. 378–9.
13. Howard to Foreign Office, 19 April 1947: PRO FO 371/67867, Z3862/3/41; Gil-Robles, *Monarquía*, pp. 203, 219; Heine, *Oposición*, pp. 379–80.
14. Alba, *Resistencia Antifranquista*, pp. 261–2; Heine, *Oposición*, pp. 380, 386–7.
15. Millard to Hogg, 6 September 1947: PRO FO 371/67873, Z8130/16/41; see also Jiménez de Asúa to Prieto, 1 November 1948: FPI ALJA 419–38.
16. Duff Cooper to Foreign Office, 4 August 1947: PRO FO 371/67873, Z7204/16/41; Martínez to Dixon, 8 August 1947: PRO FO 371/67870, Z8152/3/41; Gibaja, *Prieto*, pp. 401–2; Martínez Cobo, *¿República? ¿Monarquía?*, pp. 132–41. For the text of the resolutions adopted by the Assembly, see FPI ALJA 419–34.
17. The appeal, in English translation, is in Martínez to Dixon, 11 September 1947: PRO FO 371/67873, Z8277/16/41.
18. Hood to Bevin, 23 September 1947: PRO FO 371/67877A, Z8524/20/41.
19. 'Conversation with Sr. Indalecio Prieto (Spanish Socialist Leader)', Bevin to Howard, 29 September 1947: PRO FO 371/67873, Z8652/16/41.
20. 'Mi entrevista con Bevin', 28 September 1947, in I. Prieto, *Convulsiones de España*. Vol. II (Mexico, D.F: Oasis, 1968), pp. 176–7; 'Entrevista Prieto-

Bevin': MAE *leg.* R3514, *exp.* 14; AGA AE *caja* 7283 (Q.18.n); Birley, BBC, to Curle, 29 September 1947: PRO FO 371/67873, Z8589/16/41.

21. Prieto to Araquistain, 27 August 1947: FPI ALA 98–39; Millard to Hogg, 6 September 1947: PRO FO 371/67873, Z8130/16/41; Sainz, *Reinado*, pp. 176–7.
22. Hoyer Millar to Howard, 24 March 1947: PRO FO 371/67875, Z3121/20/41; A. Fernández to Prieto, 26 March 1947: FPI ALJA 419–34; Gil-Robles, *Monarquía*, pp. 203–4.
23. M. García-Nieto and J. Donezar, *La España de Franco, 1939–1973: Bases Documentales de la España Contemporánea.* XI (Madrid: Guadiana, 1975), pp. 237–40. In February 1947 Don Juan's elder brother, Don Jaime, momentarily revived his claim to the Spanish throne, having taken the title of Duke of Anjou: Gil-Robles, *Monarquía*, pp. 220–1.
24. Tusell, *Carrero*, pp. 167–73.
25. Gil-Robles, *Monarquía*, pp. 388–90.
26. Ibid., pp. 390–3.
27. Ibid., pp. 210, 212–15, 220; Kindelán, *Relaciones*, pp. 333–8; Tusell, *Oposición Democrática*, pp. 161–9; see also Cantabro to Clarín, 10 June 1947: FUE P 799.3.
28. 'Gil-Robles in London', Horsfall Carter, 15 July 1947: PRO FO 371/67908A, Z6765/6677/1.
29. Crosthwaite's minute to McNeil, 15 July, Gil-Robles to Horsfall Carter, received 18 July, Gil-Robles to Horsfall Carter, 22 July 1947: PRO FO 371/67908A, Z6764/4047/41.
30. Gil-Robles, *Monarquía*, pp. 229–33, 394–6; Sainz, *Reinado*, pp. 249–51, 337–9.
31. Gil-Robles, *Monarquía*, pp. 233–9.
32. In his diary Gil-Robles mentions only three meetings: Gil-Robles, *Monarquía*, pp. 240–1; see also Martínez Cobo, *¿República? ¿Monarquía?*, p. 171.
33. 'Conversation with Señor Gil-Robles (Spanish Monarchist Leader)', Bevin to Howard, 17 October 1947: PRO FO 371/67908A, Z9162/6677/41.
34. 'Memorandum by Gil-Robles' (Translation), 18 October 1947: PRO FO 371/67908A, Z9382/6677/41.
35. Ibid.
36. Prieto's memorandum, 19 October 1947: PRO FO 371/67908A, Z9381/6677/41.
37. 'Gil Robles se ha entrevistado con Bidault', Radio Paris broadcast, 22 November 1945, referred to in AGA AE *caja* 7283 (Q.18.n).
38. For Portuguese and Spanish press cuttings on the visit, see MAE *leg.* R3510, *exp.* 1; reports by EFE, the official Spanish news agency, are in AGA AE *caja* 7283 (Q.18.n); see also D. Galán and F. Lara, 'España 1947: las Conversaciones entre Gil Robles e Indalecio Prieto', *Tiempo de Historia*, III-35 (1977) 102–17; Howard to Foreign Office, 28 October 1947: PRO FO 371/67870, Z9444/3/41.
39. Martínez Cobo, *¿República? ¿Monarquía?*, pp. 175–6; Gibaja, *Prieto*, pp. 407–8.
40. Gil-Robles, *Monarquía*, pp. 246–8.
41. Prieto to Araquistain, 25 October 1947: FPI ALA 98-39; AGA AE *caja* 7283 (Q.18.n); Curle's memorandum, 'Prieto-Gil–Robles Talks', 31 October 1947: PRO FO 371/67908A, Z9201/6677/41; Crossley to Curle, 29 October, Overton's minute, 19 November 1947: PRO FO 371/67871, Z9990/3/41.

42. See Prieto's letter to de los Ríos, 12 January 1948 (wrongly dated 1946) in Gil-Robles, *Monarquía*, pp. 404–9.

43. De los Ríos to Prieto, 28 November, 12 December, Prieto to Jiménez de Asúa, 2 December, Vejarano to de los Ríos, 10 December, Prieto to de los Ríos, 13 December 1947: FPI ALJA 419–35.

44. Bevin's memorandum, 'United Nations General Assembly: Report on Second Part of First Session', 6 January 1947: PRO CAB 129/16, CP (47) 16.

45. 'Memorandum by the Secretary of State for Foreign Affairs', 13 March 1946, Annex: PRO CAB 132/2, DO (46) 40.

46. Oversea Defence Committee, 'The Role of the Colonies in War', 11 April 1947: PRO CAB 132/2, ODC (47) 10; 'The Overall Strategic Plan'. Retained: DO (47) 44, 22 May 1947, in Lewis, *Changing Direction*, pp. 324, 370–87.

47. See, for example, Bevin's memorandum, 'Economic Sanctions against Spain', 3 January 1947: PRO CAB 129/16: CP (47) 2; see also PRO CAB 128/9, CM 2(47)2, 6 January 1947; Foreign Office Economic Intelligence Department, 'Spain: Vulnerability to Import Embargo', 23 April 1947: PRO FO 371/67868, Z4313/3/41.

48. The agreement is in PRO FO 371/67895, Z3318, 3320/521/41; for the supplementary monetary agreement of June 1947, see PRO FO 371/67895, Z5761/521/41; see also F. Guirao, *Spain and the Reconstruction of Western Europe, 1945–57* (London: Macmillan, 1998), pp. 44–5.

49. Hogg's minute, 25 February 1947: PRO FO 371/67879, Z19941/521/41; for the reaction of the Spanish republican opposition, see 'Nota para el Sr. Presidente sobre el Acuerdo de Pagos Anglo-Español', 21 April 1947: FUE 501.3.

50. For a Foreign Office survey of the Spanish anti-Franco opposition groups in 1947, see Hogg's minute, 20 May 1947: PRO FO 371/67876, Z4980/20/41.

51. Duff Cooper to Foreign Office, 8, 20 February 1947: PRO FO 371/67872, Z1579, 1950/16/41; Howard to Bevin, 14 February 1947: PRO FO 371/67872, Z1768/16/41; Hoyer Millar to Howard, 24 March 1947: PRO FO 371/67875, Z3121/20/41.

52. Minutes by Horsfall Carter and Hogg, 1, 3 March 1947: PRO FO 371/67872, Z2138/16/41; Hoyer Millar's minutes, 8, 13 March 1947: PRO FO 371/67874, Z2161/20/41; see also 'Párrafos de una carta de Luis Araquistain fechada en Londres el 27 de marzo de 1947': FPI ALJA 419–34.

53. Hogg's minute, 11 [?] September 1947: PRO FO 371/67873, Z8019/16/41.

54. Howard to Foreign Office, 4, 30 January, 28 February 1947: PRO FO 371/67874, Z191, 1213, 2282/20/41; minutes by Hogg, Hoyer Millar, Harvey, 4 February 1947: PRO FO 371/67874, Z1213/20/41; Hoyer Millar to Howard, 24 March 1947: PRO FO 371/67875, Z3121/20/41; Howard to Bevin, 31 March, minutes by Hogg and Hoyer Millar, 23 April 1947: PRO FO 371/67875, Z3594/20/41.

55. Horsfall Carter's minute, 8 February 1947: PRO FO 371/60371, Z10726/36/41.

56. Hoyer Millar's minute, 21 February 1947: PRO FO 371/67874, Z1946/20/41; see also Hoyer Millar to Howard, 24 March 1947: PRO FO 371/67875, Z3121/20/41.

57. McNeil's minute, 1 April 1947: PRO FO 371/6787, Z3383/3/41.

58. Minutes by Sloan and Hoyer Millar, 4, 9 April 1947: PRO FO 371/67867, Z3383/3/41.
59. Inverchapel to Foreign Office, 3 April 1947: PRO FO 371/67867, Z3373/3/41.
60. The Acting Secretary of State to the Embassy in the United Kingdom, 7 April 1947: *FRUS, 1947*, III, pp. 1068–9; 'Summary of Department's Top Secret Telegram No. 1531, April 7, 1947': PRO FO 371/67867, Z3617/3/41.
61. Minutes by Sloan and McNeil, 11 April 1947: PRO FO 371/67867, Z3617/3/41.
62. Howard to Foreign Office, 15 April 1947: PRO FO 371/67867, Z3740/3/41.
63. Mallet's minute, 17 April 1947: PRO FO 371/67868, Z3888/3/41.
64. UK Delegation to Council of Foreign Ministers, Moscow, to Foreign Office, 25 April 1947: PRO FO 371/67868, Z4093/3/41; Douglas to Secretary of State, 1 May 1947: *FRUS, 1947*, III, pp. 1074–5.
65. Acheson to US Embassy, London, 15 May 1947: *FRUS, 1947*, III, pp. 1069–73; Inverchapel to Foreign Office, 13 May 1947: PRO FO 371/67868, Z4613/3/41.
66. Harvey's minute, 12 June 1947: PRO FO 371/67868, Z5600/3/41.
67. Crosthwaite's minute, 3 July, Foreign Office to Washington, 26 July 1947: PRO FO 371/67869, Z7004/3/41.
68. Sloan's minute, 26 March 1947: PRO FO 371/67867, Z2917/3/41.
69. Cordier and Foote, *Trygve Lie*, p. 84.
70. Howard to Foreign Office, 8 July 1947: PRO FO 371/67876, Z6476/20/41; Hood to Foreign Office, 2 August, 23 September 1947: PRO FO 371/67877A, Z7321, 8524/20/41.
71. Minutes by Crosthwaite and Sargent, 9 August, 3 September 1947: PRO FO 371/67873, Z7379/16/41; Crosthwaite's minute, 13 August 1947: PRO FO 371/67870, Z7461/3/41.
72. Millard to Hogg, 6 September 1947: PRO FO 371/67873, Z8130/16/41; Curle's brief for Bevin, 16 September, Healey to Foreign Office, 23 September: PRO FO 371/67873, Z7379/16/41; see also Prieto to Araquistain, 27 August 1947: FPI ALA 98–39.
73. Gómez, accompanied by Giral, had travelled to London on 22 July, ostensibly to discuss the question of Spanish refugees in England: Spanish Embassy, Paris, to *Ministerio de Asuntos Exteriores*, 20 July 1946: APG: JE *leg.* 9, *exp.* 1, *no.* 1.
74. 'Conversation with Sr. Indalecio Prieto (Spanish Socialist Leader)', Bevin to Howard, 29 September 1947: PRO FO 371/67873, Z8652/16/41. In a letter to Bevin of 21 October, which accompanied his memorandum of 19 October, Prieto asked Bevin to find an opportunity in Parliament or elsewhere to say a word of encouragement to the PSOE for the position it had taken in its search for a solution to the Spanish question: Prieto to Bevin, no date: FPI ALA 98–39, 100–13 (Araquistain's name has been erroneously added to the ALA 100–13 copy of the letter); Prieto to Bevin, 21 October 1947: PRO FO 371/67908A, Z9201/6677/41.
75. 'Conversation with Señor Gil Robles (Spanish Monarchist Leader)', Bevin to Howard, 17 October 1947: PRO FO 371/67908A, Z9162/6677/41.
76. Curle's memorandum, 'Prieto–Gil Robles Talks', 31 October 1947; PRO FO 371/67908A, Z9201/6677/41.
77. Minutes by Crosthwaite, Sargent, Harvey, 11, 12 November, 'Future Régime in Spain: Prieto–Gil Robles Talks', Bevin to Howard, Bevin to Prieto, 22 November 1947: PRO FO 371/67908A, Z9382/6677/41; 'Mensaje del Sr. Bevin

para el Sr. Prieto', no date: FPI ALJA 419–35. See also Prieto to Bevin, 25 November 1945: FPI ALJA 419–35; Prieto to Bevin, 25 November, Curle's memorandum, 'Señor Indalecio Prieto', 5 December 1947: PRO FO 371/67908A, Z10501/6677/41.

78. Araquistain to Curle, 20 November 1947: FPI ALA 100–29; Araquistain to Curle, 20 November, minutes by Crosthwaite and Bevin, 21 November 1947: PRO FO 371/67908A, Z10244/6677/41; see also Prieto to de los Ríos, 13 December 1947: FPI ALJA 419–35.

79. Dixon to Western Department, 'Don Juan', 27 November 1947: PRO FO 800/504, Sp/47/1; see also Xanthaky's memorandum, 2 November 1948: *FRUS, 1948*, III, (Washington DC: Government Printing House, 1974), pp. 1062–3.

80. A Lleonart y Anselem, *España y ONU, II (1947): La «Cuestión Española»*. *Estudio Introductorio y Corpus Documental* (Madrid: Consejo Superior de Investigaciones Científicas, 1983), pp. 89–104, 256, 273.

81. Ibid., pp. 107–8, 271–2, 277–9.

82. *UNGA, Second Session, Vol. 2. 1947*, Annex 25, pp. 1610–12; R. Sanders, *Spain and the United Nations, 1945–1950* (New York: Vantage Press, 1966) p. 71.

83. Bevin's memorandum, 'Proceedings of the General Assembly of the United Nations, 1947', 17 December 1947: PRO CAB 129/22, CP (47) 335; Hogg's minute, 14 November 1947: PRO FO 371/67871, Z9880/3/41.

84. Curle's minute, 'Policy Towards Spain', 3 December 1947: PRO FO 371/67871, Z10300/3/41.

85. Howard to Crosthwaite, 25 November 1947: PRO FO 371/67871, Z10300/3/41.

86. On the damage to French economic interests, see Bidault's speech to the National Assembly of 11 March 1948: Assemblée Nationale, *Journal Officiel de la République Française. Débats Parlementaires. Assemblée Nationale, 1948* (Paris: Imprimerie des Journaux Officiels, 1948) no. 34, pp. 1657–8; see also Guirao, *Reconstruction*, pp. 41–3; A. Viñas, J. Viñuela, F. Eguidazu, C.F. Pulgar, S. Florensa, *Política Comercial Exterior en España, 1931–1975*, 2 (Madrid: Banco Exterior de España, 1979), p. 571.

87. Dulphy, 'La Politique de la France', 130–1; Martínez Lillo, *Introducción*, pp 25–7; 'Aproximación', pp. 573–82, 593–5.

88. Brundu, 'L'Espagne Franquiste', 179–80; Martínez Lillo, 'Aproximación', 583–6; Suárez, *Franco*, IV, pp. 188, 201–2, 225–6.

89. *Débats Parlementaires. Assemblée Nationale*, p. 6541; *Annales du Conseil de la République. Débats. Vol 4. Session de 1947. Du 28 Octobre au 31 Décembre* (Paris: Imprimerie des Journaux Officiels, 1948), pp. 2781, 2790–1.

90. Lleonart, *España y ONU (1947)*, pp. 114–15.

91. Howard to Foreign Office, 21 January 1947: PRO FO 371/67874, Z952/20/41.

92. Undated police report: MAE *leg*. 3510, *exp*. 1.

93. *Nota Verbal, Ministerio de Asuntos Exteriores* to British Embassy, Madrid, 26 May; *Ministerio de Asuntos Exteriores* to Santa Cruz, 29 June; Spanish Embassy, London, to *Ministerio de Asuntos Exteriores*, 16 July; British Embassy, Madrid, to *Ministerio de Asuntos Exteriores*, 19 July 1947: MAE *leg*. R3510, *exp*. 1; see also 'Actividades ilícitas Francisco López Fernández y Santiago Rojo García – protesta de la Embajada británica en Madrid' and 'Actividades Colquihouen [*sic*]': AGA AE *caja* 6848 (A-740, A-755).

94. *Hansard* (Commons), 5th Ser. Vol. 433, cs. 1152–3; Foreign Office to Howard, 30 July 1947: PRO FO 371/67876, Z6712/20/41; Santa Cruz to Aguirre, 13 December 1947: AGA AE *caja* 6727 (A-813).
95. *Ministerio de Asuntos Exteriores* to British Embassy, Madrid, 22 October 1947: MAE *leg.* R3510, *exp.* 1; Howard to Foreign Office, 23 October 1947: PRO FO 371/67870, Z9304/3/41; Foreign Office to Howard, 12 November 1947: PRO FO 371/67871, Z9841/3/41. See also 'El conturbenio Prieto-Gil Robles', Erice to Santa Cruz, 25 October 1947: AGA AE *caja* 7283 (Q.18.n); *Ministerio de Asuntos Exteriores'* memorandum, 28 October 1947: MAE *leg.* R3510, *exp.* 1; also in AGA AE *caja* 7283 (Q.18.n).
96. British Embassy, Madrid, to *Ministerio de Asuntos Exteriores*, 14 November; 'Nota para su Excelencia', Erice to Martín Artajo, 15 November; *Nota Verbal*, *Ministerio de Asuntos Exteriores* to British Embassy, Madrid, 22 November 1947: MAE *leg.* R3510, *exp.* 1; also in AGA AE *caja* 7283 (Q.18.n); Howard to Foreign Office, 15, 23 November 1947: PRO FO 371/67871, Z9926, 10137, 10190/3/41.

6   1948–1950: the Frustration of the Anti-Franco Impulse

1. Martínez Cobo, *¿República? ¿Monarquía?*, pp. 374, 379; see also Prieto to Fernando de los Ríos, 12 January 1948: Gil-Robles, *Monarquía*, pp. 404–9.
2. Gibaja, *Prieto*, pp. 409–10.
3. 'Record of a conversation between Don Indalecio Prieto and P.M. Crosthwaite, Head of Western Department, on March 16th, 1948', PRO FO 371/73358, Z2694/1027/41.
4. Prieto's correspondence with the PSOE Special Committee is kept in the archives of the Fundación Pablo Iglesias, Madrid. See also Martínez Cobo, *¿República? ¿Monarquía?*, pp. 177–85; Gibaja, *Prieto*, pp. 409–45.
5. Sainz, *Reinado*, pp. 169–70.
6. Prieto to de los Ríos, 12 January 1948: FPI ALJA 419–36; Prieto to Bevin, 13 January 1948: PRO FO 371/73358, Z1027/1027/41.
7. Prieto to Jiménez de Asúa, 10 April 1948: FPI ALJA 419–36; Gibaja, *Prieto*, pp. 432–5.
8. Monarchists' memorandum, 31 May, Prieto to Vejarano, 2 July, monarchists' memorandum, 13 July, Prieto to Jiménez de Asúa, 27 July, monarchists' memorandum, 9 August 1948: FPI ALJA 419–36; also in PRO FO 371/73359, Z7414/1027.
9. Monarchists' memorandum, 13 July, Prieto's replies, 25 July, 21, 27 August 1948: FPI ALJA 419–36; also in PRO FO 371/73359, Z7414/1027/41.
10. PSOE Special Committee to British Embassy, Paris, 6 October 1948: PRO FO 371/73359, Z8130/1027/41; the Spanish text is in PRO FO 371/73359, Z8063/1027/41.
11. Jiménez de Asúa to Prieto, 5 December 1948: FPI AAVV-AAPG 143–20.
12. Note by the PSOE-in-exile's executive committee, 29 August 1948: FPI AAVV-AAPG 143–30; see also Gibaja, *Prieto*, pp. 422, 427; Heine, *Oposición*, pp. 397, 401.
13. Prieto to Gil-Robles, 25 May, Gil-Robles' memorandum, 31 May, Prieto's

reply, 8 June 1948: FPI ALJA 419–36; PRO FO 371/7338, Z5113, 5146/
1027/41. See also Gibaja, *Prieto*, pp. 414–15; Martínez Cobo, *¿República?*
¿Monarquía?, pp. 370–88.

14. Gil-Robles to Vejarano, 3 September, Prieto to Vejarano, 4 September 1948:
    FPI ALJA, 419–37; Harvey to Foreign Office, 6 October 1948: PRO FO 371/
    73359, Z8062, 8130/1027/41; Howard to Foreign Office, 1 November 1948:
    PRO FO 371/73360A, Z8892/1027/41; Caffery to Marshall, 28 September, 8
    October 1948: *FRUS, 1948*, III, pp. 1051–2, 1054–5; Gibaja, *Prieto*, pp. 425–6;
    Martínez Cobo, *¿República? ¿Monarquía?*, pp. 389–90.

15. Prieto to Vejarano, 8 October 1948: FPI ALJA 419–37; Pérez to Jiménez
    de Asúa, 27 October 1948: FPI AAVV-AAPG 143–12; Ronald to Foreign Office,
    9 October 1948: PRO FO 371/73359, Z8156/1027/41; Gil-Robles to Bevin,
    6 October 1948: PRO FO 371/73360A, Z8406/1027/41.

16. Gil-Robles, *Monarquía*, pp. 258–9.

17. Anson, *Don Juan*, pp. 272–5. Prieto described Danvila as a 'persona insig-
    nificante' suffering 'manía de exhibicionismo': Prieto to Jiménez de Asúa,
    25 September 1948: FPI ALA 98–39.

18. De la Cierva, *Don Juan de Borbón*, pp. 551–3; Sainz, *Reinado*, pp. 220–2.

19. Kindelán was banished to the Fort of Guadalupe, near San Sebastián, for two
    months for an anti-Franco lecture he gave in the house of the Marqués de
    Aledo, a prominent Asturian banker, on 16 April 1948: Gil-Robles, *Monar-
    quía*, pp. 261–2; Kindelán, *Relaciones*, pp. 137–40, 351–5.

20. Gil-Robles, *Monarquía*, pp. 269–73; Parkes, 'Don Juan's Meeting with Franco',
    13 September 1948: PRO FO 371/73363, Z7593/1380/41; 'Report of the
    Meeting between the King and Franco', undated: PRO FO 371/73363,
    Z7977/1380/41; MacVeagh to Marshall, 21 September, Xanthaky's memo-
    randum, 2 November 1948: *FRUS, 1948*, III, pp. 1050–1, 1059–63.

21. Howard to Foreign Office, 2 September 1948: PRO FO 371/73363, Z7184/
    1380/41.

22. Gil-Robles, *Monarquía*, pp. 265–6; Ronald to Foreign Office, 28 August 1948:
    PRO FO 371/73363, Z6993/1380/41.

23. Gil-Robles, *Monarquía*, pp. 272–4.

24. Johnston to Foreign Office, 14 October 1948: PRO FO 371/73359,
    Z8320/1027/41; Gil-Robles, *Monarquía*, pp. 279–87; Kindelán, *Relaciones*, pp.
    359–66. For a brief account of Juan Carlos' secondary education in Spain,
    see C. Powell, *Juan Carlos of Spain. Self-Made Monarch* (Macmillan: London,
    1996), pp. 11–15.

25. Prieto to Meana, 17 September 1948: FPI ALJA 419–37; Prieto's letter, 21
    September 1948: PRO FO 371/73359, Z7973/1027/41. According to Preston,
    the socialists had been taken in by an 'elaborate exercise in duplicity':
    Preston, 'The Anti-Francoist Opposition', p. 137.

26. ANFD declaration, 21 November 1948: FPI ALJA 419–38; Prieto to Gómez,
    Jiménez de Asúa, Pérez, 27 November 1948: FPI AAVV-AAPG 143–14;
    Fernández Vargas, *Resistencia Interior*, p. 147; Martínez Cobo, *¿República?*
    ¿Monarquía?, pp. 202–5.

27. Gibaja, *Prieto*, pp. 435–7; Martínez Cobo, *¿República? ¿Monarquía?*, p. 205.

28. CIC, *Acta I, Acta III*: FPI ALJA 419–39; 'Boletín de Actividades Monárquicas',
    no. 417, 27 December 1949: APG JE *Secretaría del Ministro Subsecretario*
    (henceforth cited as SMS) *leg.* 63, *exp.* 25; Howard to Shuckburgh, 17 March

1949: PRO FO 371/79685, Z2580/10155/41; Heine, *Oposición*, p. 401; Tusell, *Oposición Democrática*, pp. 209–12.

29. Prieto to PSOE Executive Committee, 15 March 1949: FPI ALJA 419–40.
30. Prieto to PSOE Executive Committee, 15 March 1949: FPI ALJA 419–40; Gibaja, *Prieto*, pp. 438–40; Gil-Robles, *Monarquía*, pp. 298–9; Martínez Cobo, *¿República? ¿Monarquía?*, pp. 208–11.
31. Gibaja, *Prieto*, pp. 441–2; Heine, *Oposición*, pp. 402–5; Martínez Cobo, *¿República? ¿Monarquía?*, pp. 211–13; Malley, 'Conversation with General Aranda on August 31st, 1949', Howard to Bevin, 1 September 1949: PRO FO 371/79711, Z6011/1054/41.
32. Prieto to Vejarano, 6 September 1949: FPI ALJA 419–43; Culbertson to Acheson, 9 November 1949: *FRUS, 1949*, IV (Washington DC: Government Printing House, 1975) pp. 766–8; Gibaja, *Prieto*, pp. 441–2; Gil-Robles, *Monarquía*, p. 302; Martínez Cobo, *¿República? ¿Monarquía?*, pp. 200–1, 395–9.
33. Gibaja, *Prieto*, pp. 443–7, 450–2; Heine, *Oposición*, pp. 406–8; Martínez Cobo, *¿República? ¿Monarquía?*, pp. 214–19.
34. Gil-Robles, *Monarquía*, pp. 294–5, n. 93.
35. Ibid., p. 299; Malley, 'Conversation with General Aranda on July 17th, 1949', 20 July 1949: PRO FO 371/79686, Z5301/10156/41; Xanthaky's memorandum, 27 July 1949: *FRUS, 1949*, IV, pp. 754–6.
36. Gil-Robles, *Monarquía*, pp. 304–6; Sainz, *Reinado*, p. 369.
37. Ibid., pp. 306–12.
38. Kindelán, *Relaciones*, p. 366.
39. Gil-Robles, *Monarquía*, pp. 315–17; Suárez, *Franco*, IV, pp. 372–4.
40. Gil-Robles, *Monarquía*, pp. 317–19; López Rodó, *Larga Marcha*, pp. 725–31; Hankey to Foreign Office, 10 August 1950: PRO 371/89621, WS1942/4.
41. For the improvement in Franco-Spanish relations in this period, see P. Martínez Lillo, 'Las Relaciones Hispano-Francesas entre 1948–1952' in *España, Francia y la Comunidad Europea* (Madrid: Consejo Superior de Investigaciones Científicas, 1989), pp. 150–2.
42. Ibid., pp. 153–4, 158.
43. V. Auriol, *Journal du Septennat 1947–1954: Tome II* (Paris: Armand Colin, 1974), pp. 518–19.
44. See, for example, Acheson to US Embassy, Madrid, 18 December, Culbertson to Marshall, 30 December 1947: *FRUS, 1947*, III, pp. 1096–7, 1099–1101; Liedtke, *Embracing a Dictatorship*, pp. 40–1; A. Marquina Barrio, *España en la Política de Seguridad Occidental 1939–1986* (Madrid: Servicio de Publicaciones del Estado Mayor del Ejército, 1986), pp. 127–34, 139.
45. Chancery (Washington) to Foreign Office, 16 February 1948: PRO FO 371/73333, Z1343/84/41.
46. Foreign Office to Inverchapel, 1 April 1948: PRO FO 371/73335, Z2791/84/41.
47. The sum available for 1948 was $5.3 billion: Rob's minute, 20 May 1948: PRO FO 371/73336, Z3775/84/41.
48. Lovett to Culbertson, 2 April 1948: *FRUS, 1948*, III, pp. 1035–6.
49. Achilles to Culbertson, 5 January, Culbertson's memorandum of conversation with Martín Artajo, Culbertson's notes, 2 February 1948: *FRUS, 1948*, III, pp. 1017–25.
50. Policy Statement by the Department of State on Spain, 26 July 1948: *FRUS, 1948*, III, pp. 1041–5.

51. A. Viñas, *Guerra, Dinero, Dictadura: Ayuda Fascista y Autarquía en la España de Franco* (Bareclona: Grupo Editorial Grijalbo, 1984), pp. 283–4.
52. Acheson to US Embassy (Madrid), 13 April 1949: *FRUS, 1949*, IV, pp. 735–7.
53. Chancery (Washington) to Western Department, 16 February 1948: PRO FO 371/79710, Z1632/1054/41; Marshall to Diplomatic and Consular Offices in the American Republics, 28 July 1948: *FRUS, 1948*, III, pp. 1045–7.
54. Dunham's memorandum of 1 March 1949 was concurred in by the Policy Planning Staff, the Office of European Affairs and the Office of American Republic Affairs: *FRUS, 1949*, IV, pp. 731–4.
55. Shuckburgh, 'The question of Spain at the United Nations General Assembly Meeting in April', 5 March 1949: PRO FO 371/79695, Z2810/1025/41.
56. Portero, *Franco Aislado*, pp. 318–19.
57. Kirkpatrick, 'Draft Brief for the U.K. Delegation to the Third Session of General Assembly', 25 September 1948: PRO FO 371/73338, Z7994/84/41.
58. 'Extract from Record of Meeting with Monsieur Schuman at the Quai d'Orsay on October 2nd at 10 a.m.', 2 October 1948: PRO FO 800/504, SP/48/2; 'Extract from Record of Conversation between the Secretary of State and Mr. Marshall at the U.S. Embassy in Paris on 4th October, 1948, at 11 a.m.', PRO FO 800/504, SP/48/4; 'Extract from Record of Meeting at the Quai d'Orsay on 4th October, 1948, at 3.30 p.m.', 4 October 1948: PRO FO 800/504, SP/48/3 (all also in PRO FO 371/73337, Z8133/84/41); 'Extract From the Record of a Meeting of the Consultative Council Held at the Quai d'Orsay at 10 a.m. on October 26th, 1948', 26 October 1948: PRO FO 800/504, SP/48/5; 'Extract From Meeting Held at the Quai d'Orsay on 27th October, 1948, at 4 p.m.': PRO FO 800/504, SP/48/6 (also in PRO FO 371/73338, Z8938, 8939/84/41).
59. US Representative at the United Nations to Acheson, 13 April, Acheson to United States Mission at the United Nations, 20 April 1949: *FRUS, 1949*, IV, pp. 737–40.
60. McNeil's minute, 14 March, United Kingdom Delegation, New York, to Foreign Office, 19 April 1949: PRO FO 371/79695, Z2810, 3159/1025/41.
61. US Representative at the United Nations to Acheson, 13 April 1949: *FRUS, 1949*, IV, pp. 737–9.
62. A.J. Lleonart y Anselem, *España y ONU, III, (1948–49) La Cuestión Española* (Madrid: Consejo Superior de Investigaciones Científicas, 1985), p. 56.
63. Lleonart, *España y ONU (1948–49)*, pp. 57, 145–51. For the American attitude towards the Polish and Brazilian resolutions, see Edwards, *Anglo-American Relations and the Franco Question*, pp. 137–43.
64. Lleonart, *España y ONU (1948–49)*, pp. 152–372; *United Nations: Official Records of the Third Session of the General Assembly, Part II, First Committee, 1949*, pp. 60–1, 84–5, 170–8, 185–246; *United Nations: Official Records of the Third Session of the General Assembly, Part II, Plenary Meetings, 1949*, pp. 356–66, 456–504.
65. *Hansard* (Commons), 5th Ser. Vol. 438, c. 2342.
66. Bullock, *Ernest Bevin*, pp. 395–8.
67. Clarke to Foreign Office, 22 April 1948: PRO FO 371/73335, Z3572/84/41; Howard to Kirkpatrick, 30 April, minutes by Crosthwaite and Kirkpatrick, 11, 23 May 1948: PRO FO 371/73336, Z3775, Z3775/84/41.
68. Crosthwaite's minute, 12 May 1948: PRO FO 371/73358, Z4210/1027/41.

69. Crosthwaite's memorandum, 'Spain', 6 March 1948: PRO FO 371/73334, Z1804/84/41.
70. 'Record of a conversation between Don Indalecio Prieto and P.M. Crosthwaite, Head of Western Department, on March 16th, 1948', PRO FO 371/73358, Z2694/1027/41.
71. Horsfall Carter's minute, 8 May, Parkes' minute, Bevin's comment, 15 June, minutes by Horsfall Carter and Parkes, 30 June, 1 July 1948: PRO FO 371/73358, Z4210, 5113, 5146/1027/41.
72. Crosthwaite's minute, 28 August 1948: PRO FO 371/73363, Z7054/1380/41.
73. Prieto's letter, 21 September 1948: PRO FO 371/73359, Z7973/1027/41; Gil-Robles to Bevin, 6 October 1948: PRO FO 371/73360A, Z8406/1027/41.
74. Howard to Foreign Office, 2 September, Johnston to Russell, 14 October 1948: PRO FO 371/73363, Z7184, 8384/1380/41; Howard, 'Spain: Annual Review for 1948', 9 February 1948: PRO FO 371/79665, Z1464/596/41.
75. Howard to Mallet, 10 May 1948: PRO FO 371/79710, Z3906/1054/41.
76. Mallet's minute, 28 May 1949: PRO FO 371/79711, Z4322/1054/41.
77. Russell's minute, 29 March 1949: PRO FO 371/79685, Z2580/10155/41.
78. Minutes by Russell and Shuckburgh, 7, 13 May 1949: PRO FO 371/79685, Z3429/10155/41; Hoyer Millar to Mallet, 8 June 1949: PRO FO 371/79686, Z74291/10156/41.
79. Mallet, 'Policy Towards Spain', 8 August 1949: PRO FO 371/79711, Z5454/1054/41.
80. Russell's minute, 6 August 1949: PRO FO 371/79686, Z5312/10156/41; Shuckburgh, 'Spain', 12 October 1949: PRO FO 371/79698, Z7409/1025; Strang's memorandum, 13 August, Howard to Foreign Office, 1 September 1949: PRO FO 371/79711, Z5454, 5827/1054/41.
81. Bevin's minute, undated, minutes by McNeil and Bevin, 15 August 1949: PRO FO 371/79711, Z5454/1054/41.
82. Hankey's minute, 1 November 1949; 'Policy of His Majesty's Government towards the Present Government of Spain', Bevin to Hankey, 14 November 1949: PRO FO 371/79698, Z7409/1025/41.
83. M. Bundy, *The Pattern of Responsibility* (Cambridge, Massachusetts: The Riverside Press, 1952), pp. 130–1.
84. Marquina, *España en la Política de Seguridad*, pp. 279, 282–3, 296–304.
85. Hankey, 'Spain: Annual Review for 1949', 27 January 1950: PRO FO 371/89479, Z1380/1011/41; Hankey to Bevin, 1 February, minutes by Laurence and Russell, 11, 16 February 1950: PRO FO 371/89482, WS1016/6.
86. Western Department, 'Policy towards Spain, United Kingdom's attitude at the next meeting of the United Nations General Assembly', 27 March, minute by E. Tomkins, Bevin's Private Secretary, 26 April 1950: PRO FO 371/89497, WS10345/19.
87. Mallet, 'Policy towards Spain', 2 August, Younger to Bevin, 3 August, Strang, 'Spain', 9 August, Bevin's minute, 10 August 1950: PRO FO 371/89502, WS1051/39.
88. 'Relations with Spain', memorandum by the Secretary of State for Foreign Affairs, 23 August 1950: PRO CAB 129/41, CP (50) 192.
89. PRO CAB 128/18, CM 56 (50) 8, 6 September 1950.

90. Sanders, *Spain and the United Nations*, pp. 88–92.
91. *United Nations: Official Records of the Fifth Session of the General Assembly, Vol. 1, 1950*, pp. 371–81; Portero, *Franco Aislado*, pp. 399–403.
92. PRO CAB 128/18, CM 73 (50) 1, 11 November 1950.
93. Stanton Griffis, the American Ambassador, presented his credentials to Franco on 1 March 1950; the new Spanish Ambassador to Washington, Lequerica, had presented his credentials to Truman two days earlier: Edwards, *Anglo-American Relations and the Franco Question*, pp. 172–4; Preston, *Franco*, pp. 603–6. In March 1951 the French Chargé d'Affaires in Madrid, Bernard Hardion, became France's Ambassador to Spain, and Manuel Aguirre de Cárcer, Spain's Chargé d'Affaires in Paris, Spain's Ambassador to France: Dulphy, 'La Politique de la France', 140. Martínez Lillo, 'Las Relaciones Hispano-Francesas', pp. 156–7.
94. Howard to Mallet, 10 May 1948: PRO FO 371/79710, Z3906/1054/41; minutes by Laurence and Russell, 11 October 1948: PRO FO 371/73337, Z8154/84/41; see also Guirao, *Spain and the Reconstruction of Western Europe*, pp. 57–61. For the Spanish perspective, see Juan de la Cosa, *Spain and the World*, pp. 178–86.
95. Johnston to Russell, 14 October 1948: PRO FO 371/73363, Z8384/1380/41; Kirkpatrick's minute, 9 October 1948: PRO FO 371/73360A, Z8735/1027/41; Foreign Office to Madrid, 14 October 1948: PRO FO 371/73359, Z8168/1027/41. Measures were also taken against the British Consul in Las Palmas and a Vice-Consul in Zaragoza: Howard, 'Spain: Annual Review for 1948', 9 February 1949: PRO FO 371/79665, Z1464/596.
96. In an unusual reversal of roles, Santa Cruz wrote a private letter to J. Chuter Ede, British Home Secretary, on 1 January 1948 pleading for the life of Victoriano Martínez, a Spanish national, sentenced to be hanged for the murder of his illegitimate new-born child; following his intervention the Spaniard was reprieved: Santa Cruz to Ede, 1, 7 January, Santa Cruz to Erice, 14 January 1948: AGA AE, *caja* 6730.

7 Conclusion

1. Luis Araquistain's speech to the PSOE Congress in Toulouse of 1955, quoted in Abellán, *Exilio Español*, 1, p. 23.
2. Brundu goes so far as to blame the weakness and 'personalism' of the Spanish opposition for actually preventing a number of British and French projects for Franco's removal: Brundu, *Ostracismo*, pp. 196–7.
3. Mallet, Britain's Ambassador to Spain in 1945, suggested, for example, that Spain's Moorish past rendered it 'sterile ground for the growth of healthy democratic institutions of an Anglo-Saxon type': Mallet to Foreign Office, 6 October 1945: PRO FO 371/49590, Z11432/233/41.
4. This calls into question Tusell's assertion that the *consistent* aim of British policy towards the Spanish opposition was to bring together the various oppositions of the Spanish opposition to accept a formula of collaboration under the monarchy: J. Tusell, *España del Siglo XX*, p. 637.
5. On 10 July 1951 Don Juan wrote to Franco offering to cooperate with him in establishing a stable regime which would, under the ægis of the monar-

chy, remain true to those principles 'on which Spain's existence was dependent': Sainz, *Reinado*, p. 41.

6. If Barston's condition is accepted that for 'action to constitute *policy* it must essentially take the form of concrete measures, other than merely verbal statements, carried out by a government with a view to solving a particular problem', then it might be asked whether Britain had a policy towards Spain at all: R. Barston (ed.), *The Other Powers. Studies in the Foreign Policy of Small States* (London: George Allen & Unwin, 1973), p. 14.

7. Ahmad, *Britain, Franco Spain and the Cold War*, pp. 14, 153–85. The ease with which Britain could have switched to alternative supplies of oranges has nevertheless been questioned in Edwards, *Anglo-American Relations and the Franco Question*, pp. 106–7.

8. This claim to moral leadership of the West was articulated in 'The First Aim of British Foreign Policy', memorandum by the Secretary of State for Foreign Affairs, 4 January 1948: PRO CAB 129/23, CP (48) 6.

9. That socialism is not necessarily republican is argued in Martínez Cobo, *¿República? ¿Monarquía?*, pp. 22–4. For accounts of the post-Franco transition, see, for example, R. Carr and J. Fusi, *Spain: Dictatorship to Democracy*, 2nd edn (London: Allan & Unwin, 1981); D. Gilmour, *The Transformation of Spain from Franco to the Constitutional Monarchy* (London: Quartet Books, 1985); P. Preston, *The Triumph of Democracy in Spain* (London: Methuen, 1986).

References

Unpublished primary sources

Archivo General de la Administración, Alcalá de Henares (AGA):
Sección de Asuntos Exteriores

Bodleian Library, Oxford:
Attlee papers

Fundación Pablo Iglesias, Madrid (FPI):
AAVV–AAPG: Archivos Varios – Archivo Antonio Pérez García
AE: Archivo del Exilio
AFLC: Archivo Francisco Largo Caballero
ALA: Archivo Luis Araquistain
ALJA: Archivo Luis Jiménez de Asúa

Fundación Universitaria Española, Madrid (FUE):
Archivo de la II República Española en el Exilio

Harry S. Truman Library, Independence, USA:
President Secretary's Files, Box no. 259

Ministerio de Asuntos Exteriores, Madrid (MAE):
Archivo General: Archivo Renovado

Ministerio de la Presidencia, Madrid (APG JE):
Archivo de la Presidencia del Gobierno; Fondos de la Jefatura del Estado

Public Record Office, Kew (PRO):
CAB 65, 66, 121, 127, 128, 129, 130, 131, 132, 134
HS 3, 6
FO 185, 371, 425, 800, 954
PREM 4, 8

Published primary sources

Annales du Conseil de la République. Débats. Vol 4. Session de 1947. Du 28 Octobre au 31 Décembre (Paris: Imprimerie des Journaux Officiels, 1948)
Assemblée Nationale, *Journal Officiel de la République Française. Débats Parlementaires. Assemblée Nationale* (Paris: Imprimerie des Journaux Officiels, 1948)
Centro Republicano Español de México, *México y la República Española: Antología de Documentos. 1931–1977* (Mexico: Centro Republicano Español de México, 1978)
Cordier, A. and Foote, W. (eds) *Public Papers of the Secretaries-General of the United Nations. Vol. I: Trygve Lie 1946–1953* (New York & London: Columbia University Press, 1969)

Díaz-Plaja, F. *La Posguerra Española en sus Documentos* (Barcelona: Plaza & Janés, 1970)

Djonovich, D. (ed.) *United Nations Resolutions. Series II: Resolutions and Decisions of the Security Council, Vol. I, 1946–1947* (New York: Oceana, 1988)

Documents on British Foreign Policy 1919–1939, Second Series
   Vol. XVII (London: HMSO, 1979)

Documents on British Policy Overseas, Series 1
   Vol. I (London: HMSO, 1984)
   Vol. V (London: HMSO, 1990)
   Vol. VII (London: HMSO, 1995)

Fundación Nacional Francisco Franco, *Documentos Inéditos para la Historia del Generalísimo Franco*
   Vol. II-1 (Madrid: Azor, 1992)
   Vol. II-2 (Madrid: Azor, 1992)
   Vol. III (Madrid: Azor, 1993)
   Vol. IV (Madrid: Azor, 1994)

Hansard, *Parliamentary Debates. Fifth Series. House of Commons*

Hansard, *Parliamentary Debates. Fifth Series. House of Lords*

Hudson, W. and Way, W. (eds) *Documents on Australian Foreign Policy 1937–49*, Vol. VIII (Canberra: Australian Government Publishing House, 1989)

Nelson, A. (ed.) *The State Department Policy Planning Staff Papers. 1947–1949* (New York: Garland, 1983)

The State Department Policy Planning Papers, Vol. I, 1947 (Washington, DC: Government Printing House, 1983)

Suárez Fernández, L. *Franco: la Historia y sus Documentos*, 20 vols (Madrid: Urbión, 1986)

United Nations, *Official Records of the General Assembly: First Session, Part 1, 1946*
   Official Records of the General Assembly: Plenary Meetings of the General Assembly 1946–1950
   Official Records of the General Assembly: First Committee Meetings 1946–1949
   Official Records of the General Assembly: Ad Hoc Political Committee 1950

United Nations (Security Council), *Official Records First Year: Second Series Special Supplement. Report of the Sub-Committee on the Spanish Question, 1946*

United Nations, *Yearbook of the United Nations 1946–47* (New York: Department of Public Information, 1947)

United Nations Secretary General, Public Papers of the Secretaries General of the UN.
   Vol. 1. Trygve Lie, 1946–1953 (1969)

United States Department of State, *Conference of Berlin*, Vols I, II (Washington, DC: Government Printing House, 1960)

United States Department of State: *Foreign Relations of the United States*
   1944, V (Washington, DC: Government Printing House, 1965)
   1945, I, II, V (Washington, DC: Government Printing House, 1967)
   1946, V (Washington, DC: Government Printing House, 1969)
   1947, III (Washington, DC: Government Printing House, 1972)
   1948, III (Washington, DC: Government Printing House, 1974)
   1949, IV (Washington, DC: Government Printing House, 1975)
   1950, I, III (Washington, DC: Government Printing House, 1977)

Contemporary books and articles

Calvocoressi, P. *Survey of International Affairs 1947–48* (Oxford University Press, 1952)
Survey of International Affairs 1949–50 (Oxford University Press, 1953)
Carrero Blanco, L. *España ante el Mundo (Proceso de un Aislamiento)* (Madrid: Publicaciones Españolas, 1950)
De la Cosa, J. *Spain and the World (Exposure of an Isolation)* (Madrid: Publicaciones Españolas, 1954)
Doussinague, J. *España Tenía Razón (1939–1945)* (Madrid: Espasa-Calpe, 1950)
De Erice, J. 'España y las Naciones Unidas', *Cuadernos de Política Internacional*, 4 (1950) 9–49
De Foronda y Gómez, M. *Notas Diplomáticas de Política Internacional (1949–1954)* (Madrid: publisher unnamed, 1955)
Grant, H. 'The Situation in Spain', *International Affairs*, XII (1946) 401–7
Hamilton, T. *Appeasement's Child: the Franco Regime in Spain* (London: Victor Gollancz, 1943)
—— 'Spanish Dreams of Empire', *Foreign Affairs*, XXII, 3 (1944) 458–68
Ibáñez de Ibero, C. *Política Mediterránea de España, 1704–1951* (Madrid: Instituto de Estudios Africanos, 1952)
Loveday, A. 'Spain and Persecution', *The Quarterly Review*, 284 (1946) 169
—— 'Spain, U.N.O., and Giral', *The Quarterly Review*, 285 (1947) 18–31
De Madariaga, S. *Spain. A Modern History* (London: Jonathan Cape, 1972; first published, 1942)
Martín Artajo, A. *La Política de Aislamiento de España Seguida por las Naciones Aliadas durante el Quinquenio 1945–1950* (Madrid: Oficina de Información Diplomática, 1950)
—— 'Las Constantes de Nuestra Política Exterior', *Arbor* (July–August 1958) 336–46
De la Mata, G. *Impresiones de la Postguerra, 1945–1948* (Bilbao: publisher unnamed, 1948)
Mayhew, C. 'British Foreign Policy since 1945', *International Affairs*, XXVI, 4 (1950) 477–86
De Palencia, I. *Smouldering Freedom: the Story of the Spanish Republicans in Exile* (London: Gollancz, 1946)

Diaries, letters, memoirs, collected papers

Acheson, D. *Present at the Creation: My Years in the State Department* (London: Hamish Hamilton, 1970)
Alvarez del Vayo, J. *The Last Optimist* (London: Putman, 1950)
Ansaldo, J. *¿Para qué . . . ? (De Alfonso XIII a Juan III)* (Buenos Aires: Editorial Vaska Ekin, 1951)
Areilza, J. *Así Los He Visto. Testimonios de la España de Nuestro Tiempo* (Barcelona: Planeta, 1974)
Attlee, C. *As It Happened* (London: Heinemann, 1954)
Auriol, V. *Journal du Septennat 1947–1954*, Vol. I (Paris: Armand Colin, 1970)

Vol. II (Paris: Armand Colin, 1974)

Vol. III (Paris: Armand Colin, 1977)

Barclay, R. *Ernest Bevin and the Foreign Office, 1932–69* (London: published by Sir Roderick Barclay, 1975)

Bidault, G. *Resistance: the Political Autobiography of Georges Bidault* (London: Weidenfeld & Nicolson, 1967)

Bonnet, G. *Quai d'Orsay: 45 Years of French Foreign Policy* (Isle of Man: Times Press & Anthony Gibbs & Phillips, 1965)

Bundy, M. *The Pattern of Responsibility* (Cambridge, Massachusetts: Riverside Press, 1952)

Campbell, T. and Herring, G. (eds) *The Diaries of Edward R. Stettinius, JR., 1943–1946* (New York: New Viewpoints – a Division of Franklin Watts, Inc., 1975)

Carrero Blanco, L. *Discursos y Escritos (1943–1973)* (Madrid: I.E.P., 1974)

Chauvel, J. *Commentaire. D'Alger à Berne (1944–1952)* (Paris: Fayard, 1972)

Churchill, W. *The War Speeches of Winston Churchill (compiled by Charles Eade)*, 2 (London: Purnell & Cassell, no date)

——*The Dawn of Liberation: War Speeches by the Right Hon. Winston S. Churchill C.H., M.P. 1944 (compiled by Charles Eade)* (London: Cassell, 1945)

Cooper, D. *Old Men Forget* (London: Rupert Hart-Davis, 1953)

Delegación Nacional de Organizaciones del Movimiento, *25 Años de Política Española* (Madrid: Departamento Nacional de Prensa y Publicaciones, 1961)

Dilks, D. (ed.) *The Diaries of Sir Alexander Cadogan 1938–1945* (London: Cassell, 1971)

Dugdale, J. (ed.) *War Comes to Britain: Speeches of the Rt. Hon. C. R. Attlee, M.P.* (London: Gollancz, 1940)

Eccles, D. *By Safe Hand: Letters of Sybil and David Eccles 1939–1942* (London: Bodley Head, 1983)

Franco, F. *Franco Ha Dicho* (Madrid: publisher unnamed, 1947)

——*Textos de Doctrina Política: Palabras y Escritos de 1945 a 1950* (Madrid: Publicaciones Españolas, 1951)

——*Pensamiento Político*, 2 vols (Madrid: Ediciones del Movimiento, 1975)

——*Manuscritos de Franco (seleccionados por el Profesor Luis Suárez)* (Madrid: Otero, 1990)

Franco Salgado-Araujo, F. *Mi Vida Junto a Franco* (Barcelona: Planeta, 1977)

De Gaulle, C. *Mémoires de Guerre: le Salut 1944–1946* (Paris: Plon, 1959)

——*Discours et Messages: Pendant la Guerre, 1940–1946* (Paris: Plon, 1970)

——*Discours et Messages: Dans l'Attente, Février 1946–Avril 1958* (Paris: Plon, 1970)

Gil-Robles, J. *La Monarquía por la que Luché. Páginas de un Diario (1941–1954)* (Madrid: Taurus, 1976)

Hayes, C. *Wartime Mission in Spain, 1942–1945* (Toronto: Macmillan, 1945)

Hoare, S. *Ambassador on Special Mission* (London: Collins, 1946)

Hull, C. *The Memoirs of Cordell Hull*, 2 vols (London: Hodder & Stoughton, 1948)

Kimbell, W. (ed.) *Churchill & Roosevelt. The Complete Correspondence. III. Alliance Declining* (Princeton: Princeton University Press, 1984)

Kindelán, A. *La Verdad de Mis Relaciones con Franco* (Barcelona: Planeta, 1981)

——*Mis Cuadernos de Guerra* (Barcelona: Planeta, 1982)

Martínez Barrio, D. *Memorias* (Barcelona: Planeta, 1983)

Mera, C. *Guerra, Exilio y Cárcel de un Anarcosindicalista* (Paris: Ruedo Ibérico, 1976)

Pemán, J. *Mis Encuentros con Franco* (Barcelona: Dopesa, 1976)
Peterson, M. *Both Sides of the Curtain: an Autobiography* (London: Constable, 1950)
Philby, K. *My Silent War* (London: MacGibbon & Kee, 1968)
Piétri, F. *Mes Années d'Espagne, 1940–1948* (Paris: Plon, 1954)
Prieto, I. *Convulsiones de España,*
  Vol. I (Mexico, D.F: Oasis, 1967)
  Vol. II (Mexico, D.F: Oasis, 1968)
  Vol. III (Mexico, D.F: Oasis, 1969)
Prieto, I. *Discursos Fundamentales* (Madrid: Turner, 1975)
——*Cartas a un Escultor* (Barcelona: Planeta, 1989)
——*Epistolario Prieto-Negrín: Puntos de Vista sobre el Desarrollo y Consecuencias de la Guerra Civil Española* (Barcelona: Planeta, 1990)
——*Discursos en América: Con el Pensamiento puesto en España,* 2 vols (Barcelona: Planeta, 1991)
——*Epistolario, 1941–1946* (Eibarko: Udala, 1991)
Sainz Rodríguez, P. *Testimonio y Recuerdos* (Barcelona: Planeta, 1978)
——*Un Reinado en la Sombra* (Barcelona: Planeta, 1981)
Saña, H. *El Franquismo sin Mitos: Conversaciones con Serrano Suñer* (Barcelona: Grijalbo, 1982)
Serrano Suñer, R. *Entre Hendaya y Gibraltar* (Madrid: Ediciones Nauta 1973; first edition, 1947)
——*Entre el Silencio y la Propaganda; la Historia Como Fue. Memorias* (Barcelona: Planeta, 1977)
Truman, H. *Memoirs by Harry S. Truman. 2. Years of Trial and Hope, 1946–1952* (New York: Doubleday, 1956)
Vegas Latapié, E. *Memorias Políticas: El Suicidio de la Monarquía y la Segunda República* (Barcelona: Planeta, 1983)
——*Los Caminos del Desengaño* (Madrid: Tebas, 1987)
——*La Frustración en la Victoria: Memorias Políticas 1938–1942* (Madrid: Actas, 1995)
Williams, F. *A Prime Minister Remembers: the War and Post-War Memoirs of the Rt. Hon. Earl Attlee* (London: Heinemann, 1961)
Young, K. (ed.) *The Diaries of Sir Robert Bruce Lockhart 1939–1965* (London: Macmillan, 1980)

Articles

Adamthwaite, A. 'Britain and the World 1945–49: the View from the Foreign Office', *International Affairs*, 91, 2 (1985) 223–35
Aken, M. 'Don Albert Martín Artajo "el Canciller de la Resistencia"', *Política Internacional*, 30 (1957) 9–13
Alpert, M. 'Las Relaciones Hispano-Británicas en el Primer Año de la Posguerra: los Acuerdos Comerciales y Financieros de Marzo 1940', *Revista de Política Internacional*, 147 (1976) 13–29
Angoustures, A. 'L'Opinion Publique Française et l'Espagne 1945–75', *Revue d'Histoire Moderne et Contemporaine*, 37 (1990) 672–86
——'Les Réfugiés Espagnols en France de 1945 à 1981', *Revue d'Histoire Moderne et Contemporaine*, 44, 3 (1997) 457–83

Arranz, M. 'La Pobreza Ideológica del General Franco', *Historia 16*, 99 (1984) 11–20

Avilés Farré, J. 'Lequerica, Embajador Franquista en París', *Historia 16*, 160 (1989) 12–20

——'L'Ambassade de Lequerica et les Relations Hispano-Françaises 1939–1944', *Guerres Mondiales et Conflits Contemporains*, 158 (1990) 65–78

——'Un Alba en Londres: la Misión Diplomática del XVII Duque (1937–1939)', *Historia Contemporánea*, 15 (1996) 163–77

Bennett, G. 'Britain's Relations with France after Versailles: the Problem of Tangier, 1919–1923', *European History Quarterly*, 24, 1 (1994) 53–84

Benton, K. 'The ISOS Years: Madrid 1941–3', *Journal of Contemporary History*, 30, 3 (1995) 359–410

Biddiscombe, P. 'The French Resistance and the Chambéry Incident of June 1945', *French History*, II, 4 (1997) 438–60

Blinkhorn, M. 'Spain: The "Spanish Problem" and the Imperial Myth', *Journal of Contemporary History*, 15 (1980) 5–25

Brundu, P. 'L'Espagne Franquiste et la Politique Étrangère de la France au Lendemain de la Deuxième Guerre Mondiale', *Relations Internationales*, 50 (1987) 165–81

Buchanan, T. 'A Far Away Country of which We Know Nothing'? Perceptions of Spain and its Civil War in Britain, 1931–1939', *Twentieth Century British History*, 4, 1 (1993) 1–24

Buñuel Salcedo, L. 'La Embajada del Duque de Alba en Londres', *Historia 16*, 108 (1985) 11–24

——'La Génesis del "Cerco" Internacional al Régimen del General Franco (1945–1947)', *Espacio, Tiempo y Forma*, 1 (1987) 313–40

Cabeza Sánchez-Albornoz, S. 'Posición de la República Española en el Exilio ante el Ingreso de España en la ONU', *Cuadernos de Historia Contemporánea*, 17 (1995) 147–68

Castiella, F. 'Política Exterior de España (1898–1960)', *Cuadernos Hispano-Americanos*, 124 (1960) 5–18

Collado Seidel, C. '¿De Hendaya a San Francisco? Londres y Washington contra Franco y la Falange (1942–1945)', *Espacio, Tiempo y Forma, Serie V Historia Contemporánea*, 7 (1994) 51–84

Cowan, A. 'The Guerrilla War against Franco', *European History Quarterly*, 20, 2 (1990) 227–53

Croft, S. 'British Policy towards Western Europe, 1947–9: the Best of Possible Worlds', *International Affairs*, 64, 4 (1988) 617–29

Deighton, A. 'The "Frozen Front": the Labour Government, the Division of Germany and the Origins of the Cold War, 1945–7', *International Affairs*, 3, 2 (1987) 449–65

Delaunay, J-M. 'L'Espagne et la France, 1940–1945', *Guerres Mondiales et Conflits Contemporains*, 162 (1991) 99–103

Dreyfus-Armand, G. 'Les Réfugiés Républicains au Cœur des Relations Franco-Espagnols, 1945–1962', *Relations Internationales*, 74 (1993) 153–69

Dulphy, A. 'La Politique de la France à l'égard de l'Espagne Franquiste 1945–1949', *Revue d'Histoire Moderne et Contemporaine*, XXXV (1988) 123–40

Dunthorn, D. 'The Prieto–Gil-Robles Meeting of October 1947: Britain and the Failure of the Spanish Anti-Franco Coalition, 1945–50', *European History Quarterly*, 30, 1 (2000) 49–76

Fernández García, A. and Pereira Castañares, J. 'La Percepción Española de la ONU (1945–1962)', *Cuadernos de Historia Contemporánea*, 17 (1995) 121–46

Galán, D. and Lara, F. 'España 1947: las Conversaciones entre Gil Robles e Indalecio Prieto', *Tiempo de Historia*, 35 (1977) 102–17

García Durán, J. 'La CNT y Alianza Nacional de Fuerzas Democráticas' in *Cuadernos de Ruedo Ibérico* (supplement), *El Movimiento Libertario Español, Pasado, Presente y Futuro* (Paris: Ruedo Ibérico, 1974), pp. 123–28

Gilmour, J. 'Reliving an Imperialist Past – the Extreme Right, Franco and the Catholic Monarchs', *Tesserae*, 1, 2 (1995) 201–21

Gordon, R. 'France and the Spanish Civil War', unpublished PhD thesis (Columbia University, 1971)

Graham, H. 'Spain and Europe: the View from the Periphery', *History Journal*, 35, 4 (1992) 969–83

Greenwood, S. 'Ernest Bevin, France and "Western Union": August 1945–February 1946', *European History Quarterly*, 14, 3 (1984) 319–37

Guerrero, A. and Mateos, A. 'Algunas Notas sobre el Hispanismo Británico del *Laberinto Español* de Brenan al *Franco* de Preston', *Spagna Contemporanea*, 8 (1995) 133–47

Hamilton, K. 'Non-Intervention Revisted: Great Britain, the United Nations and Franco's Spain in 1946', *Foreign & Commonwealth Office Historians. Occasional Papers*, 10 (1995) 46–63

Johnson, E. 'Britain and the United Nations, 1946', *Foreign & Commonwealth Office Historians. Occasional Papers*, 10 (1995) 5–21

Jover, J. 'La Percepción Española de los Conflictos Europeos: Notas Históricas para su Entendimiento', *Revista de Occidente*, 57 (1986) 5–42

Leitz, C. ' "More Carrot than Stick", British Economic Warfare and Spain, 1941–1944', *Twentieth Century British History*, 9, 2 (1998) 246–73

De León-Portilla, A. 'El Primer Año del Exilio Español en México', *Historia 16*, 94 (1984) 11–22

Lleonart y Anselem, A. 'El Ingreso de España en la ONU: Obstáculos e Impulsos', *Cuadernos de Historia Contemporánea*, 17 (1995) 101–19

Marquina Barrio, A. 'Conspiración contra Franco. El Ejército y la Injerencia Extranjera en España: el Papel de Aranda 1939–45', *Historia 16*, 72 (1982) 21–30

—— 'El Servicio Secreto Vasco', *Historia 16*, 97 (1984) 11–26

—— 'La Neutralidad o la Pérdida de la Neutralidad en la Segunda Guerra Mundial. Cuestiones Pendientes de un Debate Todavía Inconcluso', *Espacio, Tiempo y Forma, Serie V, Historia Contemporánea*, 7 (1994) 313–22

Martínez Lillo, P. 'Una Aproximación al Estudio de las Relaciones Bilaterales Hispano-Francesas durante la Posguerra. El "Affaire" Fronterizo en la Perspectiva del Quai d'Orsay (1946–1948)', *Revista de Estudios Internacionales*, 6, 3 (1985) 567–99

—— 'La Normalización de las Relaciones Diplomáticas Hispano-Francesas después de la IIª Guerra Mundial (Septiembre de 1950–Enero de 1951)', *Mélanges de la Casa de Velázquez* (École des Hautes Études Hispaniques), XXIX, 3 (1993) 307–25

Moradiellos García, E. 'El Franquismo: Cuarenta Años de la Historia Contemporánea de España', *Revista de Extremadura*, 18 (1995) 3–19
—— 'Juan Negrín: un Socialista en la Guerra Civil', *Sistema*, 125 (1995) 23–31
Morales Lezcano, V. 'Les Relations de l'Espagne avec ses Voisins', *Relations Internationales*, 37 (1984) 141–47
—— 'La Cuestión del Reajuste de Fronteras Interzonales en el Protectorado Hispano-Francés en Marruecos', *Revista de Estudios Internacionales*, 6, 2 (1985) 357–77
—— 'L'Espagne de l'Isolationnisme à l'Intégration Internationale', *Relations Internationales*, 50 (1987) 147–55
Mugnaini, M. 'Recenti Studi sulla Politica Estera della Spagna Contemporanea', *Storia delle Relazioni Internazionali*, 2 (1989) 371–85
Payne, S. 'El Régimen de Franco en Perspectiva', *Historia 16*, 122 (1986) 11–19
Pereira Castañares, J. and Cervantes Conejo, A. 'La Política Exterior del Franquismo: un Reto para la Historiografía Española', *Cuadernos de Historia Contemporánea*, 12 (1990) 175–82
Pereira Castañares, J. and Moreno Juste, A. 'La Spagna Franchista di fronte al Processo di Costruzione Europea (1945–1970), *Storia delle Relazioni Internazionali*, 7, 1 (1991) 53–88
Von Petersdorff, E. 'Las Relaciones Internacionales de España en los Años 1945 a 1955', *Revista de Política Internacional*, 58, 88 (1971) 51–88
Pike, D. 'Franco and the Axis Stigma', *Journal of Contemporary History*, 17 (1982) 369–409
—— 'Franco et l'Admission aux Nations Unies', *Guerres Mondiales et Conflits Contemporains*, 162 (1991) 105–14
Pollis, A. 'United States Foreign Policy towards Authoritarian Regimes in the Mediterranean', *Millennium. Journal of International Studies*, 4, 1 (1975) 28–51
Portero, F. 'La Política Española del Reino Unido en la Postguerra Mundial', *Espacio, Tiempo y Forma*, 1 (1987) 341–59
—— 'Artajo, Perfil de un Ministro en Tiempos de Aislamiento', *Historia Contemporánea*, 15 (1996) 211–24
Preston, P. 'The Dilemma of Credibility: the Spanish Communist Party, the Franco Régime and After', *Government and Opposition: a Journal of Comparative Politics*, 11, 1 (1976) 65–83
—— 'Franco et ses Généraux (1939–1945)', *Guerres Mondiales et Conflits Contemporains*, 162 (1991) 7–28
—— 'Franco y la Elaboración de una Política Exterior Personalista (1936–1953)', *Historia Contemporánea*, 15 (1996) 193–210
De Rivas, E. 'Azaña en Montauban', *Historia 16*, 178 (1991) 12–30
Romero Maura, J. 'Spain: the Civil War and After', *Journal of Contemporary History*, 2 (1967) 157–68
Del Rosal, A. 'El Tesoro de *Vita*', *Historia 16*, 95 (1984) 11–24
Sánchez Férriz, R. 'Cánovas y la Constitución de 1876', *Revista de Estudios Políticos*, 101 (1998) 9–43
Smith, R. and Zametica, J. 'The Cold Warrior: Clement Attlee Reconsidered, 1945–7', *International Affairs*, 61, 2 (1985) 237–52
Smyth, D. 'Screening "Torch": Allied Counter-Intelligence and the Spanish Threat to the Secrecy of the Allied Invasion of French North Africa in November, 1942', *Intelligence and National Security*, 4, 2 (1989) 335–56

—— ' "Les Chevaliers de Saint-George": la Grande-Bretagne et la Corruption des Généraux Espagnols (1940–1942)', *Guerres Mondiales et Conflits Contemporains*, 162 (1991) 29–54

—— 'Franco Cunctator', *The International History Review*, XVIII, 3 (1996) 629–40

Stone, G. 'Britain, France and Franco's Spain in the Aftermath of the Civil War', *Diplomacy and Statecraft*, 6, 2 (1995) 373–407

Sueiro, S. 'España en Tánger durante la Segunda Guerra Mundial: la Consumación de un Viejo Anhelo', *Cuadernos de Historia Contemporánea*, 17 (1995) 135–63

Tusell, J. 'La Autarquía Cuartelera: las ideas Económicas de Franco a partir de un Documento Inédito' in *Franco, Diez Años Después, Historia 16, número especial*, 115 (1985) 41–9

Viñas, A. 'Autarquía y Política Exterior en el Primer Franquismo 1939–1959', *Revista de Estudios Internacionales*, I, 1 (1980) 61–92

—— 'La Política Exterior Española en el Franquismo', *Cuenta y Razón*, 6 (1982) 61–76

—— 'La Historia de la Contemporaneidad Española y el Acceso a los Archivos del Franquismo', *Sistema*, 78 (1987) 17–36

Walton, J. 'British Perceptions of Spain and their Impact on Attitudes to the Spanish Civil War. Some additional Evidence', *Twentieth Century British History*, 5, 3 (1994) 283–99

Secondary works

Abellán, J. (ed.) *El Exilio Español de 1939, 1, La Emigración Republicana; 2, Guerra y Política* (Madrid: Taurus, 1976)

Aguado Sánchez, F. *El Maquis en España. Su Historia* (Madrid: San Martín, 1975)

Ahmad, Q. *Britain, Franco Spain and the Cold War, 1945–1950*, revised edn (Kuala Lumpur: A S Noordeen, 1995)

—— 'Britain and the Isolation of Franco 1945–1950' in Leitz, C. and Dunthorn, D. (eds) *Spain in an International Context, 1936–1959* (New York & Oxford: Berghahn, 1999)

Alba, V. *1936–1976: Historia de la II República Española* (Barcelona: Planeta, 1976)

—— *Historia de la Resistencia Antifranquista 1939–1955* (Barcelona: Planeta, 1978)

Aldrich, R. and Connell, J. (eds) *France in World Politics* (London: Routledge, 1989)

Aldrich, R. 'Unquiet in Death: the Post-War Survival of the "Special Operations Executive", 1945–51' in Gorst, A., Johnman, L. and Scott Lucas W. (eds) *Contemporary British History 1931–61: Politics and the Limits of Policy* (London & New York: Pinter Publishers, 1991)

—— *British Intelligence, Strategy and the Cold War, 1945–51* (London: Routledge, 1992)

Alexander, M. 'France, the Collapse of Republican Spain and the Approach of General War: National Security, War Economics and the Spanish Refugees, 1938–1940' in Leitz, C. and Dunthorn, D. (eds) *Spain in an International Context, 1936–1959* (New York & Oxford: Berghahn, 1999)

Alfaya, J. 'Españoles en los Campos de Concentración' in Abellán, J. *El Exilio Español de 1939, 2, Guerra y Política* (Madrid: Taurus, 1976)

Allardt, E. and Littunen, Y. (eds) *Cleavages, Ideologies and Party Systems: Contribu-*

tions to Comparative Political Sociology (Helsinki: UNESCO & Finnish Ministry of Education, 1964)

Alpert, M. 'Don Juan Negrín en Londres, 1940–1956' in Tusell, J., Alted, A., Mateos, A. *et al. La Oposición al Régimen de Franco: Estado de la Cuestión y Metodología de la Investigación: Actas del Congreso Internacional que, organizado por el Departamento de Historia Contemporánea de la UNED, tuvo lugar en Madrid del 19 al 22 de Octubre de 1988*, Vol. I-I (Madrid: UNED, 1990)

Alted Vigil, A. 'La Oposición Republicana, 1939–1977' in Townson, N. (ed.) *El Republicanismo en España (1830–1977)* (Madrid: Alianza Universitaria, 1994)

Amalric, J-P. and Pech, R. 'L'Équilibre Impossible: les Échanges Agro-Alimentaires Franco-Espagnols avant l'Élargissement du Marché Commun (1945–1985)' in *España, Francia y la Comunidad Europea* (Madrid: Consejo Superior de Investigaciones Científicas, 1989)

Anderson, C. *The Political Economy of Modern Spain, Policy Making in an Authoritarian Regime* (Madison: University of Wisconsin Press, 1970)

Andrews, C. *Secret Service: the Making of the British Intelligence Service* (London: Sceptre, 1986)

Andrews, C. and Noakes, J. (eds) *Intelligence and International Relations 1900–1945* (University of Exeter, 1987)

Anson, L. *Don Juan* (Barcelona: Plaza & Janés, 1994)

Armero, J. *La Política Exterior de Franco* (Barcelona: Planeta, 1978)

Aróstegui, J. 'Nuevas Aportaciones al Estudio de la Oposición en el Exterior: Largo Caballero y la Política de "Transición y Plebiscito"' in García Delgado, J. (ed.) *El Primer Franquismo: España durante la Segunda Guerra Mundial* (Madrid: Siglo Veintiuno Editores, 1989)

——'La Oposición al Franquismo. Represión y Violencia Políticas' in Tusell, J., Alted, A., Mateos, A. *et al. La Oposición al Régimen de Franco: Estado de la Cuestión y Metodología de la Investigación: Actas del Congreso Internacional que, organizado por el Departamento de Historia Contemporánea de la UNED, tuvo lugar en Madrid del 19 al 22 de Octubre de 1988*, Vol. I-I (Madrid: UNED, 1990)

Avilés Farré, J. *Pasión y Farsa. Franceses y Británicos ante la Guerra Civil Española* (Madrid: Eudema, 1994)

Badía, J. *El Régimen de Franco* (Madrid: Tecnos, 1984)

Balfour, S. and Preston, P. (eds) *Spain and the Great Powers in the Twentieth Century* (London & New York: Routledge, 1999)

Barker, E. *Britain in a Divided Europe 1945–1970* (London: Weidenfeld & Nicolson, 1971)

——*The British between the Superpowers 1945–50* (London: Macmillan, 1983)

Barnett, C. *The Audit of War: the Illusion and Reality of Britain as a Great Nation* (London: Macmillan, 1986)

——*The Lost Victory: British Dreams, British Realities 1945–1950* (London: Macmillan, 1995)

Barston, R. (ed.) *The Other Powers: Studies in the Foreign Policy of Small States* (London: Allen & Unwin, 1973)

Bayod, A. *Franco Visto por sus Ministros* (Barcelona: Planeta, 1981)

Becker, J. and Knipping, F. (eds) *Power in Europe?: Great Britain, France, Italy and Germany in a Postwar World, 1945–1950* (Berlin: de Gruyter, 1986)

Ben Amí, S. *La Revolución desde Arriba: España 1936–1979* (Barcelona: Ríopiedras Ediciones, no date)

Bermejo, J. *et al*. *1812–1992, el Arte de Gobernar: Historia del Consejo de Ministros y de la Presidencia del Gobierno* (Madrid: Edición preparada por el Ministerio de Relaciones con las Cortes y de la Secretaría del Gobierno, Tecnos, 1992)

Berrington, H. *Backbench Opinion in the House of Commons 1945–55* (Oxford: Pergamon, 1973)

De Blaye, E. *Franco ou la Monarchie sans Roi* (Paris: Stock, 1974)

Blescas Ferrer, J. and Tuñón de Lara, M. *Historia de España. X. España bajo la Dictadura Franquista (1939–1975)* 2nd edn (Madrid: Editorial Labor, 1990)

Blinkhorn, M. *Carlism and Crisis in Spain 1931–1939* (Cambridge University Press, 1975)

——'Right-wing Utopianism and Harsh Reality: Carlism, the Republic and the "Crusade"' in Blinkhorn, M. (ed.) *Spain in Conflict 1931–1939: Democracy and Its Enemies* (London: Sage, 1986)

——(ed.), *Spain in Conflict 1931–1939: Democracy and Its Enemies* (London: Sage, 1986)

Bolloten, B. and Esenwein, G. 'Anarchists in Government: a Paradox of the Spanish Civil War, 1936–1939' in Lannon, F. and Preston, P. (eds) *Élites and Power in Twentieth Century Spain. Essays in Honour of Sir Raymond Carr* (Oxford: Clarendon Press, 1990)

Borràs Betriu, R. *El Rey de los Rojos: Don Juan de Borbón. Una Figura Tergiversada*, 3rd edn (Barcelona: Plaza & Janés, 1996)

Borras Llop, J. *Política de los Exiliados Españoles 1944–1950* (Paris: Ruedo Ibérico, 1976)

——'Relaciones entre los Gobiernos de París y Burgos al final de la Guerra Civil; la Firma del Convenio Jordana-Bérard' in Castillo, S., Forcadell, C., García-Nieto, M., Sisino Pérez Garzón, J. (eds) *Estudios sobre Historia de España. Homenaje a Manuel Tuñon de Lara*, II (Madrid: Universidad Internacional 'M Pelayo', 1981)

Botín, L. *Españoles en el Reino Unido. Breve Reseña, 1810–1988* (Madrid: Ministerio de Trabajo y Seguridad Social, 1988)

Boyce, R. and Robertson, E. (eds) *Paths to War: New Essays on the Origins of the Second World War* (London: Macmillan, 1989)

Brinkley, D. (ed.) *Dean Acheson and the Making of U.S. Foreign Policy* (London: Macmillan, 1993)

Brundu, P. *Ostracismo e Realpolitik: gli Alleati e la Spagna Franchista negli Anni del Dopoguerra* (Università di Cagliari, Pubblicazioni della Facoltà di Scienze Politiche: Instituto Storico Politico, C.E.L.T. Editrice, 1984)

Buchanan, T. *The Spanish Civil War and the British Labour Movement* (Cambridge University Press, 1991)

Bullock, A. *Ernest Bevin: Foreign Secretary, 1945–1951* (London: Heinemann, 1983)

Cabanellas, G. *Cuatro Generales*, 2 vols (Barcelona, Planeta, 1977)

Cabeza Sánchez-Albornoz, S. *Historia Política de la Segunda República en el Exilio* (Madrid: Fundación Universitaria Española, 1997)

Cairncross, R. *Years of Recovery: British Economic Policy 1945–51* (London: Methuen, 1985)

Calvo Serrer, R. *Franco frente al Rey: el Proceso del Régimen* (Paris: publisher unnamed, 1972)

Cappelle, R. *The MRP and French Foreign Policy* (New York: Praeger, 1963)

De Carmoy, G. *Les Politiques Étrangères de la France, 1944–66* (Paris: La Table Ronde, 1967)

Carr, R. *Modern Spain 1875–1980* (Oxford University Press, 1980)
——*Spain, 1808–1975* 2nd edn (Oxford: Clarendon Press, 1982)
Carrillo, S. *Juez y Parte. 15 Retratos Españoles* (Barcelona: Plaza & Janés, 1996)
Castillo, S., Forcadell, C., García-Nieto, M., Sisino Pérez Garzón, J. (eds) *Estudios sobre Historia de España: Homenaje a Manuel Tuñon de Lara*, II (Madrid: Universidad Internacional 'M Pelayo', 1981)
Catterall, P. and Morris, C. (eds) *Britain and the Threat to Stability in Europe, 1918–45* (Leicester University Press, 1993)
Caudet, F. *Hipótesis sobre el Exilio Republicano de 1939* (Madrid: Fundación Universitaria Española, 1997)
Cava Mesa, M. *Los Diplomáticos de Franco. J.F. de Lequerica, Temple y Tenacidad (1880–1963)* (Bilbao: Universidad de Deusto, 1989)
Cerny, P. *The Politics of Grandeur: Ideological Aspects of de Gaulle's Foreign Policy* (Cambridge University Press, 1980)
Chastagnaret, G. 'Une Histoire Ambigüe: les Relations Commerciales entre l'Espagne et les Onze de 1949 à 1982' in Consejo Superior de Investigaciones Científicas, *España, Francia y la Comunidad Europea* (Madrid: Casa de Velázquez, CSIC, Departamento de Historia Contemporánea, 1989)
Churchill, W. *The Second World War. V. Closing the Ring* (London: Cassell, 1952)
De la Cierva, R. *Francisco Franco: un Siglo de España*, 2 vols (Madrid: Editora Nacional, 1973)
——*Historia del Franquismo. Orígenes y Configuración (1939–1945)* (Barcelona: Planeta, 1975)
——*Historia del Franquismo. Aislamiento, Transformación, Agonía (1945–1975)* (Barcelona: Planeta, 1978)
——*Pro y Contra Franco. Franquismo y Antifranquismo* (Barcelona: Planeta, 1985)
——*La Conversión de Indalecio Prieto* (Barcelona: Plaza & Janés, 1988)
——*Victoria Eugenia; el Veneno en la Sangre* (Barcelona: Planeta, 1995)
——*Don Juan de Borbón: Por Fin Toda la Verdad. Las Aportaciones Definitivas* (Madrid: Fénix, 1997)
Clemente, J. *El Carlismo en la España de Franco (Bases Documentales 1936–1977)* (Madrid: Editorial Fundamentos, 1994)
Consejo Superior de Investigaciones Científicas, *Españoles y Franceses en la Primera Mitad del Siglo XX* (Madrid: Consejo Superior de Investigaciones Científicas, 1986)
——*España, Francia y la Comunidad Europea* (Madrid: Consejo Superior de Investigaciones Científicas, 1989)
Cortada, J. *Two Nations over Time: Spain and the United States, 1776–1977* (London: Greenwood Press, 1978)
——(ed.) *Spain in the Twentieth Century. Essays on Spanish Diplomacy, 1898–1978* (London: Aldwych Press, 1980)
Cross, J. *Sir Samuel Hoare: a Political Biography* (London: Jonathan Cape, 1977)
Crozier, B. *Franco: a Biographical History* (London: Eyre & Spottiswoode, 1967)
Dahl R. (ed.) *Regimes and Oppositions* (Newhaven and London: Yale University Press, 1973)
Deighton, A. *Britain and the First Cold War* (London: Macmillan, 1990)
Descloa, J. *Oh España* (Barcelona: Argos-Vergara, 1976), translated from *O Espagne* (Paris: Albin Michel, 1976)

Díaz Barrado, M. 'El Partido Socialista en el Exilio Americano: Indalecio Prieto' in Tusell, J., Alted, A., Mateos, A. *et al*. *La Oposición al Régimen de Franco: Estado de la Cuestión y Metodología de la Investigación: Actas del Congreso Internacional que, organizado por el Departamento de Historia Contemporánea de la UNED, tuvo lugar en Madrid del 19 al 22 de Octubre de 1988*, Vol. I-I (Madrid: UNED, 1990)

Díaz-Plaja, F. *La España Política del Siglo XX* (Barcelona: Plaza & Janés, 1972)

Dockrill, M. and Young, J. (eds) *British Foreign policy, 1945–56* (London: Macmillan, 1989)

Domínguez Ortiz, A. (ed.) *Historia de España, Alfonso XIII y la Segunda República (1902–1939)*, Vol. II (Barcelona: Planeta, 1991)

Duroselle, J-B. 'Le Général de Gaulle et l'Espagne (1940–1944)' in *Españoles y Franceses en la Primera Mitad del Siglo XX* (Madrid: Consejo Superior de Investigaciones Científicas, 1986)

Edwards, J. *The British Government and the Spanish Civil War* (London: Macmillan, 1979)

——*Anglo-American Relations and the Franco Question 1945–1955* (Oxford: Clarendon Press, 1999)

Ellwood, S. *Spanish Fascism in the Franco Era* (New York: St. Martin's Press, 1987)

——*Franco* (London: Longman, 1994)

Espada Burgos, M. *Franquismo y Política Exterior* (Madrid: Rialp, 1988)

Estruch Tobella, J. *El PCE en la Clandestinidad, 1939–1956* (Madrid: Siglo Veintiuno de España Editores, 1982)

Fagen, P. *Exiles and Citizens: Spanish Republicans in Mexico* (Austin & London: University of Texas Press, 1973)

Feis, H. *The Spanish Story: Franco and the Nations at War* (Westport, Connecticut: Greenwood Press, 1966)

Feld, W. (ed.) *The Foreign Policy of the West European Socialist Parties* (New York & London: Praeger, 1978)

Fernández, A. *La España de los Maquis* (Mexico: Ediciones Era, 1971)

——'Las Formaciones Políticas del Exilio' in Abellán, J. (ed.) *El Exilio Español en 1939, 2, Guerra y Política* (Madrid: Taurus, 1976)

Fernández, C. *El General Franco* (Barcelona: Argos Vergara, 1983)

——*Tensiones Militares durante el Franquismo* (Barcelona: Plaza & Janés, 1985)

Fernández Vargas, V. *La Resistencia Interior en la España de Franco* (Madrid: Ediciones Istmo, 1981)

Ferrary, A. *El Franquismo: Minorías Políticas y Conflictos Ideológicos (1936–1956)* (Pamplona: Ediciones Universidad de Navarra, 1993)

Fondo de Cultura Económica, *El Exilio Español en México* (Mexico: Salvat, 1982)

Fontana, J. (ed.) *España bajo el Franquismo* (Barcelona: Grijalbo, 1986)

Foot, M. and Langley, J. *M19: The British Secret Service that Fostered Escape and Evasion: 1939–1945 and its American Counterpart* (London: Bodley Head, 1979)

Footitt, H. and Simmonds, J. *France 1943–1945* (Leicester University Press, 1988)

Frankel, J. *British Foreign Policy 1945–1973* (London: published for the Royal Institute of International Affairs by Oxford University Press, 1975)

Fuente, I. *Don Juan de Borbón: Hijo de Rey, Padre de Rey, Nunca Rey* (Barcelona: Prensa Ibérica, 1992)

Fusi, J. *Franco: Autoritarismo y Poder Personal* (Madrid: Ediciones El País, 1985), translated as *Franco: a Biography* (London: Unwin Hyman, 1987)

Gallo, M. *Histoire de l'Espagne Franquiste* (Paris: Laffon, 1969), translated as *Historia de la España Franquista* (Paris: Ruedo Ibérico, 1971)

García Delgado, J. (ed.) *El Primer Franquismo. España durante la Segunda Guerra Mundial* (Madrid: Siglo Veintiuno Editores, 1989)

García Escudero, M. *Vista a la Derecha* (Madrid: Ediciones Rialp, 1988)

García-Nieto, M. and Donezar, J. *La España de Franco, 1939–1973. Bases Documentales de la España Contemporánea*. Vol. XI (Madrid: Guadiana, 1975)

Garriga, R. *La España de Franco. De la División Azul al Pacto con los Estados Unidos (1943 a 1951)* (Puebla, Mexico: Editorial José M Cajica JR, 1971)

——*Nicolás Franco, el Hermano Brujo* (Barcelona: Planeta, 1980)

——*Los Validos de Franco* (Barcelona: Planeta, 1981)

Georgel, J. *Le Franquisme: Histoire et Bilan (1939–1969)* (Paris: Éditions du Seuil, 1970)

Gibaja Velázquez, J. *Indalecio Prieto y el Socialismo Español* (Madrid: Editorial Pablo Iglesias, 1995)

Gillespie, R. *The Spanish Socialist Party: a History of Factionalism* (Oxford: Clarendon Press, 1989)

Giral, F. 'Actividad de los Gobiernos y de los Partidos Republicanos (1939–1976)' in Abellán, J. (ed.) *El Exilio Español de 1939, 2, Guerra y Política* (Madrid: Taurus, 1976)

Giral, F. and Santidrian, P. *La República en el Exilio* (Madrid: Historia Secreta del Franquismo Ediciones, 1977)

González-Doria, F. *Don Juan de Borbón* (Madrid: Mirasierra, 1976)

Gordon, M. *Conflict and Consensus in Labour's Foreign Policy 1914–1965* (Stanford University Press, 1969)

Gorst, A., Johnman, L., and Scott Lucas, W. (eds) *Contemporary British History 1931–61: Politics and the Limits of Policy* (London & New York: Pinter Publishers, 1991)

Graham, H. *Socialism and War: the Spanish Socialist Party in Power and Crisis, 1936–1939* (Cambridge University Press, 1991)

——'War, Modernity and Reform; the Premiership of Juan Negrín 1937–1939' in Preston, P. and MacKenzie, A. (eds) *The Republic Besieged: Civil War in Spain 1936–1939* (Edinburgh University Press, 1996)

Graham, H. and Preston, P. (eds) *The Popular Front in Europe* (London: Macmillan, 1987)

Grosser, A. *La IVe République et sa Politique Extérieure*, 3rd edn (Paris: Armand Colin, 1961)

Guirao, F. *Spain and the Reconstruction of Western Europe, 1945–57* (London: Macmillan, 1998)

Harper, J. *American Visions of Europe* (Cambridge University Press, 1994)

Harris, K. *Attlee* (London: Weidenfeld & Nicolson, 1982)

Harrison, J. *An Economic History of Modern Spain* (Manchester University Press, 1978)

——*The Spanish Economy in the Twentieth Century* (London & Sydney: Croom Helm, 1985)

Heine, H. *La Oposición Política al Franquismo de 1939 a 1952* (Barcelona: Editorial Crítica, 1983)

Hermet, G. *Les Communistes en Espagne: Étude d'un Mouvement Politique Clandestin* (Paris: Armand Colin, 1971)

Hills, G. *Franco: the Man and His Nation* (London: Robert Hale, 1967)

Hinsley, F. *British Intelligence in the Second World War: Its Influence on Strategy and Operations*, I (London: HMSO, 1979)

Hogan, M. *The Marshall Plan: America, Britain and the Reconstruction of Western Europe, 1947–1952* (New York: Cambridge University Press, 1987)

Jáuregui, F. and Vega, P. *Crónica del Anti-Franquismo. Los Hombres que Lucharon por Devolver la Democracia a España*, I (Madrid: Argos Vergara, 1983)

Jensen, E. and Fisher, T. (eds) *The United Kingdom – The United Nations* (London: Macmillan, 1990)

Jérez Mir, M. *Elites Políticas y Centros de Extracción en España, 1938–1957* (Madrid: Centro de Investigaciones Sociológicas, 1982)

Jiménez de Aberasturi, J. *La Huelga General del 1º de Mayo de 1947* (San Sebastián: Eusko Ikaskuntza, 1991)

Jones, M. *Britain, the United States and the Mediterranean War* (Oxford: Clarendon Press, 1996)

Judt, T. (ed.) *Resistance and Revolution in Mediterranean Europe, 1938–1948* (London: Routledge, 1989)

Karsh, E. *Neutrality and Small States* (London: Routledge, 1988)

Langhorne, R. (ed.) *Diplomacy and Intelligence during the Second World War. Essays in Honour of F.H. Hinsley* (Cambridge University Press, 1985)

Lannon, F. *Privilege, Persecution and Prophesy: the Catholic Church in Spain, 1875–1975* (Oxford University Press, 1987)

Lannon, F. and Preston, P. (eds) *Elites and Power in Twentieth Century Spain. Essays in Honour of Sir Raymond Carr* (Oxford: Clarendon Press, 1990)

Leffler, M. and Painter, D. (eds) *Origins of the Cold War: an International History* (London: Routledge, 1994)

Leitz, C. *Economic Relations between Nazi Germany and Franco's Spain 1936–1945* (Oxford University Press, 1996)

Leitz, C. and Dunthorn, D. (eds) *Spain in an International Context, 1936–1959* (New York & Oxford: Berghahn, 1999)

Lewis, J. *Changing Direction: British Military Planning for Post-War Strategic Defence, 1942–1947* (London: Sherwood Press, 1988)

Lieberman, S. *The Contemporary Spanish Economy: a Historical Perspective* (London: Allen & Unwin, 1982)

Liedtke, B. *Embracing a Dictatorship: US Relations with Spain* (London: Macmillan, 1998)

Linz, J. 'An authoritarian Régime: Spain' in Allardt, E. and Littunen, Y. (eds) *Cleavages, Ideologies and Party Systems: Contributions to Comparative Political Sociology* (Helsinki: UNESCO & Finnish Ministry of Education, 1964)

——'Opposition in and under an Authoritarian Regime: the Case of Spain' in Dahl, R. (ed.) *Regimes and Oppositions* (Newhaven & London: Yale University Press, 1973)

Little, D. *Malevolent Neutrality: the United States, Great Britain, and the Origins of the Spanish Civil War* (Ithaca, New York: Cornell University Press, 1985)

Lleonart y Anselem, A. and Castiella y Maiz, F. *España y ONU, I (1945–1946). La «Cuestión Española». Documentación Básica, Sistematizada y Anotada* (Madrid: Consejo Superior de Investigaciones Científicas, 1978)

Lleonart y Anselem, A. *España y ONU, II (1947). La «Cuestión Española». Estudio introductorio y Corpus Documental* (Madrid: Consejo Superior de Investigaciones Científicas, 1983)
——*España y ONU, III (1948–49). La «Cuestión Española»* (Madrid: Consejo Superior de Investigaciones Científicas, 1985)
De Llera, L. and Andrés-Gallego, J. *La España de Posguerra: un Testimonio* (Madrid: Consejo Superior de Investigaciones Científicas, 1992)
Llorens, V. 'La Emigración Republicana de 1939' in Abellán, J. (ed.) *El Exilio Español de 1939, 1, La Emigración Republicana* (Madrid: Taurus, 1976)
López Rodó, L. *La Larga Marcha hacia la Monarquía* (Barcelona: Plaza & Janés, 1979; first published Barcelona: Noguer, 1977)
Luard, E. *A History of the United Nations. Vol. I: The Years of Western Domination 1945–1955* (London: Macmillan, 1982)
MacLachlan, D. *Room 39: Naval Intelligence in Action* (London: Weidenfeld & Nicolson, 1968)
McLellan, D. *Dean Acheson: the State Department Years* (New York: Dodd, Mead & Company, 1976)
Maier, C. 'Hegemony and Autonomy within the Western Alliance' in Leffler, M. and Painter, D. (eds) *Origins of the Cold War: an International History* (London: Routledge, 1994)
Maldonado, V. 'Vías Políticas y Diplomáticas del Exilio' in Fondo de Cultura Económica, *El Exilio Español en México* (Mexico: Salvat, 1982)
Malerbe, P. *La Oposición al Franquismo 1939/1975* (Madrid: Ediciones Naranco, 1977)
Marichal, J. 'Juan Negrín y la Continuidad de la Segunda República' in Tusell, J., Alted, A., Mateos, A. *et al. La Oposición al Régimen de Franco: Estado de la Cuestión y Metodología de la Investigación: Actas del Congreso Internacional que, organizado por el Departamento de Historia Contemporánea de la UNED, tuvo lugar en Madrid del 19 al 22 de Octubre de 1988*, Vol. I-I (Madrid: UNED, 1990)
Marquina Barrio, A. *La Diplomacia Vaticana y la España de Franco (1936–1945)* (Madrid: Consejo Superior de Investigaciones Científicas, 1983)
——*España en la Política de Seguridad Occidental 1939–1986* (Madrid: Servicio de Publicaciones del Estado Mayor del Ejército, 1986)
Martínez Cobo, C. and Martínez Cobo, J. *La Primera Renovación. Intrahistoria del PSOE, Volumen I (1939–1945)*, (Barcelona: Plaza & Janés, 1989)
——*¿República? ¿Monarquía? En busca del Consenso. Intrahistoria del PSOE. Volumen II (1946–1954)* (Barcelona: Plaza & Janés, 1992)
Martínez Lillo, P. *Une Introducción al Estudio de las Relaciones Hispano-Francesas (1945–1951)* (Madrid: Fundación Juan March, 1985)
——'Francia y la Cuestión Española en el Tercer Período de Sesiones de la Asamblea General en las Naciones Unidas' in Lleonart y Anselem, A. *España y ONU, III (1948–49). La «Cuestión Española»* (Madrid: Consejo Superior de Investigaciones Científicas, 1985)
——'La Perspectiva de la Ruptura Diplomática con la España Franquista en la Política Francesa (Noviembre–Diciembre de 1945–Enero de 1946)' in Tusell, J., Sueiro, S., Marín, J., Casanova, M. *El Régimen de Franco: Política y Relaciones Exteriores*, II (Madrid: UNED, 1993)
Martínez Nadal, R. *Antonio Torres y la Política Española del Foreign Office (1940–1944)*, I (Madrid: Casariego, 1989)

——*Antonio Torres de la* BBC *a* The Observer: *Republicanos y Monárquicos en el Exilio 1944–1956*, II (Madrid: Casariego, 1996)

Medhurst, K. *Government in Spain: the Executive at Work* (Oxford, Pergamon Press, 1973)

Miaja de Liscy, T. and Maya Nava, A. 'Creación de Organismos, Mutualidades, Centros de Reunión, Instituciones Académicas' in Fondo de Cultura Económica, *Exilio Español en México* (Mexico: Salvat, 1982)

De Miguel, A. *Sociología del Franquismo* (Barcelona: Editorial Euros, 1975)

Milward, A. *The Reconstruction of Western Europe, 1945–51* (London: Routledge, 1984)

Mir Curcó, C. 'Violencia Política, Coacción Legal y Oposición Interior' in Sánchez Recio, G. (ed.) *El Primer Franquismo (1936–1959)* (Madrid: *Ayer*, 33, Marcial Pons, 1999)

Miscamble, W. *George F. Kennan and the Making of American Foreign Policy 1947–1950* (Princeton University Press, 1992)

Montero, J. 'Los Católicos Ideológicos de la ANCP durante la Primera Etapa del Franquismo' in Fontana, J. (ed.) *España bajo el Franquismo* (Barcelona: Editorial Crítica, Grijalbo, 1986)

Montero, M. *Historia de la Asociación Católica Nacional de Propagandistas. La Construcción del Estado Confesional 1936–1945.* II (Pamplona: Ediciones Universidad de Pamplona, 1993)

Moradiellos García, E. *Neutralidad Benévola* (Oviedo: Pentalfa, 1990)

——'El General Apacible. La Imagen Oficial Británico de Franco durante la Guerra Civil' in Tusell, J., Sueiro, S., Marín, J., Casanova, M. *El Régimen de Franco: Política y Relaciones Exteriores*, II (Madrid: UNED, 1993)

——'Appeasement and Non-Intervention: British Policy during the Spanish Civil War' in Catterall, P. and Morris, C. (eds) *Britain and the Threat to Stability in Europe, 1918–45* (Leicester University Press, 1993)

——*La Perfidia de Albión; el Gobierno Británico y la Guerra Civil Española* (Madrid: Siglo XXI de España, 1996)

——'La Conferencia de Potsdam de 1945 y el Problema Español' in Tusell, J., Avilés, J., Pardo, R., Casanova, M., Mateos, A., Sepúlveda, I., Soto, A. (eds) *La Política Exterior de España en el Siglo XX* (Madrid: UNED, 1997)

——'The British Government and General Franco during the Spanish Civil War' in Leitz, C. and Dunthorn, D. (eds) *Spain in an International Context, 1936–1959* (New York & Oxford: Berghahn, 1999)

Morales Lezcano, V. *Historia de la No-Beligerencia Española durante la Segunda Guerra Mundial (VI. 1940–X. 1943)* (Mancomunidad de Cabildos de las Palmas: Plan Cultural, 1980)

Morán, G. *Miseria y Grandeza del Partido Comunista de España* (Barcelona: Planeta, 1976)

Moreno Juste, A. 'La Ruptura del Principio de Unidad de Acción Exterior en el Caso Español y las Organizaciones Regionales Europeas (1949–1962)' in Comisión Española de la Historia de Relaciones Internacionales, *La Historia de las Relaciones Internacionales: una Visión desde España* (Madrid: Dirección General de Investigación Científica y Técnica del Ministerio de Educación y Ciencia, 1994)

Moreno Gómez, F. 'La Represión en la España Campesina' in García Delgado, J. (ed.) *El Primer Franquismo. España durante la Segunda Guerra Mundial* (Madrid: Siglo Veintiuno Editores, 1989)

Morgan, K. *Labour in Power 1945–1951* (Oxford: Clarendon Press, 1984)

Mujal-León, E. *Communism and Political Change in Spain* (Bloomington: Indiana University Press, 1983)

Muniesa, B. *Dictadura y Monarquía en España: de 1939 hasta la Actualidad* (Barcelona: Editorial Ariel, 1996)

Nadal, E. *Todos contra Franco – la Alianza Nacional de Fuerzas Democráticas 1944/1947* (Madrid: Queimada Ediciones, 1982)

Neila Hernández, J. 'The Foreign Policy Administration of Franco's Spain: from Isolation to International Realignment (1945–1957)' in Leitz, C. and Dunthorn, D. (eds) *Spain in an International Context, 1936–1959* (New York & Oxford: Berghahn, 1999)

Northedge, F. (ed.) *The Foreign Policies of the Powers* (London: Faber & Faber, 1968)

Ovendale, R. (ed.) *The Foreign Policy of the British Labour Governments, 1945–51* (Leicester University Press, 1984)

Packard, J. *Neither Friend Nor Foe: the European Neutrals in World War II* (New York: Macmillan, 1992)

Payne, S. *Politics and the Military in Modern Spain* (Stanford University Press, 1967), translated as *Los Militares y la Política en la España Contémporanea* (Paris: Ruedo Ibérico, 1967)

——*The Franco Regime 1936–1975* (Madison, Wisconsin: University of Wisconsin Press, 1987)

——*Franco. El Perfil de la Historia* (Madrid: Espasa-Calpe, 1992)

——*A History of Fascism 1914–45* (London: University College London Press, 1995)

Pecharromán, J. *Conservadores Subversivos: la Derecha Autoritaria Alfonsina (1913–1936)* (Madrid: Eudema, 1994)

Pelling, H. *The Labour Governments, 1945–51* (London: Macmillan, 1984)

Pereira, J. *Introducción al Estudio de la Política Exterior de España en los Siglos XIX y XX* (Madrid: Akal, 1983)

Pérez Mateos, A. *El Rey que Vino del Exilio* (Barcelona: Planeta, 1981)

Pike, D. *Jours de Gloire, Jours de Honte: le Parti Communiste d'Espagne en France depuis son Arrivée en 1939 jusqu'à son Départ en 1950* (Paris: Sedes, 1984)

——*In the Service of Stalin: the Spanish Communists in Exile, 1939–1945* (Oxford: Clarendon Press, 1993)

Pollack, B. and Hunter, G. *The Paradox of Spanish Foreign Policy* (London: Pinter Publishers, 1987)

Pons Prades, E. *Republicanos Españoles en la 2ª Guerra Mundial* (Barcelona: Planeta, 1975)

——*Los Derrotados y el Exilio* (Barcelona: Bruguera, 1977)

——*Guerrillas Españolas 1936–1960* (Barcelona: Planeta, 1977)

Portero, F. *Franco Aislado: La Cuestión Española (1945–1950)* (Madrid: Aguilar, 1989)

——'Spain, Britain and the Cold War' in Balfour, S. and Preston, P. (eds) *Spain and the Great Powers in the Twentieth Century* (London & New York: Routledge, 1999)

Portero, F. and Pardo, R. 'Las Relaciones Exteriores como Factor Condicionante del Franquismo' in Sánchez Recio G. (ed.) *El Primer Franquismo (1936–1959)* (Madrid: *Ayer*, 33, Marcial Pons, 1999)

Powell, C. *Juan Carlos of Spain: Self-Made Monarch* (London: Macmillan, 1996)

Pozharskaia, S. *Breve Historia del Franquismo* (Barcelona: L'Eina, 1987)

Preston, P. 'The Anti-Francoist Opposition: the Long March to Unity' in Preston, P. (ed.) *Spain in Crisis: the Evolution and Decline of the Franco Regime* (Hassocks: Harvester Press, 1976).

——(ed.) *Spain in Crisis: the Evolution and Decline of the Franco Regime* (Hassocks: Harvester Press, 1976)

——'Alfonsist Monarchism and the Coming of the Spanish Civil War' in Blinkhorn, M. (ed.) *Spain in Conflict 1931–1939: Democracy and Its Enemies* (London: Sage, 1986)

——*The Politics of Revenge: Fascism and the Military in Twentieth Century Spain* (London: Unwin Hyman, 1990)

——*Franco* (London: Harper Collins, 1993)

——*The Coming of the Spanish Civil War: Reform, Reaction and Revolution in the Second Republic,* 2nd edn (London: Routledge, 1994)

——'Mussolini's Spanish Adventure: from Limited Risk to War' in Preston, P. and MacKenzie, A. (eds), *The Republic Besieged: Civil War in Spain 1936–1939* (Edinburgh University Press, 1996)

——*¡Comrades! Portraits from the Spanish Civil War* (London: HarperCollins, 1999)

Preston, P. and MacKenzie, A. (eds), *The Republic Besieged: Civil War in Spain 1936–1939* (Edinburgh University Press, 1996)

Ramírez, L. *Franco – la Obsesión de Ser; la Obsesión de Poder* (Paris: Ruedo Ibérico, 1976)

Richards, M. 'Terror and Progress: Industrialisation, Modernity, and the Making of Francoism' in Graham, H. and Labanyi, J. (eds) *Spanish Cultural Studies: an Introduction. The Struggle for Modernity* (Oxford University Press, 1995)

——*A Time of Silence: Civil War and the Culture of Repression in Franco's Spain, 1936–1945* (Cambridge University Press, 1998)

Rioux, J-P. *La France de la Quatrième République, Vol. 1, L'Ardeur et la Nécessité 1944–1952* (Paris: Seuil, 1980)

Rodríguez Cruz, R. 'Relaciones Franco-Españolas al Término de la Segunda Guerra Mundial: de la Tirantez al Cierre de la Frontera' in *Españoles y Franceses en la Primera Mitad del Siglo XX* (Madrid: Consejo Superior de Investigaciones Científicas, 1986)

Rodríguez-Moñino Soriano, R. *La Misión Diplomática del XVII Duque de Alba: en la Embajada de España en Londres (1937–1945)* (Valencia: Castalia, 1971)

Rojas, C. *La Guerra Civil Vista por los Exiliados* (Barcelona: Planeta, 1975)

Romeu Alfaro, F. 'Panorámica Socio-Política de los Primeros Movimientos Guerrilleros en la España del 39 al 46' in García Delgado, J. (ed.) *El Primer Franquismo: España durante la Segunda Guerra Mundial* (Madrid: Siglo Veintiuno Editores, 1989)

Del Rosal, A. *El Oro del Banco de España y la Historia del Vita* (Barcelona: Grijalbo, 1977)

Rothwell, V. *Britain and the Cold War 1941–1947* (London: Cape, 1982)

Rubottom, R. and Carter-Murphy, J. *Spain and the United States since World War Two* (New York: Praeger, 1984)

Ruhl, K-J. *Spanien im Zweiten Weltkrieg: Franco, die Falange und das 'Dritte Reich'* (Hamburg: Hoffmann & Campe, 1975)

Sainz Ortega, L. 'Las Cortes de la II República entre Francia y México: su Doble Impacto Institucional e Internacional' in Comisión Española de la Historia de

Relaciones Internacionales, *La Historia de las Relaciones Internacionales: una Visión desde España* (Madrid: Dirección General de Investigación Científica y Técnica del Ministerio de Educación y Ciencia, 1994)

Saiz Valdivieso, A. *Indalecio Prieto. Los Tres Exilios* (Madrid: Fundación Españoles en el Mundo, 1993)

Sánchez Recio, G. 'La Coalición Reaccionaria y la Confrontación Política dentro del Régimen Franquista' in Tusell, J., Pecharromán, J., Montero, F. *Estudios sobre la Derecha Española Contemporánea* (Madrid: UNED, 1993)

—— 'Líneas de Investigación y Debate Historiográfico' in Sánchez Recio, G. (ed.) *El Primer Franquismo (1936–1959)* (Madrid: Ayer, 33, Marcial Pons, 1999)

—— (ed.) *El Primer Franquismo (1936–1959)* (Madrid: Ayer, 33, Marcial Pons, 1999)

Sanders, R. *Spain and the United Nations, 1945–1950* (New York: Vantage Press, 1966)

Sanz, M. *Los Guerrilleros Españoles en Francia, 1940–1945* (Havana: Editorial de Ciencias Sociales del Instituto Cubano del Libro, 1971)

Saville, J. *The Politics of Continuity: British Foreign Policy and the Labour Government, 1945–46* (London: Verso, 1993)

Schor, R. *L'Opinion Française et les Étrangers en France 1919–1939* (Paris: Publication de la Sorbonne, 1985)

Séguéla, M. *Franco Pétain: los Secretos de una Alianza* (Barcelona: Prensa Ibérica, 1994), translated from *Pétain–Franco: les Secrets d'une Alliance* (Paris: Éditions Albin Michel, 1992)

De la Serre, F., Leruez, J., Wallace, H., (eds) *Les Politiques Étrangères de la France et de la Grande-Bretagne depuis 1945: l'Inévitable Ajustement* (Paris: Presses de la Fondation Nationale des Sciences Politiques & Berg, 1990)

Sinova, J. *La Censura de Prensa durante el Franquismo (1936–1951)* (Madrid: Espasa-Calpe, 1989)

Smith, R. *OSS: The Secret History of America's First Central Intelligence Agency* (Berkeley: University of California Press, 1972)

Smyth, D. 'The Politics of Asylum, Juan Negrín and the British Government in 1940' in Langhorne, R. (ed.) *Diplomacy and Intelligence during the Second World War: Essays in Honour of F.H. Hinsley* (Cambridge University Press, 1985)

—— *Diplomacy and Strategy of Survival: British Policy and Franco's Spain, 1940–41* (Cambridge University Press, 1986)

Solé Tura, J. 'Unidad y Diversidad en la Oposición Comunista al Franquismo' in Fontana, J. (ed.) *España bajo el Franquismo* (Barcelona: Editorial Crítica, Grijalbo, 1986)

Sorel, A. *Búsqueda, Reconstrucción e Historia de la Guerrilla Española del Siglo XX, a través de sus Documentos, Relatos y Protagonistas* (Paris: Librairie du Globe, 1970)

Stafford, D. *Britain and European Resistance, 1940–1945: a Survey of the Special Operations Executive, with Documents* (London: Macmillan, 1980)

—— *Churchill and Secret Service* (London: John Murray, 1997)

Stein, L. *Beyond Death and Exile: the Spanish Republicans in France, 1939–1955* (Cambridge, Massachusetts & London: Harvard University Press, 1979)

Stone, G. 'The European Great Powers and the Spanish Civil War, 1936–1939' in Boyce, R. and Robertson, E. (eds) *Paths to War: New Essays on the Origins of the Second World War* (London: Macmillan, 1989)

—— 'The Degree of British Commitment to the Restoration of Democracy in

Spain, 1939–1946' in Leitz, C. and Dunthorn, D. (eds) *Spain in an International Context, 1936–1959* (New York & Oxford: Berghahn, 1999)

Suárez Fernández, L. *Francisco Franco y Su Tiempo*, Vols. I–IV (Madrid: Fundación Francisco Franco, 1984)

——*Franco y la URSS* (Madrid: Rialp, 1987)

——*Franco y su Época* (Madrid: Actas, 1993)

——*España, Franco y la Segunda Guerra Mundial desde 1939 hasta 1945* (Madrid: Actas, 1997)

Sueiro, D. and Díaz Nosty, B. *Historia del Franquismo* (Madrid: Sarpe, 1986)

Swain, G. 'Stalin and Spain, 1944–1948' in Leitz, C. and Dunthorn, D. (eds) *Spain in an International Context, 1936–1959* (New York & Oxford: Berghahn, 1999)

Table Ronde de l'Équipe Défense et Diplomatie des Moyennes Puissances, *La Moyenne Puissance au XXᵒ Siècle. Recherche d'une Définition* (Paris: Institut d'Histoire des Conflits Contemporains, 1989)

Tamames, R. *La República: La Era de Franco* (Madrid: Alfaguara, 1973)

Tierno Galván, E. *Cabos Sueltos* (Madrid: Brughera, 1981)

Tint, H. *French Foreign Policy since the Second World War* (London: Weidenfeld & Nicolson, 1972)

Togores, L. and Neila, J. *La Escuela Diplomática: Cincuenta Años de Servicio al Estado (1942–1992)* (Madrid: Escuela Diplomática, 1993)

Toquero, J. *Franco y Don Juan: la Oposición Monárquica al Franquismo* (Barcelona: Plaza & Janés, 1989)

——'La Oposición Monárquica. La política del Conde de Barcelona' in Tusell, J., Alted, A., Mateos, A. *et al. La Oposición al Régimen de Franco: Estado de la Cuestión y Metodología de la Investigación: Actas del Congreso Internacional que, organizado por el Departamento de Historia Contemporánea de la UNED, tuvo lugar en Madrid del 19 al 22 de Octubre de 1988*, Vol. I–I (Madrid: UNED, 1990)

——*Don Juan de Borbón, el Rey Padre* (Barcelona: Plaza & Janés, 1992)

Townson, N. (ed.) *El Republicanismo en España (1830–1977)* (Madrid: Alianza Universitaria, 1994)

Trythall, J. *Franco, a Biography* (London: Rupert Hart-Davis, 1970)

Tuñón de Lara, M. 'Los Españoles en la II Guerra Mundial y su Participación en la Resistencia Francesa' in Abellán, J. (ed.) *El Exilio Español de 1939, 2, Guerra y Política* (Madrid: Taurus, 1976)

——*Historia de España. XII. Textos y Documentos de Historia Moderna y Contemporánea (Siglos XVIII–XX)* (Barcelona: Labor, 1985)

——'Sobre la Historia de la Oposición al Franquismo: Balance y Perspectivas' in Tusell, J., Alted, A., Mateos, A. *et al. La Oposición al Régimen de Franco: Estado de la Cuestión y Metodología de la Investigación: Actas del Congreso Internacional que, organizado por el Departamento de Historia Contemporánea de la UNED, tuvo lugar en Madrid del 19 al 22 de Octubre de 1988*, Vol. I-I (Madrid: UNED, 1990)

Tuñón de Lara, M., Miralles, R., Díaz Chico, B. *Juan Negrín López, el Hombre Necesario* (Las Palmas: Gobierno de Canarias, 1996)

Tusell, J. *Historia de la Democracia Cristiana en España. I. Los antecedentes. La Ceda y la II República. II. Los nacionalismos Vasco y Catalán. Los Solitarios* (Madrid: Editorial Cuadernos para el Diálogo, Edicusa, 1974)

——*La España del Siglo XX. Desde Alfonso XIII a la Muerte de Carrero Blanco* (Barcelona: Dopesa, 1975)

——*La Oposición Democrática al Franquismo (1939–1962)* (Barcelona: Planeta, 1977)

——*Franco y los Católicos: La Política Interior Española entre 1945–57* (Madrid: Alianza, 1984)

——*Carrero. La Eminencia Gris del Régimen de Franco* (Madrid: Ediciones Temas de Hoy, 1993)

Tusell, J., Alted, A., Mateos, A. *et al. La Oposición al Régimen de Franco: Estado de la Cuestión y Metodología de la Investigación: Actas del Congreso Internacional que, organizado por el Departamento de Historia Contemporánea de la UNED, tuvo lugar en Madrid del 19 al 22 de Octubre de 1988*, Vol. I-I (Madrid: UNED, 1990)

Tusell, J., Pechorromán, J., Montero, F. *Estudios sobre la Derecha Española Contemporánea* (Madrid: UNED, 1993)

Tusell, J., Sueiro, S., Marín, J., Casanova, M. *El Régimen de Franco: Política y Relaciones Exteriores*, 2 vols (Madrid: UNED, 1993)

——*Juan Carlos I. La Restauración de la Monarquía* (Madrid: Temas de Hoy, 1995)

——*Franco, España y la II Guerra Mundial. Entre el Eje y la Neutralidad* (Madrid: Temas de Hoy, 1995)

Tusell, J., Avilés, J., Pardo, R., Casanova, M., Mateos, A., Sepúlveda, I., Soto, A. (eds) *La Política Exterior de España en el Siglo XX* (Madrid: UNED, 1997)

Universidad Complutense de Madrid: *Perspectivas de la España Contemporánea. Estudios en Homenaje al Profesor Vicente Atard* (Madrid: Universidad Complutense, 1986)

Various contributors, *Eugenio Vegas Latapié (1907–1985)* (Madrid: Speiro, 1960)

Del Valle, J. *Las Instituciones de la República Española en el Exilio* (Paris: Ruedo Ibérico, 1976)

Vidal Sales, J. *Don Juan de Borbón: Biografía. Hijo de Rey, Padre de Rey, Jamás Rey* (Madrid: Editorial Mitre, 1984)

Vilar, J. (ed.) *Las Relaciones Internacionales en la España Contemporánea* (Murcia: Servicio de Publicaciones, 1989)

Vilar, S. *La Oposición a la Dictadura: Protagonistas de la España Democrática* (Barcelona: Aymá, 1976)

——*Historia del Anti-Franquismo 1939–1975* (Barcelona: Plaza & Janés, 1984)

Viñas, A., Viñuela, J., Eguidazu, F., Pulgar, C., Florensa, S. *Política Comercial Exterior en España, 1931–1975*, 3 vols (Madrid: Banco Exterior de España, 1979)

Viñas, A. *Los Pactos Secretos de Franco con Estados Unidos* (Barcelona: Grijalbo, 1981)

——*Guerra, Dinero, Dictadura: Ayuda Fascista y Autarquía en la España de Franco* (Barcelona: Grijalbo, 1984)

——'La Política Exterior del Franquismo' in Vilar, J. (ed.) *Las Relaciones Internacionales en la España Contemporánea* (Murcia: Servicio de Publicaciones, 1989)

Watt, D. 'Britain, the United States and the Opening of the Cold War' in Ovendale, R. (ed.) *The Foreign Policy of the British Labour Governments, 1945–51* (Leicester University Press, 1984)

——'British Military Perceptions of the Soviet Union as a Strategic Threat, 1945–50' in Becker, J. and Knipping, F. (eds) *Power in Europe?: Great Britain, France, Italy and Germany in a Postwar World, 1945–1950* (Berlin: de Gruyter, 1986)

Welles, B. *Spain: The Gentle Anarchy* (London: Pall Mall Press, 1965)

West, N. *MI6: British Secret Intelligence Operations, 1909–45* (London: Weidenfeld & Nicolson, 1983)

Wheeler-Bennett, J. and Nicholls, A. *The Semblance of Peace: the Political Settlement after the Second World War* (London: Macmillan, 1972)

Whitaker, A. *Spain and the Defence of the West: Ally and Liability* (New York: Harper & Bros, 1961)

Woodward, L. *British Foreign Policy in the Second World War*
Vol I (London: HMSO, 1970)
Vol II (London: HMSO, 1971)
Vol IV (London: HMSO, 1975)

Young, J. *Britain, France and the Unity of Europe, 1945–1951* (Leicester University Press, 1984)

——*France, the Cold War and the Western Alliance, 1944–1949: French Foreign Policy and Post-War Europe* (Leicester University Press, 1990)

——'Duff Cooper and the Paris Embassy, 1945–47' in Zametica, J. (ed.) *British Officials and British Foreign Policy, 1945–50* (Leicester University Press, 1990)

——*Cold War Europe, 1945–1989: a Political History* (London: Edward Arnold, 1991)

Zametica, J. (ed.) *British Officials and British Foreign Policy 1945–50* (Leicester University Press, 1990)

Index